commercial re ...ships

commercial relationships

Mark Moore MBA BA(Hons) MCIPS

TUDOR

©M. Moore 1999

First published in Great Britain by Tudor Business Publishing Limited.

A CIP catalogue for this book is available from the British Library

ISBN 1 872807 37 2

The right of Mark Moore to be identified as the author
of this work has been asserted by him in accordance with the
Copyright, Designs and Patents Act 1988.

Typeset by Bitter & Twisted, N. Wales

Printed and Bound in Great Britain by
Athenaeum Press Ltd, Newcastle upon Tyne

To Jackie and my mother - for their help and support over the years.

Foreword

I first met Mark whilst he was at the University of North London as Programme Director for Purchasing and Logistics. At the time, I encouraged him to produce a book based on the experience of both his educational background and his management training/consultancy projects. Mark moved to Achilles Information (an IT and consultancy group specialising in procurement) in 1997 and has indeed produced a title which is a useful contribution to the expanding number of texts on supply chain management. It will prove of use, I am sure, to both students of the Chartered Institute of Purchasing and Supply's professional stage diploma, the Certificate of Competence and to practitioners wanting a practical insight into contemporary supply chain management.

The book highlights an area of expanding importance in modern business life. Greater attention is now focused on the relationships between customer and supplier and this is reflected in the syllabus for the CIPS professional stage with the Commercial Relationships Unit, which has become a very popular choice amongst CIPS students.

Key features of this book are:

- The importance of managing external resources and commercial relationships with suppliers
- A guide to contracts both in terms of the law relating to agreements established with suppliers and their role in commercial relationships
- The management of relationships with internal customers
- Important features of both structures and strategies for effective procurement
- New innovations in relationship management such as partnership sourcing and lean supply
- The implications of procurement in the public sector
- A practical guide to IT systems relating to procurement, including the use of the Internet and data base systems.

I hope that you will enjoy the read!

David Jessop

Contents

chapter one

Purchasing and Commercial Relationships

No organisation exists in isolation. Businesses will usually inter-connect to produce outputs of goods and services and, in so doing, form commercial relationships with other organisations. The networks of linkages between different organisations has given rise to the term 'supply chain management' which is concerned with the management of the flows of materials and information between the different operations involved in the production of goods or services (see Slack et al, *Operations Management*). This network includes customers, who may of course be individual consumers or commercial customers. There will also be suppliers of goods and services to the organisation. There may be tiers of both suppliers and customers, as suppliers will be dependent on other suppliers and customers may not be the final customer.

Tiers of Customers and Suppiers

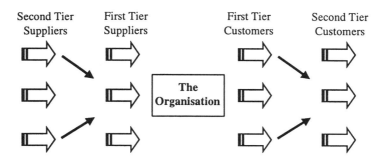

Michael Porter in *Competitive Strategy* produced a model for understanding the environment in which organisations operate. He refers to four external influences on the organisation.

Bargaining Power of Suppliers and Buyers

Michael Porter's Structural Analysis of the Competitive Environment

Michael Porter Competitive Strategy (1980)

Porter's analysis highlights the possible threats to business competitiveness of the actions of suppliers. It is argued that supplier power is likely to be high when:

- There is a concentration of suppliers rather than a fragmented supplier base. This point is best illustrated in oligopolistic supply markets, when a number of key suppliers dominate the market.
- The costs of changing from one supplier to another is expensive. Again, this point can be true when the supplier in dealing with a particular purchaser has built up a large body of expertise and, perhaps, specialist plant and equipment. In addition, it would be very time consuming and risky for the purchasing organisation to switch the source of supply.
- There is a risk that the supplier could affect the buyer's operating environment directly by influencing the supply chain. This can be referred to as forward or 'downstream' vertical integration where the supplier takes greater control of the environment in which the purchasers operate.
- The supplier's customers are of little importance to the supplier, and so the supplier is not overtly concerned about long-term relationships with the purchasing organisation.

Porter's analysis therefore highlights the possible threat to business performance of its external resources. Equally, the power of the purchasing organisation is likely to be high:

- When there is a high concentration of buyers, particularly when the quantities or spend of the purchaser is high.
- When there are many suppliers operating in a competitive market place enabling the purchaser to switch suppliers with little or no disruption to operations.
- If the suppliers product or service supplied amounts to a high percentage of the purchaser's costs, the purchaser will be able to source competitively to obtain the best price from suppliers, thereby squeezing their margins.
- Where they may be threat of upstream vertical integration if the purchaser is dissatisfied with supplier performance.

Apart from the power of buyers and suppliers, Porter also highlights:

The Threat of Entry

The threat of entry is very much dependent on the extent of barriers to entry which refers to the difficulty of new producers entering the industry. Barriers to entry can include factors such as:

- the extent to which there are economies of scale;
- the amount of capital needed;
- the existence of legal and protective barriers through intellectual property rights;
- the level of customer switching costs;
- access to distribution channels.

Threat of Substitutes

- The availability and willingness of purchasers to buy substitute products or services which have similar characteristics.
- The comparative costs of substitutes may also affect demand.

Rivalry Among Existing Competitors

Organisations will also be concerned with the degree of rivalry with other organisations operating in the same market. Essentially this aspect is concerned with an analysis of the competition in the market.

Porter's model argues that the role of the management strategist is to determine which of these four forces are of the greatest importance to the organisation, and which can then be influenced by the strategic decisions of management. The model highlights the impact of external resources on business performance.

Over the last few years, an increasing number of business leaders have come to realise the contribution that effective purchasing can make to business success. Businesses now operate in fast changing conditions and the characteristics of contemporary economic conditions are:

- Increased globalisation
- Intensified competition
- Shorter product life cycles
- Greater uncertainty of future demand
- Improvements in information through developments in information technology.

Businesses now compete in the market on the basis of quality, prices and reliability. Tom Peters, the influential American management consultant, argues that businesses will only be successful if they focus on the achievement of total customer satisfaction through creating a superior product or service giving value for money. In today's global economy, businesses have to be World Class to survive.

In this fast changing world, public and private sector organisations have called the subordinate nature of this role into question. Almost all organisations have increasingly realised their dependence on suppliers to achieve sustainable competitive advantage. Competitive advantage can be created through:

- Cost Leadership – the products/ services the company sells are competitively priced.
- Product/ Service Differentiation – the products/ services sold to the customer are different to the competition by the creation of a differential advantage (this may be real or perceived).
- Reliability – in terms of quality and delivery.

It is not surprising that suppliers can make an important contribution both in terms of cost, innovation and reliability. In terms of cost, bought in goods and services constitute between 60 and 80% of most manufacturing companies product cost.

Research conducted by Chapman et al published in the *McKinsey Quarterly* concluded that the cost of purchased goods and services accounted for significant amounts of expenditure as a proportion of total costs in a range of industries. The following chart shows the percentages of total costs generally made up of purchased goods and services.

Cost of Purchased Goods and Services

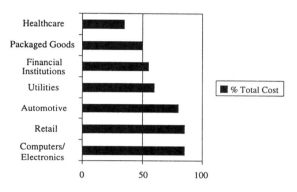

Source: McKinsey Quarterly (1997)

The graph demonstrates the significant proportion of costs which are accounted for by externally bought goods or services. In the case of a retail organisation for example, generally 80% of costs will be accounted for by the products and, to a lesser extent, the services supplied by external suppliers. The remaining 20% of cost will be accounted for by direct labour, depreciation of assets, financing costs and other purely internal costs. Many overheads will be accounted for by external services bought from suppliers – consider the supply of electricity, for example. Based on these total costs, the retail organisation will aim to charge prices which will achieve a satisfactory profit margin.

Task

Is there a reliable estimate of the proportion of costs accounted for by bought-in goods and services in your organisation?

In service organisations, this percentage will vary in accordance with the type of industry in which they operate and the dependence on external resources. In line with the ideas expressed in Peters and Waterman's *In Search of Excellence*, a dominant characteristic of organisational behaviour in the late 1980s and 1990s has been to concentrate on core business. There has been a rapid growth in the extent of outsourcing non-core businesses and services previously performed by employees of the organisation to external suppliers. More organisations are also realising the scope for savings in cost and the ability to work with suppliers to become World Class performers. The purchasing organisation will therefore be forming commercial relationships with the organisation responsible for the outsourced activity.

An Example of Outsourcing

A leading confectionery producer traditionally employed sales representatives whose responsibilities centred on merchandising stocks of confectionery for the independent retail sector throughout the UK. Many newsagents will fall into the independent sector, as they are often sole traders and not owned by a larger chain. Nevertheless, the independent sector accounts for a significant percentage of overall confectionery sales, and approximately 80% of confectionery purchase decisions made by consumers is done on impulse. The layout of confectionery in retail shops can have a major influence on consumer buying. It is vital, therefore, for the confectionery manufacturers to both promote and monitor the displays and sales of their branded products. In addition, a key aspect of merchandising is to inform retailers of special promotions and to take orders for future supply.

The decision was made in the early 1990s to outsource the merchandising role to an independent agency. The agency organisation provides people to conduct the merchandising in independent retail organisations. The benefit to the confectionery manufacturer were numerous:

- Considerable savings achieved in employing its own personnel.
- The sales representatives were an expensive overhead, as there were high costs of supplying company cars, communications, etc.
- The confectionery manufacturer would be better able to concentrate on its core business of producing and marketing its product range leaving an external supplier to concentrate on resourcing the merchandising operations with the independent retail sector.
- Greater flexibility to vary the resources involved in merchandising. At busier times of the year, or for special sales campaigns, the outsourced agency would be able to take on additional part-time workers to meet demand.

The external supplier providing the merchandising employs people on a part-time basis giving maximum flexibility. The supplier is also providing a quality service to the confectionery manufacturer as it is concentrating on its core business, the provision of a merchandising service to a manufacturer.

In this example, the relationship between the supplier and the manufacturer has to be carefully managed to maximise business performance. The supplier is almost part of the manufacturing organisation, although it does supply these types of services to other customers. The commercial relationships between the purchaser and the external supplier can have a significant impact on the manufacturer's sales, and the service has provided considerable savings in cost. As organisations have pursued outsourcing, this has increased the importance of managing external resources.

External Resources and Added Value

Michael Porter suggests that an organisation's success is achieved by the creation of competitive advantage. He argues that this can be most effectively created through achieving cost leadership or through differentiation. He states:

> Competitive advantage results from a firm's ability to perform the required activities at a collectively lower cost than rivals, or perform some activities in unique ways that create buyer value and hence allow the firm to command a premium price.
> *Competitive Advantage: Creating and Sustaining Superior Performance (1985).*

So, an organisation's ability is judged by its customers or users of its products and services produced. A firm creates competitive advantage through the way that various activities required to design, produce, market, deliver and support the product or service are performed. These are referred to as value activities and these activities are performed by different people across the organisation. It is this mix of activities which defines its competitive advantage.

The primary value chain activities of the organisation are categorised under these headings:

Value Chain Activities

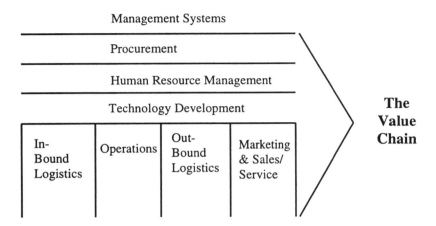

Inbound Logistics which are the activities concerned with receiving, storing and distributing the inputs to the product or service. This category includes acceptance of supplies from external suppliers, receipt and inspection, materials handling, stock control and transport.

Operations which is the area which transforms these inputs into the final product or service. Aspects of operations management will include design of the layout and flow of production, the technology used to transform the product or service, and job design and work organisation.

Outbound Logistics collects, stores and distributes the product/ service to customers. Again, much of this element is usually outsourced to a third party logistics specialist.

Marketing and Sales provides the information to prospective purchasers of the product or service. This category would include the sales support team, the merchandise personnel, and those involved in sales promotions and advertising. Again, there is an increasing tendency by organisations to outsource this work to third party agents.

Service which includes those activities that improve or maintain the value of the product or service to the customer, such as sales support, help desks, training and warranty replacement.

These primary value chain activities are coupled with support activities which include:

Management Systems which cover aspects like planning, finance, quality control.

Procurement which is the function responsible for managing external resources

Technology Development which could either be concerned with the production or design of the product or service itself. Alternatively, this can refer to business processes – the means of achieving the linkages between the firm's activities and also with external suppliers or customers.

Human Resource Management which covers all aspects of people development, such as recruitment, training, remuneration and career planning.

Porter recognised that the value chain activities will be performed not just internally but also by external organisations linked to the firm. The linkages between each activity, internally and externally, impact on competitiveness. These commercial relationships need to be managed with expertise for the organisation to improve its position in the market. The focus of this text, therefore, is on the commercial management of its external resources.

The Stages in Development of Procurement

From the brief analysis of Michael Porter's work on organisational competitiveness, a key factor is supply chain management. However, the function has been slow to develop in many organisations. There are many reasons to account for the slow development of the function:

- Many organisations have perceived that buying (placing orders) is an administrative function. The buyer's duty is to ensure that the paperwork is properly processed.
- Many businesses typically have little difficulty in selling the goods and services that they produce since effective marketing policies have enabled these organisations to be able to sell their products and services without great concern over cost. Increasing competition has, however, forced companies to concentrate on their costs because of reduced profit margins.

- In many manufacturing organisations, production was the key driving force. Since the 1970s and 1980s, though, the tendency has been for companies to concentrate on their core businesses and, as a result, the proportion of expenditures accounting for bought-in goods and services contracted out of the organisation has increased.
- There was a general feeling that no special training was necessary. Anyone could be a buyer! What needed to be learnt could be done 'on the job'. However, modern purchasing calls for an understanding of supplier management, logistics and contracts.
- There was, and still is in many organisations, limited information available because of a lack of research on the costs and scale of purchasing. Even if there were a purchasing department, little would be known about:
  the number of suppliers;
  the spend in aggregate terms and per supplier.
  With the increasing sophistication of computer software, greater attention can be focussed on purchasing through improved information.
- Purchasing people make poor sales people, and have not created a favourable impression with other departments (their internal customers) or the board room. Procedures have traditionally had the effect of creating greater bureaucracy and little real impact on improving business performance.

It can be argued that organisations have tended to concentrate on the outputs rather than inputs.

Inputs	Outputs
Purchases of stock	Price
Purchases of sub-assemblies	Produc
Procurement of services	Promotion
Inventory management	Outbound logistics
Inbound logistics	

Purchasing has been traditionally viewed as a subsidiary function in organisations – one that is relatively unimportant compared to, for example, finance and marketing. A document published by the UK Department of Trade and Industry 'Managing Into the 1990s', as part of the Enterprise Initiative campaign commented:

Purchasing and supply can no longer be treated as a second order function. The way forward lies with integrated materials management, pulling together suppliers, production and distribution. In the years ahead, those who have not got their purchasing and supply operations right will not be competitive.

The Enterprise Initiative was a scheme launched by the Government to help improve the competitiveness of British Industry, particularly manufacturing SMEs (small and medium enterprises). A similar view was expressed by the popular business commentator, Sir John Harvey Jones, who stated:

I'm amazed that actual buying decisions are made so low down in British companies when you bear in mind that buying decisions usually effect the largest single expenditure of the company. You would have thought this was an area where the chief executive would be deeply and personally concerned. But, it is very often passed a long way down the line and yet on it totally depends the success and viability of the company.
Getting it Together (1991).

The concept of 'external resource management' was first coined by Professor Richard Lamming Chair of Purchasing and Supply at Bath University in his book *Beyond Partnership-Strategies for Innovation and Lean Supply* (1993), an authoritative study of commercial relationships in the automotive sector. He commented that:

It is no longer sufficient to see this function (purchasing) dealing with suppliers- as a matter of spending money, of buying parts and services. The suppliers are now part of the extended organisation of the assembler- intrinsic parts of the value-added process... Purchasing and supply thus becomes a matter of external resource management... and a change of title for the function may well be necessary to focus strategic attention (and imagination) accordingly.

The quotations from both Sir John Harvey Jones and Professor Richard Lamming highlight the point that there is a range of levels of sophistication of purchasing in organisations. Many organisations still have under-developed purchasing functions, whereas others utilise very sophisticated processes, and have established sound commercial relationships.

A number of models have been prescribed to enable our understanding of the stage of development of a purchasing function. By identifying the current stage of development achieved by a purchasing function, this helps to focus attention on the necessary change to further development.

Adapted from Reck and Lang: A Four Stage Purchasing Development Model

Non-existent

No function or person is appointed to take responsibility for managing external resources. Purchasing decisions are made by non-experts in the organisation and the control of external resources is patchy, depending on the competence of the individuals concerned.

Passive

A function is in existence but has no strategic direction and reacts to the requests of other functions. A high proportion of time is spent on transactional, routine placing and associated administration. Supplier selection is based, primarily, on price and availability.

Independent

The function is still reactive, but some implementation of latest techniques and practices may be evident. The function may have introduced a number of cost reduction projects. Links are established with other functions/business units but relationships are generally uncooperative.

Supportive

Top management recognises the positive contribution to corporate performance and provides the function with the necessary resources and manpower to improve performance. Improved links are made with other parts of the internal value chain. Suppliers are considered an important resource. Markets, products and services are continuously monitored and analysed and continuous improvement in quality and cost is the focus of purchasing effort.

Integrative

The purchasing function is fully integrated into the organisation's competitive strategy Suppliers are given greater prominence in the strategic planning of the organisation and cross-functional teams are established with suppliers. Purchasing's performance is measured in terms of contributions to the firm's success. Best practice procurement processes are continuously adopted.

Many organisations will not achieve the integrative stage, and many chief executives may contend that their businesses do not warrant such sophistication. Much will depend on the importance of procurement to the firm's value chain.

Baily, Farmer, Jessop and Jones propose a profiling scheme which has five stages of measurable development: infant, awakening, developing, mature and advanced. Profiles can be produced for individual purchasing organisations and this can be used as a tool for indicating the areas which need further development.

Measurement Area	Infant	Awakening	Developing	Mature	Advanced
Activity Breakdown					
Analysis					
Purchasing Organisation					
Structure					
Purchasing Services					
Functions Position in the Business					
Extent of Development of the Buyers (Training Needs)					
Relative Remuneration levels					
Measurement of Performance					
Standard of Info Systems					
IT facilities					
Operating Procedures					
Interface development					
Buying Process Involvement					
Buyer Characteristics					
Degree of Purchasing Specialism					
Supplier Interface Development					
Policy on Ethics					
Hospitality					
Quality of Buyer - Supplier Relationships					

A useful perspective on the status of purchasing is provided by Ernst and Young's document on 'Good Management of Purchasing' published in 1993.

Scenario 1: the Clerical Supply Management Function

- Supply management is a sub-section of another support department, such as operations in a manufacturing environment and finance in a service sector organisation.
- There is no head of supply management and, therefore, there is no contribution to planning.
- Internal initiators of purchase requirements decide on their needs, choose

suppliers, agree prices and other commercial terms, then simply pass this arrangement to purchasing to raise the order and generate the necessary paperwork for the payment of the invoice.

- There are minimal written procedures.
- Procurement staff have little training, if any.
- Purchase orders are usually placed over the phone and backed up with a manual copy of order. There is little regard for contractual risk.
- There is a large number of suppliers used. There is little aggregation of requirements, so no call off arrangements made with suppliers.
- There is no measurement of supplier performance.

Scenario 2: the Commercial Supply Management Function

- Supply management is now regarded as a distinct function with a head of department usually at lower middle management level.
- Procurement staff are still rarely involved with specifying requirements and are largely dependent on internal users to provide such information.
- A degree of fire-fighting is characteristic of purchasing activities with no time available to analyse the requirement, suppliers and contractual risk.
- There is little distinction between the processes used for small and large purchases.
- The battle of the forms may take place with suppliers (this is referred to in Chapter 2).
- There is some performance monitoring in terms of analysing subjective savings made on purchases.

Scenario 3: the Supportive Supply Management Function

- The function is now recognised in policy planning and makes a contribution to the overall aims and objectives of the organisation.
- A functional head reports to senior management.
- A manual exists with documented procedures. Standard contractual terms exist for the procurement of both products and services.
- Training is provided for all procurement staff.
- Specifications are developed which allow competitive procurement.
- The function is still largely dependent on fragmented information systems, so analysis of data on suppliers is cumbersome.
- Lead buyers may be established for different products and series and efforts are made to aggregate requirements for these areas to improve purchasing power.

Scenario 4

- Supply management is a core activity staffed by qualified professionals with a functional head at board level.
- The function is recognised by its internal customers and suppliers as a centre of expertise.
- Agreements exist with suppliers which include agreed goals and regular performance reviews.
- The total costs of acquisition are measured rather than basing decisions on price and availability.
- Databases allow fast extraction of data on the supplier base.
- Procurement is committed to working to meet customer requirements.
- Supplier development programmes are developed which focus on continuous improvement.

Given that an effective purchasing function can play a major role in the success of an organisation it is clear that it must have a high status in order to achieve its objectives. The status of purchasing is important for the following reasons:

- The status given to it by senior management will reflect the esteem with which it is held at lower organisational levels.
- The status of the function will affect the status of individuals within the function and their ability to influence decision making.

Where purchasing has a high status the following factors are usually present:

- It will have strong support from senior management.
- There will be equality of standing between purchasing and other department's such as finance.
- Purchasing will be consulted at all critical stages of the procurement process with regard to the preparation of specifications, price, quality and availability of materials.
- The professionalism and expertise of purchasing staff will be high.

The status of the purchasing function can therefore be judged by the factors referred to in this section.

It can be seen that the esteem with which the purchasing function is viewed in any organisation will impact on its ability to use the best procurement practices and to get benefit from their application. Where purchasing has a low status there is a danger that it will be bypassed and not be consulted with regards to the preparation of specifications, sources of supply or high-value, high-risk procurements. In organisations where purchasing is held in low esteem buyers will tend to do what is requested of them by other departments and the professionalism and expertise of the purchasing staff will be low.

The Objectives of Purchasing/ External Resource Management

A traditional definition of purchasing objectives is to obtain the five rights:

The Five Rights of Purchasing

The Aim of Effective Purchasing Will Be to Obtain:

- The Right *Quality*

- Delivery/ Performance on *Time*

- Delivery at the Right *Location*

- The Right *Quantities*

- At the Desired *Cost*

A traditional definition of purchasing or external resource management in an organisational context is the function responsible for obtaining equipment, materials, supplies and services required by an organisation, through purchase, lease, hire or other legal means.

This definition using the five rights is very much a traditional view of purchasing activities. Baily, Farmer, Jessop and Jones provide a more helpful definition:

The Objectives of Purchasing

1. To supply the organisation with a steady flow of materials and services to meet its needs

2. To ensure continuity of supply by maintaining effective relationships with existing sources of supply and by developing other sources either as alternatives or to meet emerging or planned needs

3. To buy efficiently and wisely, obtaining by ethical means the best value for every unit of currency spent

4. To maintain sound co-operative relationships with other departments (internal customers), providing information and advice as necessary to ensure the effective operation of the organisation as a whole

5. To develop staff, policies, procedures and organisation to ensure the achievement of these objectives

6. To select the best suppliers in the market

7. To help generate the effective development of new products

8. To protect the organisation's cost structure

9. To monitor supply market trends

10. To negotiate effectively in order to work with suppliers who will seek mutual benefit through superior performance

Very often, departments have mission statements and statements of goals/ objectives which state what roles the purchasing department are trying to perform. An example is provided overleaf:

BA's Purchasing Mission and Goals

Mission:
Improved Profitability Through the Effective Management of the Airline's External Resources

Goals:
To Minimise the Life - Time Cost of Providing Goods and Services, Meeting the Company's Needs for Quality, Timing and Contractual Protection

Means:
Recruit and Develop a Highly Professional Team Qualified and Committed to Deliver a Consistently High Level of Performance

Exploit Opportunities Where Our Business Skills Add Maximum Value

Fully Develop Our Relationship With Suppliers to Stimulate Innovation and Optimise Performance For BA

Further Develop Relationships With Client Departments

In addition to those aims stated in the diagram, other means of achieving the intended goals are through:

- constantly monitoring the performance of the purchasing team against measurable business targets in the areas of cost, quality and service;
- maintaining the highest ethical and professional standards;
- constantly evaluating new developments in the purchasing field.

Another example is taken from British Telecom in their 'Supply Management Vision' statement:

- BT will be recognised as an industry leader in obtaining competitive advantage through Supply Chain Management.
- BT will achieve increased profitability through the establishment and operation of end to end supply chains which cross all organisation boundaries.

The mission/vision statement is a generalised objective or expression of an organisation's or department's purpose. It is worth mentioning the Chartered Institute of Purchasing and Supply's mission statement:

To be the centre of excellence for purchasing and supply chain management by:

18

- continuously improving the professional standards of practitioners;
- raising awareness of their contribution to corporate, national and international prosperity;
- representing the interests of individuals within the profession.

The Institute's objective is to promote the highest standards of professionalism in the purchasing, supply and logistics function. The CIPS acts as the central reference point on all matters affecting:

- the setting, testing and assessment of professional standards;
- the arrangement of appropriate supporting educational and training facilities;
- advice to individuals, businesses, government, other national bodies, and to the European Commission;
- maintenance of a strict ethical code to which all members are required to adhere.

The Purchase Decision-Making Unit

Whilst the objectives of purchasing departments have been outlined, there are numerous other people in the organisation who have roles in the procurement process. A very useful model for understanding the industrial buying process was produced by the authors, Webster and Wind. They argue that a purchasing organisation, whether it be large or small, has a number of people who will participate in the purchasing decision-making process. Members of the organisation can play any of six roles in the purchasing decision process:

Users: the members of an organisation who actually use the goods, equipment or service. In many cases, the users initiate the buying proposal and help define the specification.

Influencers: those people within the organisation who influence the buying decision. They often help define specifications and also provide information for evaluating alternatives. Technical personnel are particularly important as influencers.

Deciders: the people who have the power to decide on product requirements and/ or suppliers.

Approvers: those who have delegated authority to authorise the proposed actions of deciders or buyers.

Buyers: persons with formal authority for placing the contract with the supplier and arranging the terms of purchase. This role can be limited to the clerical activities involved in processing the transaction, although the buyer may contribute to the development of specifications.

Gatekeepers: those who have the power to prevent sellers or information from reaching other members of the decision-making unit within the purchasing organisation. For example, buyers, secretaries and receptionists may prevent suppliers' sales personnel from talking directly to users or deciders.

The decision-making unit model helps us to identify the roles of key personnel who may be involved in a purchase. A look at procurement procedures will demonstrate that in most organisations, the procurement department will be attempting to pursue the roles of decider, approver, buyer and gatekeeper; although this creates a great volume of work!

TASK

Analyse the decision-making unit in your organisation. Who are the various decision makers. Are there differences between buying goods and services? Which of these roles do you perform?

Purchasing's Roles

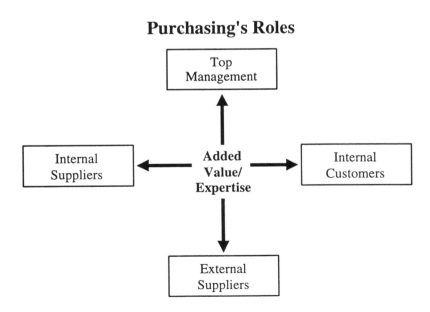

In addition to the organisational actors referred to in Webster and Wind's model, it is also important to note that procurement has a number of client groups. These are: top management, internal customers and suppliers within the purchasing organisation, and external suppliers/ contractors. All of these groupings need to be convinced of the mission of the purchasing department. This requires strong leadership by the procurement managers.

Top Management

The executive of the organisation, responsible for strategic decision making.

Internal Customers

This grouping will consist of those individuals and departments requiring a service from procurement. The service may consist of purchasing a requirement from an external supplier or, alternatively, the service may be help and advise on aspects of procurement.

Internal Suppliers

Procurement will also depend on other individuals and departments in the organisation to achieve their service. For example, by seeking advice from a technical section to help develop a specification, the section will be acting as an internal supplier of information.

External Suppliers

In accordance with our earlier analysis of Porter's work on value chains, the central role of procurement is to provide added value to the procurement process. By adding value, procurement will be providing a service which will improve some aspect of the purchase. In best practice organisations, such as IBM, Nissan and Rover, only a small proportion of the buyers' time is spent on administrative activities. The aim should be to reduce the burden of administrative work through the adoption of information technology and refined processes.

SmithKline Beecham

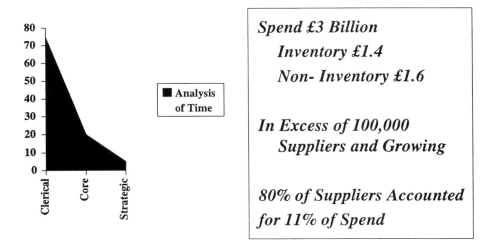

Spend £3 Billion
    Inventory £1.4
    Non- Inventory £1.6

In Excess of 100,000
    Suppliers and Growing

80% of Suppliers Accounted
for 11% of Spend

An example of an organisation which is undergoing the transition from a low status function to one that provides improved added value is SmithKline Beecham.

SmithKline Beecham is one of the top 12 UK listed companies. In 1993, it had £6 billion of sales and operated in four business sectors: pharmaceuticals, consumer health, animal health and clinical laboratories.

Consultants were commissioned by the Group in 1993 to discover their expenditure on outside goods and services. The firm of consultants reported that the spend was approximately £1 billion. A second firm of management consultants were also used, and they provided a more accurate figure – £3 billion. For years, the company did not have a true picture of the amount of money spent on outside suppliers! This is typical of many organisations.

An analysis of the use of time of purchasing personnel in the UK found that approximately 75% of the typical buyer's time was spent carrying out clerical tasks. As part of their purchasing initiative, a five-year goal was set to reduce this time to 10%. The other 90% should be spent on 'core' activities negotiating requirements with internal customers; selecting sources of supply; supplier negotiation; supplier management; as well as 'strategic' activities – long-term improvements to the service provided by the function and achieving long-term improvements from the supplier base.

As their ex-Purchasing Director, Mark Ralf, commented in 'Strategic Procurement in the 1990s: Concepts and Cases' (1995):

> The demand from the customer is incredible: year on year cost improvement, year on year service improvement, year on year quality and innovation transfer. Every time we, as customers, buy a new car we expect more free features and higher standard quality, or we become irritated when things break. The resulting demands down the supply chain are therefore for quality, innovation and value to the customer.

SmithKline Beecham

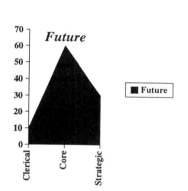

Means:

Widening the Horizon & Scope of Purchasing.

Focus on Non-Production Spend

Select Appropriate Supplier Relationships

Standardise Purchasing Processes

Improved Supply Chain Management

For further detail of SmithKline Beecham's purchasing strategy see Professor Richard Lamming and Professor Andrew Cox 'Strategic Procurement in the 1990s: Concepts and Cases' (1995).

The Varying Nature of Purchasing and Supply

Practitioners are quick to point out that not all organisations operate in the same way. A lot of attention has tended to focus on manufacturing purchasing strategies, particularly on Just in Time and, latterly, the concept of 'lean supply' (discussed later in this book). Equally, many of the theories are not applicable to many sectors or many smaller organisations.

Just as there are dangers in treating all purchasing solutions as universally applicable, there are equally faults in treating every situation as totally different. Many of the principles of purchasing are capable of being transferred to different sectors and sizes of organisations. There are a number of sectors in which purchasing and supply operates:

Primary Sector Extractive Organisations

These organisations are in the business of extracting a product or material, such as the mining of ores or the extraction of oil.

Manufacturing Sector

The key function of this sector is to manufacture by processing, transforming, converting, fabricating or assembling parts or sub-assemblies into finished or intermediate products for sale to external customers. Non-manufacturing parts or subassemblies bought from outside suppliers include consumables (often called maintenance, repair and operating supplies (MRO)), capital equipment and services.

Tertiary Sector - Wholesale or Retail Organisations

The principal business of firms operating in this sector is distribution of products whether to consumers or industrial customers. The key difference is that there is a small internal transformation process converting inputs received from suppliers into completed products. Products bought in this sector are referred to as 'goods for resale'.

Tertiary Sector - Service Organisations

There is obviously a wide variety of service-type organisations. The category includes local and central government organisations (note that they are there to provide services to the public), educational institutions, utilities such as water, gas and electricity, financial institutions, and professional service organisations (consultants).

In addition to the type of sector in which an organisation operates, size also can have an impact on the techniques deployed by the purchasing function to achieve value for money. Size can be related to the purchasing spend. Larger organisations will generally:

- have more opportunity to employ specialists in the function: titles such as Purchasing Analyst or Procurement Policy Adviser are becoming more common;

- have greater power and influence over the supplier base.

What should matter is not necessarily size itself since many of the best practices exercised by the larger organisations can be adopted by small organisations because of the scale of their purchases relative to individual suppliers and the market as a whole. Some examples of best practice purchasing adopted by SMEs (Small, Medium Sized Enterprises) will be identified in this text.

TASK

Which sector does your organisation operate in? Is it unique? In what ways? How do these factors have an impact on the management of external resources?

Training and Development

The new challenges of improved external resource management have placed demands for higher numbers of skilled and trained professionals. There is no doubt that careers and qualifications in purchasing and supply have received greater recognition over the last decade. Training and education in procurement has a crucial role to play in ensuring that relationships with procurement's client groups – top management, internal and external suppliers and customers – are managed effectively. Paul Cousins of Bath University in research published in 1995 found that the qualification levels of purchasing personnel are increasing. The major professional qualification is run by the Chartered Institute of Purchasing and Supply. There are two stages to the Institute's scheme:

Foundation Stage which provides a broad background to the business environment and the subjects assessed through examination are:

- Introduction to Purchasing and Supply Chain Management
- Management Principles and Practice
- Economics
- Quantitative Studies
- Business Accounting.

Students having degrees, higher national diplomas or other management qualifications can apply to the Institute for exemptions from this stage.

Professional Stage: purchasers can move on to the professional stage of CIPS which provides a detailed analysis of best practice procurement. The units of the professional stage are as follows:

PROFESSIONAL STAGE - CORE SUBJECTS
PSCM I: Strategy
PSCM II: Tactics and Operations
PSCM III: Legal Aspects
Case Study

PROFESSIONAL STAGE - SPECIALIST OPTIONS
Purchasing
Stores and Inventory Management
Distribution
Commercial Relationships

PROFESSIONAL STAGE - ELECTIVE SUBJECTS
The Project
Operations Management
Marketing
Project and Contract Management
Retail Merchandise Management
International Purchasing

In addition to the compulsory units, four subjects are taken from the list of optional and elective subjects.

NVQ/SVQ: another choice for training is provided through vocational qualifications. The Purchasing and Supply Lead Body have established competence-based qualifications which are designed to show the individual's ability in the workplace. The Lead Body is composed of senior practitioners selected to represent the interest and requirements of those working in the purchasing and supply function.

Degrees/ Masters Programmes: a number of leading universities have introduced degree programmes specialising in purchasing management. These include Coventry, Glamorgan and the University of North London. In addition, a research-based masters programme is offered at Bath University, under Professor Richard Lamming, and

Birmingham University offers a specialist MBA in Strategic Procurement. The increasing number of programmes and their level indicate the improving academic standing of the discipline.

Central Unit on Procurement 'Certificate of Competence': the certificate programme was launched in 1990 for public sector procurement staff. It provides a framework for professional training and career development and exempts delegates from the foundation stage of the Chartered Institute of Purchasing and Supply's scheme.

In addition to these taught programmes, organisations often use consultants to provide specialist in-house training. What is important is that people are being trained and educated in ever increasing numbers to meet the challenges of contemporary purchasing and supply management. This will help to improve the management of external resources.

References/ Further Study

Baily, Farmer, Jessop and Jones *Purchasing Principles and Management* 7th Edition (1994) Pitman Publishing

Chapman et al 'Purchasing: No Time for Lone Rangers' *McKinsey Quarterly* Number 2 (1997)

Ernst and Young *Good Management of Purchasing* (1993)

Jones *Getting it Together* (1991) Heinemann

Peters *A Passion for Excellence* (1985) New York

Peters and Waterman *In Search of Excellence* (1982) Harper and Row

Porter *Competitve Strategy* (1980) Free Press

Porter *Competitve Advantage: Creating and Sustaining Superior Performance* (1985) The Free Press

Professor Richard Lamming *Beyond Partnership: Strategies for Innovation and Lean Supply* (1993) Prentice Hall

Professor Richard Lamming and Professor Andrew Cox *Strategic Procurement in the 1990s: Concepts and Cases* (1995) Chartred Institute of Purchasing and Supply

Slack, Chambers, Harland, Harrison and Johnston *Operations Management* (1995) Pitman Publishing

Webster and Wind 'Modelling the Industrial Buying Process' *Journal of Purchasing and Materials Management* (Summer) (1982)

chapter two
Contract Management

Most commercial relationships rely on written contracts to establish the rights and duties of both purchaser and supplier organisations. In essence, contract management is a process which ensures that a contract is performed to a standard which fully meets the objectives and expectations agreed between the supplier and the purchasing organisation. Effective contract management runs from the identification of the requirement through to the completion of the contract.

The objectives of contract management need to be set for each particular contract, but may include some or all of the following:

- To manage all aspects of the relationship between the supplier and the purchaser's customers.
- To ensure the delivery of cost-effective and reliable goods and services to cost and agreed performance standards.
- To achieve maximum effort from the supplier and to seek continual improvements throughout the duration of the contract.
- To focus on future requirements and so explore developments in the supply market to then improve subsequent contracts.

The Benefits of Contract Management

- Improved Control in the Execution of the Contract

- Improved Performance by the Supplier so that we Obtain the Product/ Service that we Want, when we Want it

- Better Value for Money through Improved Control of Costs and Quality

- Better Anticipation of Risks (What Can Go Wrong in the Performance of the Contract)

- Better Management of the Legal and Commercial Issues

It is difficult to predict where problems might arise, but effective contract management with regular communication with the supplier should help to identify the potential for problems.

By anticipating problems, effective contract management can prevent disputes. Areas of risk need to be identified first, but some will be more likely to occur than others, and much of this will depend on what the contract is actually for, the time period and also the state of the supply market. In a recession, for example, more companies are likely to face cash flow problems because of the shortage of business that is likely to occur. Under such conditions, a major risk is that the supplier chosen could fall into insolvency. If this happens, the purchaser may not be supplied with the products or services required at all. The risks present in each contract will vary. The contract manager needs to evaluate these risks, the likelihood that they may occur, and then manage these accordingly.

Anticipation of Problems

- The Purchaser Wants to Minimise Costs whilst the Supplier will Want to Maximise Profits - this is usually the Main Cause of Conflict
- The Contract is not properly Prepared for eg. the Specification is Prepared in a Rush and Is Incomplete
- Changed Requirements Result in Changes Being Made to the Contract. This will normally Cost more Money and Take a longer than Planned Completion Time
- The Supplier Might Experience Cash Flow Difficulties and then ultimately, Cash Flow Problems
- The Supplier Fails to Comply with Requirements Stated in the Contract
- A Lack of Communication Results in unnecessary Work and Cost
- Prices for Materials and Labour Spiral Upwards - Resulting in Increased Costs

The skills of a contract manager include a knowledge of specific aspects.

Skills of a Contract Manager

- Products/ Services Required
- Contractual Terms
- Writing Contracts & Specifications
- Forming Relationships with Customers & Suppliers
- Negotiation Skills

To achieve effective contracts management, the purchaser should aim to be an intelligent customer. An 'intelligent' customer is a general description applied to a business area rather than to an individual. A business area would be described as an intelligent customer when its culture and procedures successfully enable the procurement of a product or service for value for money.

The Intelligent Customer

Define Business Needs

Review

What to Buy

Obtain Performance

Determine Value/ Cost

Manage the Relationship

Know the Market

Make the Agreement

Business Needs

The purchaser needs to ensure that the needs of the business are being optimised. The use of purchase portfolio analysis referred to earlier can help identify supplier strategy.

What to Buy

The requirements of the service have to be specified by the use of a performance or conformance specification.

Value/ Cost

The purchaser needs to analyse the full life-cycle costs of the requirement. There will be trade-offs between cost and service levels – very high service levels, such as extremely short and consistent response times for a service, can be very expensive to procure.

Knowing the Market

A knowledge of the market place is necessary, but this can be difficult to achieve in practice. The intelligent customer needs to be aware of what suppliers can offer, and what developments are taking place in the market.

Contracts

A contract forms the link between the organisation's requirements and the actual service provision. It must be flexible enough to allow change but rigorous enough to give adequate protection. A sound contract provides a useful reference point for both parties and reduces the risk of dispute.

Managing the Relationship

The intelligent customer will have a clear understanding of what the supplier is capable of providing. Experience suggests that a close partnership can be a most successful approach.

Service Quality

The product or service supplied should have agreed measures of performance set up. These need to maintained and improved upon.

Monitor/ Review

The effectiveness of the service needs to be monitored by the intelligent customer, to ensure that the customer is satisfied with the service quality.

The relationship with the supplier has a great deal of impact on the actual results achieved. Teamwork is necessary to achieve the results that are required. There needs to be collaboration with the supplier and the problems that can often arise in contracts need to be solved. Communication between the organisations involved is important.

Managing the Supplier Relationship

Improve Aspects of Performance

Competitive Tendering

A buying method common to many larger contracts is the selection of suppliers through competitive tender. Competitive tendering is designed to:

- be open and, even under the closest scrutiny, give no cause or justification to allegations of favoritism or improper conduct;
- discourage the development of cartels, monopolies or other forms of anti-competitive action;
- encourage the development of open, innovative and competitive markets with an interest in our work, so that more suppliers are able to compete for our contracts and orders so maximising our opportunities to gain value for money.

IDENTIFY THE REQUIREMENT	Specify Requirements Contract Strategy Evaluation Criteria
SOURCING THE MARKET	Research Contractors Prequalification Criteria
INVITATION TO TENDER	Contractual Terms Specification
TENDER EVALUATION	Tender Evaluation Post Tender Negotiation
AWARD OF CONTRACT & PERFORMANCE	Contract Award Contract Control

The aim of the tendering process is to select the bid proposal which represents the best overall value for money by a balance between quality, performance, delivery, risk and cost. The criteria used in making this judgment, and their relative importance, should be agreed before inviting bids (the evaluation criteria).

The tender documents completed by the supplier represent an offer which, if unconditionally accepted by the buyer, will form a legally binding contract. Sellers are also prone to make promises at this stage to win business – promises which they can be held to if their bid is accepted.

All invitations to tender must be identical so individual tenderers must not be offered different terms or information. They should also be allowed a reasonable period to prepare and submit their bids. All responses to invitations to tender should be conducted under sealed bid conditions. Each bid should therefore be kept secure until the bid opening time is reached.

The bid will need to assess the bids, making judgments on financial, technical, contractual and personnel matters. An important principle is that the assessment process must be systematic, thorough and fair and seen to be so.

In order to make a full assessment of each bid, the following factors need to be considered:

Capability Assessment which should establish whether the tenderer has the capability (including the personnel, support systems and experience) to deliver. The analysis should also consider the effects of any innovative variations proposed.

Technical Assessment which should establish whether tenders can meet the requirements included in the specification. The assessment should also consider whether there is sufficient capacity available and seek assurances manpower and facilities are adequate to meet the requirement.

Quality Assessment which should establish whether tenderers can deliver the service to the appropriate quality standards. The team should consider the adequacy of the proposed systems of quality control by contract monitoring and taking remedial actions to prevent problems from re-occurring.

Financial Assessment which should check that all relevant costs are included; establish any adjustments needed to make bids comparable; and assess the effects of any proposed changes in price formulae over the life of the contract.

An important aspect of the tender evaluation is to undertake risk analysis. There are a multitude of different risks which can be experienced in making a purchase agreement, such as the risk of an inadequate specification and supplier failure.

The contract between the purchaser and supplier forming the commercial relationship between the two organisations will generally consist of written terms of business. These should comprise a specification and the contractual terms and conditions of business.

The Specification

The purchasing organisation needs to develop a specification of requirements. A specification can be defined as a statement of requirements satisfied by the procurement of a product or service. Specifications have two functions: they communicate to a supplier the purchaser's requirements and they provide criteria against which the goods or services actually supplied can be compared. The specification therefore defines what the purchaser wishes to buy and, consequently, what the supplier is expected to provide.

A specification needs to be sufficiently tight to ensure that the supplier is contractually bound to provide the level of service required. However, if the specification is very detailed and explicit, it can prevent the supplier from using expertise to propose innovative solutions and, therefore, the opportunity to offer better value for money to the purchaser. An effective specification will:

- state the requirement clearly, concisely, logically and unambiguously;
- contain enough information for potential suppliers to decide and cost the products/services they will offer;
- permit offered products/services to be evaluated against defined criteria;
- provide equal opportunities for all potential suppliers to offer a product/service which satisfies the needs of the purchaser and which may incorporate alternative technical solutions.

A specification which is too tightly defined may of course result in less choice for the purchaser and, therefore, less competition in the market place. According to Beehan in *Purchasing in Government*, Longman (1994) other examples of specifications which may unnecessarily restrict competition are those which:

- are written around a specific product or service, and slanted towards few suppliers, thus reducing or precluding competition;
- which are too prescriptive, and over specify, not allowing potential suppliers sufficient scope to use their available expertise;
- which do not allow potential suppliers to offer alternative, innovative solutions that give better value for money.

In the use of specifications, there is a clear distinction between performance and conformance specifications.

Types of Specification

Conformance	*Performance*
• Prescribe the Exact Characteristics of the Product or Service to be Provided by the Supplier	• Leave the Precise Nature of the Characteristics of the Product or Service to be Determined by the Supplier

Performance

Performance refers to those specifications which define the standard of performance required under the contract. The performance specification should specify the purchaser's requirements in terms of: the outputs to be achieved by the supplier; the quality of the product/ service to be provided; and the requirements in terms of time.

For a cleaning contract, as an example, the specification should identify: the areas to be cleaned; the frequency and particular details about when the cleaning should be performed (the time element); and the requirements of the level of cleanliness (the quality element). The cleaning contractor would then propose appropriate levels of resources to satisfy the purchaser's requirements. The resources would include manpower and materials for the contract.

Conformance

Under a conformance specification, the purchaser would define precisely the characteristics of the contract. In the case of the cleaning contract, the purchaser would specify how the work should be done, the minimum manpower to do the work at any particular time, and also the use of certain cleaning materials. This method prescribes solutions to the supplier, whereas the use of performance specifications allows the supplier to propose solutions to the purchaser's requirements.

The development of a specification should involve close and continuous liaison between the user, who may be responsible for drafting the specification, and procurement staff. The involvement of potential suppliers can also provide a valuable input to the development of a specification.

In terms of developing specifications for service contracts, the service specification defines what the purchaser or client organisation wishes to buy, what the supplier is to provide, and there should also be an explicit statement of the work required. So the specification may indicate:

- **What Is Being Required:** in terms of the nature and scope of the service.
- **Contract Details:** the type and duration of the contract.
- **Responsibilities of the Purchaser:** this allows access and information, authorises work carried out by the supplier, payment, issues changes to the specification and monitoring of the supplier.
- **Responsibilities of the Supplier:** provision of resources for the contract (people, materials, etc.) working to timescales, responding in timely manner to queries raised, invoicing and other administration, contract monitoring, reports, etc.
- **Miscellaneous:** profiles of locations of the work, security arrangements, interfaces between purchaser and supplier, working hours and accessibility, etc.

Performance Measures

The aims of contractual performance measurement are to:

- ensure that there is a consensus between individual, departmental and corporate aims and objectives;
- compare actual with planned performance;
- ascertain the causes of poor performance and provide a basis for improvement;
- identify the contribution of purchasing to the results achieved by the organisation;
- Provide an incentive to efficient purchasing and to maintain highly-motivated staff.

It is particularly important to undertake performance measurement on contracts. Purchasing organisations need to be able to assess the outputs of the contract, and therefore determine whether or not the contract is a success. The following outputs of a contract can be measured for example.

Specifications	*Performance Measures*
A Statement of Needs to be Satisfied by the Procurement of External Resources	The Supplier's Ability to Conform to Aspects of the Specification
Should Cover Aspects of:	*Aspects of Conformance to Agreed Targets to be Quantitatively Assessed*
Quality	Proportion of Defects %
Time	Service Levels %
Communication	Response Times Number
Administration	Correct Invoicing %

Time

In almost all contracts, time is a variable. Consider a contract between a purchasing organisation and a supplier to provide professional advice. A number of aspects of the consultancy supplier's performance may be measured. An important output of the contract may be written reports which set out particular recommendations which should be adopted by the purchasing organisation. These reports may be required by a certain due date. In addition, the consultancy supplier may also be required to attend arranged meetings, perhaps with key individuals at pre-arranged times. Failure to comply with these key dates could constitute a breach of contract, and so it is important that a representative of the purchasing organisation maintains a simple data file recording aspects of the timely performance of the contract. This is obviously a simple example; in more complex contracts, timing of the supplier's outputs can obviously have great significance on the performance of the contract.

Quality

Quality is rather a general word, and can mean different things to different people. However, in this context, the supplier's performance needs to conform with any stated specification. As we saw earlier in this chapter, there is a clear distinction between performance and conformance specifications. Performance refers to those specifications which define the standard of performance required under the contract. The performance specification should specify the purchaser's requirements in terms of the outputs to be achieved by the supplier and the quality of the product/ service to be provided.

In a consultancy contract, for example, the supplier may be given certain objectives. These may include:

- the provision of relevant and appropriate advice;
- the advice given should include an implementation plan;
- the supplier should respond responsively to any queries raised by the purchasing organisation;
- objectives set to reduce operating costs.

Alternatively, under a conformance specification, the purchaser would define precisely the characteristics of the service contract. It could be argued that a conformance specification would not be relevant to our example of a consultancy contract. However, under certain conditions, it may be possible to specify the minimum manpower to do the work at any particular time, and also the use of particular grades of consultant varying from senior partner to low-level administrative support.

In the performance of the contract, the purchasing organisation will take on certain responsibilities such as allowing access and information, and authorising work carried out by the supplier. In addition, in return for the supplier's product or service offering, payments will be made.

In addition, quality can also cover non-tangible aspects of the supplier's performance. The purchaser may feel satisfied with the achievements and motivation of the supplier. The personal commitment given by individuals can of course have a significant bearing on the relationship between the two organisations. The purchaser may be able to express satisfaction with these aspects of the supplier's performance.

Cost Control

The supplier's performance can also be measured in terms of ability to conform to pre-agreed prices and other related costs. In many industries, there is considerable effort exerted by both the purchaser and supplier organisations to reduce costs. The generation of ideas to continually improve and reduce costs, whilst maintaining or improving quality, can be measured.

Once the contract is underway, the purchaser will need to monitor performance. A system needs to be established whereby the supplier reports progress, and the programme of the actual work done compared with a plan of the work.

Finally, we need to have effective administration of the contract. Changes made to contracts should be negotiated with the supplier so that any disruption is minimised. Payments should be made promptly and any disputes that do arise should be effectively dealt with.

Effective Contract Management

is achieved through:

- Managing the Supplier Relationship
  +
- Managing Risks
  +
- Contract Monitoring
  +
- Effective Administration

Contractual Terms and Conditions

The specification and related performance measures may form part of the contract. To understand the role of contracts in commercial relationships, we need to investigate the fundamentals of legal contracts. A contract can be defined as: 'A legally binding agreement made between at least two parties, by which rights are acquired by one or more to acts of forbearances on the part of the other or others', or 'An Agreement, enforceable at law, entered into freely between a willing buyer and a willing seller.' For a contract to come into being the following legal requirements are necessary:

- **Consideration:** 'the price for which a promise is bought'. In other words each party should give something that may be valued in money or money's worth, however slight. The adequacy of consideration is for agreement between the parties. Under Scottish Law, consideration is not an essential element of a contract.
- **Intention to Create Legal Relations:** a contract is not a 'gentleman's agreement'; when entering into a contract the parties must understand that the agreement is enforceable at law.
- **Capacity to Contract:** certain people, such as minors, do not have the capacity to enter into particular contracts.
- **Reality of Consent:** there must be a 'meeting of minds for a common purpose': both parties must agree and understand the objectives of the contract.
- **Lawfulness of Object:** the contract must not be for an illegal purpose or be contrary to some statute or common law. The intention of the contract must be clear and the terms certain. It must be capable of performance.

- **Agreement:** agreement between the parties consists o▮
called the 'offeror' and an unqualified acceptance of this
called the 'offeree'.

Offers

Offers must be stated in certain, clear terms with the intention on the part of the offer▮
be legally bound in the event of there being an unqualified acceptance of the offer.

An offer must be distinguished from an 'invitation to treat'. An example of an invitation to
treat is when retailers display priced articles; they are not making offers for contracts of sale
but are holding themselves ready to consider offers made to them by customers. A useful
case which illustrates this point is provided by the *Pharmaceutical Society of Great Britain
v Boots Cash Chemists (Southern) Ltd* (1953). The facts of the case were:

> Boots Edgware branch had converted to a self-service system, now familiar of course
> at most retail outlets. Customers selected their purchases from shelves on which the
> goods were displayed and put them into the basket before taking them to the till. The
> case was brought on the basis of drugs selected from a shelf which were included in
> the Poisons List referred to in Section 17 of the Pharmacy and Poisons Act 1933.
> However, the drugs were not classified as dangerous drugs and nor did they require
> a doctor's prescription. Section 18 of the Act required the sale of such drugs to take
> place in the presence of a qualified pharmacist. Boots ensured that every sale of
> drugs on the list was supervised at the till by a qualified pharmacist. The
> Pharmaceutical Society's role was to ensure that the provisions of the Act were
> enforced and brought the action against Boots because it was claimed that the
> retailer was infringing Section 18 of the Act.

> It was held that the display of goods on the shelves did not constitute an offer. The
> contract of sale was not made when the customer selected the drugs from the
> shelves, but when money was offered by the customer at the till and accepted by the
> company employee. The court held that the supervision required by the Act was
> provided at the time of purchase.

An offer is capable of being converted into an agreement by acceptance. So an offer must
be a definite promise as opposed to a mere offer to negotiate. This is what contrasts an
offer from an invitation to treat.

An example of an invitation treat is the inducement provided in suppliers' circulars or
catalogues advertising goods. This is a particularly important aspect now for many
organisations that purchase via supplier catalogues. The same is also usually the case with
advertisements published in newspapers or periodicals.

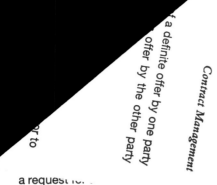

sed in a catalogue have increased in price or
 ~w offer on the basis of the increased price or

ing Offers

of goods or services, usually made in response to
a request ιc. . ɔle suppliers. Tenders can take the following forms:

- **Single Offer:** acceptance of such a tender constitutes a contract.
- **Sole Supplier:** the purchaser receiving the tender may agree to take all the requirements for the products or services supplied from the supplier submitting the tender. This agreement does not oblige them to make any orders at all, but if they do require goods from within the category agreed they must take them from the tenderer.
- **Standing Offer:** arrangements are set up with suppliers to simplify the ordering of routinely purchased items or services. Under these agreements, the purchaser makes an agreement with a supplier for a tender to supply goods or services to named people working in the purchasing organisation. The aim is to enable those customers to demand from the supplier the products or services required without the need to tender competitively for each requirement on an as and when required basis. The tender enquiry will generally contain a specification of the products or services and include estimated quantities required over the duration of the agreement. The purchaser will usually not include any guarantee that any or all of the quantities will be bought. Tenderers then submit bids on this basis. Such an arrangement is normally referred to as a framework agreement. Such agreements may also be called 'blanket contracts', or 'call off contracts' which are becoming an increasingly popular supply arrangement in commercial relationships.

Under a call-off arrangement, a new contract is actually made each time the buyer places an order on the supplier. There is usually no obligation on the supplier to deliver anything at all! The risk can be limited by paying the supplier a token sum 'in consideration' for keeping the tendered offer open until the period of the arrangement expires.

Call Off/Framework Agreements

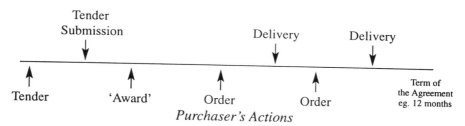

A new contract is formed each time the supplier delivers the required product or service. There is a new offer and acceptance

An interesting case is provided by the old London County Council in *Percival Ltd v LCC* (1918). Percival was awarded a contract to supply goods up to a certain amount to the LCC over a certain period. The LCC's orders did not come up to the expected amount and so Percival sued for breach of contract. The court held in favour of LCC, as they decided that each order made a separate contract. There was, therefore, no obligation for LCC to order from Percival the amount specified.

Counter Offers

An offer will terminate when the offeree (the person to whom the offer has been made) rejects it. A counter offer has the effect of cancelling the original offer. A case which highlights this point is provided in *Hyde v Wrench* (1840) where the defendant offered to sell his farm for £1,000. The plaintiff's agent made an offer of £950 and Wrench then asked for a few days to think about the offer. He subsequently wrote to Hyde saying that he could not accept it. Hyde then wrote back stating that he would accept the original offer of £1,000, but Wrench had decided that he no longer wanted to sell to Hyde. Hyde, the plaintiff, then sued on the basis of specific performance. The court held that the plaintiff could not enforce this 'acceptance' because the counter offer was a rejection of the original offer and had therefore had the effect of terminating the offer.

Acceptance

This is positive, unqualified assent to all the terms of the offer. The following rules apply:

- Acceptance must be total and unqualified, otherwise it is not an acceptance but an offer called a 'counter offer' which the other party in turn can either accept or reject.
- Acceptance must be communicated to the offeror unless the offeror when making the offer stipulated that certain course of conduct would create sufficient acceptance. However, negative instruction from the offeror is insufficient to make a contract; silence is not acceptance.

Acceptance

- Acceptance is an Agreement to all the Terms of an Offer

- A Counter Offer rejects the original Offer

- Acceptance can be made verbally/in writing/by conduct

- The Offeror can specify the mode of communication of Acceptance

---

If letters sent through the post are a proper and reasonable method of communication between the parties, then acceptance is deemed complete as soon as a letter of acceptance is posted, provided it has been properly stamped and addressed. This rule even applies if the letter is lost or destroyed in the post. This postal rule does seem a little harsh on the supplier (assuming that the buyer is accepting the supplierís offer). This was held in *Household Fire Insurance Co v Grant* (1879). The facts of this case were as follows:

The defendant handed a written application for shares in the Household Fire Insurance to their agent in Glamorgan. The application had stated that the company's bankers had been paid £5, which was a deposit of 5p per share on an application for 100 shares. It also stated that Grant would pay 95p per share within 12 months of the allocation. The agent then sent this letter of application to the insurance company which was based in London. Their company secretary wrote a letter of allotment in favour of Grant which was subsequently posted to him. However, the defendant never received the letter. The company credited him with dividends of 25p, but the company then went into liquidation. The liquidator sued for £94.75 which was the balance due on the shares allocated. It was held that Grant was liable for the sum, as acceptance was complete when the letter of allotment was posted.

Letters of Intent

An instruction to proceed (ITP) or letter of intent given to a supplier/contractor enables work to be commenced before the full contractual details have been agreed. This is now very rarely used because the letter itself, depending on its actual wording, can constitute an acceptance of a supplier's/contractor's offer. Furthermore, if a contractor commences work and later refuses to accept terms regarded as vital by the purchaser, there is a risk that the purchaser might have to stop the work and pay for abortive work carried out up to that date. The advice is that letters of intent should rarely be used due to lack of trust in many contractual relationships.

The Battle of the Forms

A leading case which demonstrates the 'battle of the forms' was provided by *Butler Machine Tool Co Ltd v ExCellO Corporation (England) Ltd* (1979). In this case, Butler quoted for terms for a machine tool on 23 May 1969, at a price of £75,535 and delivery to be within ten months from the date of order. The contractual terms included within the quotation were stated expressly to prevail over any contractual terms contained in the buyerís order. One of Butler's standard terms was a contract price adjustment or price variation clause.

Ex-Cell-O ordered the machine on 27 May 1969, but their order included their own terms of contract. These terms did not include a price variation clause and the delivery date was changed to 10-11 months. Their order form also included an acknowledgement slip. This slip was returned to Ex-Cell-O on 5 June 1969, and it stated: 'Acknowledgement: please sign and return to Ex-Cell-O. We accept your order on the terms and conditions stated therein - and undertake to deliver by.....date......signed.'

The machine was ready for delivery by September 1970, but Ex-Cell-O delayed taking delivery because of necessary arrangements to their production schedule. They eventually took delivery in November 1970, and Butler claimed £2,892 due under their contract price variation clause. Ex-Cell-O refused to pay the sum arguing that the contract was based on their terms.

The Court of Appeal held that there was indeed no price variation clause present in the contract and so Ex-Cell-O did not have to pay the additional £2,892. Butler's quote was an offer, Ex-Cell-O's order was a counter offer which was accepted by the return of the acknowledgement slip.

A similar case was provided in 1986 in *Sauter Automation v Goodman (Mechanical Services)*. Sauter tendered to supply the control panel of a boiler ordered by Goodman. The tender included a 'retention of title' clause, sometimes called a Romalpa clause (see Chapter 3). Title passes when the buyer has paid for goods, even though the buyer may have possession of them. If the clause operates, should the purchasing organisation go into receivership or liquidation, then the seller is able to recover the goods and the proceeds of resale by the purchasing organisation. Goodman had accepted Sauter's tender on the basis of their standard terms of contract which, unsurprisingly, did not include a retention of title clause. Goodman later delivered the panel which the court held was acceptance of the buyer's terms. Goodman went into liquidation leaving Sauter unable to recover the price of the goods as they were an unsecured creditor.

Mistake

Mistakes often occur in the formation of a contract. In the pricing of large-value contracts, for example, arithmetical errors may occur when the supplier fails to calculate the total price of the bid correctly. In *Higgins (W) Ltd v Northampton Corporation* (1927), the plaintiff (Higgins) entered into a contract with the corporation to construct a number of houses. The plaintiff had made an arithmetical error in arriving at the price, as a sum of money had been deducted twice. The corporation made a contract with Higgins to build the houses assuming that the price arrived at by the plaintiff was correct. It was held that the contract was binding on the parties.

However, if one of the parties takes unfair advantage of such a mistake, then the contract can be void for mistake.

Mistake

> "It is now clear that a contract will be set aside if the mistake of the one party has been induced by a material representation of the other; or if one party, knowing that the other is mistaken about the terms of the offer...lets him remain under his delusion and concludes a contract on the mistaken terms instead of pointing out the mistake."
>
> *Lord Denning*

TASK

Have you dealt with a supplier's tender or offer which included an arithmetical error? How was the situation resolved?

Implied and Express Terms

By contracting work out, an organisation has to rely on the competence and continued interest of the chosen supplier. Equally, the chosen supplier makes a risk assessment of the work to be done for the purchasing organisation. The supplier can of course underestimate the risks involved. An example of this is provided by the heavy engineering supplier, Davy Corporation, in 1991, when over £100 million was lost on the construction of an oil rig for the Emerald oil field near the Shetland Isles. Davy had agreed to complete the project for a fixed price without any progress payments (see Chapter 3). Unfortunately, they underestimated the technical and commercial risks involved in the project by a significant margin. Equally, if the purchaser fails to properly plan and execute its resources effectively, the contract will be considerably more risky and will not give value for money.

The agreements made with suppliers may or may not include written terms, and may indeed be made verbally. It would incorrect to think that if there were no contractual terms agreed with the supplier, there would be no contract. A contract will be in existence on the basis of implied terms – the body of law enforced through legislation, case law or custom.

Contract Terms

Implied	Express
Legislation:	Details of the Agreement
Sale of Goods Act 1979	
Supply of Goods & Services 1982	Purchasers/Suppliers
Unfair Contract Terms Act 1977	Contractual Terms
Precedent - Case Law	Model Form Contracts
Custom	

The most common example or form of express terms is a written contract between two parties. Purchasers and suppliers may of course have a battle of forms to establish the use of their own forms of contract. These written contract terms can have a number of important functions:

- defining the obligations of the parties;
- clarifying the agreement (the price, completion, the specification, etc);
- stating which law will apply (for example English);
- providing a system or procedures for settling disputes;
- apportioning liabilities between the parties (for example the purchaser to supply information, to provide accommodation, etc).

Most, though by no means all, agreements with suppliers are made in the form of written contracts. These, include express terms. Express terms do not necessarily need to be written. Oral statements which have an impact on the agreement can also be express terms. It is considered good practice though to record in writing that which is agreed verbally, to eliminate misunderstandings.

Express terms can also modify terms that would otherwise be implied by law. This is an important point and one which we need to concentrate on in a little more detail. Consider the last time you, as a consumer, bought a pair of shoes. It is extremely doubtful that you will have agreed upon a written contract with the retailer, unless you are an extremely pedantic person! There is obviously still a contract with the retailer and in the event of a breach of contract you are given rights as a consumer by the Sale of Goods Act 1979. This Act is an example of a set of implied terms and does not merely apply to consumer contracts; the terms can equally apply to business contracts made between organisations. Purchasers and suppliers will typically amend the terms implied by the law to make their agreements more specific to the goods or services which are being traded. There does not have to be a a written contract; a buyer could simply rely on implied terms for protection and for defining the obligations of the parties. Before we look at the implied terms of the Sale of Goods Act, we should firstly look at the rights of the parties in the event of a breach of contract.

Suppliers may not do as they promised in a contract and can therefore be in breach. Alternatively, it may be felt by the parties involved that there is no need for any written contractual terms as the relationship between the two parties may be based on trust (See Chapter 7). If a disaster should happen, where the supplier becomes insolvent for example, then terms are implied by law and these would then clarify the contractual position. In any agreement though, there are two types of term:

- **A Condition** is a vital term, one going to the root of a contract. In the event of a breach, the innocent party is entitled to treat the contract as at an end (the contract will be repudiated) and to claim damages for the breach.
- **A Warranty** is a term which is subsidiary to the main purpose of the contract, breach of which entitles the innocent party to damages only.

You might well be a little confused about the two types of terms. Written contracts are usually called 'terms and conditions'. This is mere terminology as there will be both conditions (the vital terms) and warranties (the subsidiary terms) within those written clauses. The word 'condition' in law has a specific meaning and one has to distinguish between the two types of term. The classification as a condition or warranty depends on the intention of the parties.

Remedies for Breach

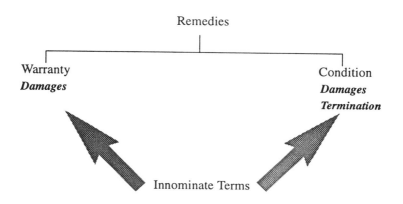

An innominate term can either be a warranty or a condition. The courts will decide whether or not the actions of the parties render the term a warranty or a condition. For example, a purchaser may have stated in a contract that 'time is of the essence' in an attempt to make delivery or completion a condition of the contract. If in the event of lateness the purchaser fails to expedite the goods or service and generally acts as though time really was not that important after all, it would then be difficult for the purchaser to terminate the contract claiming that the supplier is in breach of a condition. It is likely that such a term would be considered an innominate term, and would most probably be construed as a mere breach of warranty.

In the event of a breach of warranty or condition, the purchaser may claim for damages. The converse is of course true when a purchaser is in breach of contract. The sum of damages that may be claimed has principles laid down by case law. It is worth mentioning the leading case involving *Hadley v Baxendale* (1854).

Hadley's mill shaft broke and had to be sent to the makers in Greenwich for repair to serve as a pattern for replacement. Baxendale agreed to transport the shaft to Greenwich, but a breach of contract delayed delivery causing several days lost production at the mill. Hadley claimed £300 for loss of profit. It was held that:

1. The loss did not arise naturally since Baxendale could not foresee that the delay would have stopped the mill. It was quite possible that Hadley may have had a spare

shaft or have been able to get one.

2. The loss could not have been contemplated by both parties at the time of the contract as the probable result of the breach. If Baxendale had been told that any delay would have stopped the mill, the loss would have been in his contemplation and Hadley could have claimed for the lost profit.

The Sale of Goods Act 1979

As we have seen, terms can be implied by statute (legislation), by the courts by precedent set in cases and by custom. As regards legislation which implies terms into contracts, the Sale of Goods Act 1979 lays down important rules for commercial relationships. A contract for the sale of goods is an agreement where the seller transfers or agrees to transfer the property in goods to the buyer for a money consideration (the price). Sections 12 to 15 of the Act contain particularly important terms, and these are as follows:

Sale of Goods Act 1979

Section 12:	Title
Section 13:	Description
Section 14(2):	Satisfaction Quality
Section 14(3):	Fitness for Purpose
Section 15:	Sale by Sample

Section 12: TITLE

There is an implied condition on the part of the seller that they have the right to sell the goods.

Section 13: DESCRIPTION

Where there is a sale of goods by description, there is an implied condition that the goods shall correspond with the description. This is an important term for buyers since it is implied by the act that suppliers need to conform with specifications provided.

Section 14 (2): SATISFACTORY QUALITY

The Sale and Supply of Goods Act 1994 now amends the Sale of Goods Act 1979. Section 14(2) did imply that goods should be of 'merchantable quality'. This has now been replaced by 'satisfactory quality'. According to the new Act, goods are of satisfactory quality if:

For the purpose of this Act, the quality of goods includes their state and condition and the following (among others) are in appropriate cases aspects of the quality of goods:

i. fitness for all purposes for which goods of the kind in question are commonly supplied,
ii. appearance and finish,
iii. freedom from minor defects,
iv. safety, and
v. durability.

The term implied does not extend to any matter making the quality of goods unsatisfactory:

- which is specifically drawn to the buyer's attention before the contract is made,
- where the buyer examines the goods before the contract is made, which that examination ought to reveal, or
- in the case of a contract for sale by sample, which would have been apparent on a reasonable examination of the sample.

Section 14 (3) FITNESS FOR PURPOSE

Where the buyer, expressly or by implication, makes known to the seller any particular purpose for which goods are bought, it is an implied condition that the goods supplied under the contract are reasonably fit for the purpose, unless the circumstances show that either the buyer does not rely on, or it is unreasonable to rely on, the skill and judgment of the seller.

Section 15: SALE BY SAMPLE

In a sale by sample, there are implied conditions that: the bulk shall correspond with the sample; the buyer shall have a reasonable opportunity of comparing bulk with sample; the goods shall be free of any defect rendering them unsatisfactory which would not be apparent on a reasonable examination of the samples.

The Supply of Goods and Services Act 1982

Of particular relevance to the management of service contracts is the Supply of Goods and Services Act (rather than the Sale of Goods Act). The Supply of Goods and Services Act has the effect of extending the provisions of the Sale of Goods Act to contracts which are not just purely for goods. The Sale of Goods applies to contracts of that precise nature, unsurprisingly!

Supply of Goods and Services Act 1982

Part 1
Work and Materials

S2: Title
S3: Description
S4: Fitness for Purpose
S5: Sample

Hire of Goods

S7: Title
S8: Description
S9: Satisfaction Quality
S9: Fitness for Purpose
S10: Sample

Part 2
Supply of Services

S13: Reasonable Care and Skill
S14: Reasonable Time

S15: Reasonable Price

Many commercial contracts do not fall within the definition of a sale of goods. For example:

- Contracts for work and materials, for example a construction contract.
- Design contracts, such as those for research, marketing services, equipment, facilities, etc.
- Contracts of hire (or leasing agreements) such as those for computer hardware, property, vehicles, items of plant, etc.
- Contracts for professional advice, such as information technology services, accounting/finance, marketing and consultancy.

The problem with the Sale of Goods Act is that protection did not apply to the work supplied under such contracts. Part 1 of the Supply of Goods and Services Act relates to 'contracts for the transfer of property in goods' such as contracts for work and materials. The supply of goods is governed by Part 1 of the Act and the services supplied (or the work element) are governed by Part II of the 1982 Act. Contracts of exchange or barter, hire, rental or leasing are governed by Part 1, while contracts for services only are governed by Part II.

In Part 1 of the Act, Sections 2-5 provide for statutory implied terms on the part of the seller similar to those in S.12-15 of the Sale of Goods Act 1979. Contracts for the hire of goods are defined in Section 6 of the Act and Sections 7-10 provide for statutory implied conditions similar to S.12-15 of the Sale of Goods Act. Hire contracts are also commonly referred to as leasing agreements, and under such an arrangement property of the goods does not pass. There is an implied condition in Section 7 of the Act that the supplier has the right to transfer possession of the goods by hiring for the appropriate period. There is also a warranty that the customer will enjoy quiet possession of the goods (so the customer enjoys the use of the goods under the rental agreement).

The Supply of Goods and Services Act includes a number of implied terms relating specifically to services.

Section 13

There is an implied term that where the supplier is acting in the course of a business, the service will be carried out with reasonable care and skill.

Section 14

There is an implied term that where the supplier is acting in the course of a business and the time for the service to be carried out is not fixed by the contract or determined by the course of dealings between the parties, the supplier shall carry out the contract within a reasonable time.

Section 15

There is an implied term that where the consideration is not determined by a contract or by the course of dealings between the parties, the party contracting with the supplier shall pay a reasonable price.

The Unfair Contract Terms Act 1977

Whilst we have explored a number of terms implied by the Sale of Goods Act and the Supply of Goods and Services Act, it is a common practice for suppliers to exclude liability altogether or at least disclaim some of their liabilities implied by these important Acts of Parliament.

The use and application of exclusion clauses is subject to the provisions covered by the Unfair Contract Terms Act. This Act regulates the use of exclusion clauses and severely limits the concept of freedom of contract. In non-consumer sales (where a business is selling to another business) any exclusion clause can only be valid if it passes the test of 'reasonableness'. The Act lists a number of guidelines to help determine whether a term is indeed reasonable.

Strength of the Bargaining Position of the Parties. If one party is in a strong position and the other is weaker in terms of bargaining power, the stronger party may not be allowed to retain the exclusion clause in the contract. In non-consumer sales, the courts will deem most businesses to have equal strength, and therefore, most exclusion clauses will stand!

Availability of Other Supplies. Again, if a supplier is in a monopolistic position so that it is not possible for the buyer to purchase the goods elsewhere, the exclusion clause may not apply.

Inducements Given to Secure Agreement to Inclusion of the Clause. The concession given by the supplier may enable the clause to be deemed reasonable.

The Buyer's Knowledge of the Extent of the Clause. If the buyer is made aware of the existence of the clause then this will enhance the likelihood of its inclusion.

Customs of Trade and Previous Dealings. Exclusion clauses may be usual in the trade or may have been used in previous dealings. In such cases the court may decide that an exclusion clause should apply. In consumer transactions, it is unlikely that previous transactions will be relevant.

Whether the Goods have been Made, Processed
If the seller has been contracted to produce goods
reasonable for the seller to exclude liability for aspe

Under Section 6 of the Unfair Contract Terms Act,
cannot be excluded, and Sections 13-15 cannot
However, Sections 13-15 can be excluded in a non-c
is reasonable.

The Act lists a number of guidelines to help determine   _____nable.
Of these the strength of the bargaining positions of ... parties is the most relevant. In
commercial relationships, the courts will deem most businesses to have equal strength,
and therefore, most exclusion clauses will stand. Therefore, the implied terms of the Sale
of Goods and Supply of Goods and Services Acts can, quite correctly, be excluded.

Impact of Unfair Contract Terms Act 1977

Implied Term SOGA 79 Ammended 94		Consumer	Business
S12:	Title	X	X
S13:	Description	X	Yes
S14(2)	Satisfactory Quality	X	Yes
S14(3)	Fitness for Purpose	X	Yes
S15:	Sample	X	Yes

The Latin phrase 'caveat emptor' (let the buyer beware) has particular significance in
commercial relationships.

Further Reading

This Chapter merely provides an overview of aspects of contract law that can impact on
commercial relationships. For a more detailed analysis of contract law, you may want to
refer to:

Denis Keenan *Advanced Business Law* 8th Edition (1991) Pitman Publishing

Margaret Griffiths *Law for Purchasing and Supply* (1994) Pitman Publishing

chapter three
Key Contractual Terms

Chapter two considered the background to contractual relationships between the purchaser and supplier. Specifications and commercial terms will of course have legal effect if they are incorporated into a binding agreement. If there are no written contract terms, or for that matter no verbal promises or agreements made, then terms will be applied into the contractual relationship through implied terms – principally via legislation and case law. It is important for the buyer to be aware of these points, as enhanced commercial protection is a source of added value which purchasing can provide to the organisation.

The Use of Written Contracts

This chapter focuses on a number of more detailed contractual clauses which may be incorporated in a written agreement made with a supplier. The degree to which the parties rely on the written contract as a basis for their relationship is very much a matter of their long-term dependence and how well they work together. In chapter 7, we will see that organisations may attach far more significance to their working relationship and commitment to continuous improvement than they do to the written contract.

Most, though by no means all, agreements with suppliers are made in the form of written contracts. These, therefore, include express terms. Express terms do not necessarily need to be written. Oral statements which have an impact on the agreement can also be express terms. It is considered good practice though to record in writing that which is agreed verbally, to eliminate misunderstandings.

The contractual terms may be very detailed in their nature. For complex products or services, there may be a significant number of clauses written into a contract. The contract itself may be a standard form of agreement. Standard contracts may be drawn up by:

- either the buying or selling organisation;
- professional bodies such as the Chartered Institute of Purchasing and Supply;
- trade associations: groupings of similar suppliers often establish common contractual terms for their industry.

In a contract for the purchase of goods or services, the parties will generally agree to do the following:

Duties of the Purchaser	*Duties of the Supplier*
• Order a Quantity of Product or Service Required	• Supply the Correct Quantity of the Product or Service Required
• Pay the Supplier for the Work	• Invoice for the Work at the Price Agreed
• State any Particular Requirements Relating to Delivery	• Comply with the Purchaser's Delivery Requirements
• State any Particular Requirements Relating to Timing	• Deliver the Product or Service Required at the Agreed Time

Standard Contracts

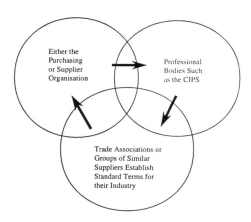

Either the Purchasing or Supplier Organisation

Professional Bodies Such as the CIPS

Trade Associations or Groups of Similar Suppliers Establish Standard Terms for their Industry

Common Contractual Terms
Control of Sub-contractors and Collateral Guarantees

The purchaser in making a contract with a supplier makes an agreement to provide a product or service. Modern industrial activity is based on specialisation and the combining of specialist skills to form an integrated whole. It follows that the supplier may sub-contract parts of work or, for that matter, purchase materials from other specialist suppliers. This is the concept of 'supply chain management'.

Privity of Contract

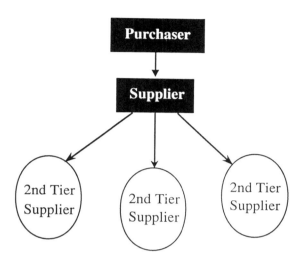

In the diagram, the supplier sub-contracts packages of work to 'second tier' suppliers. The supplier is free to decide the amount of work which can be sub-contracted – unless the purchaser restricts the ability of a supplier to sub-contract work in the contract between the purchaser and the supplier. In law, only a person party to a contract can sue on it. This issue of law is of major importance in the law relating to sub-contractors and suppliers.

Therefore, a purchaser cannot, under the terms of a contract with a supplier, sue a sub-contractor or supplier in contract for breach. Nor can a sub-contractor or supplier have an action under that contract against the purchaser. It is said that there is no privity of contract between the sub-contractor and the purchaser.

A typical contractual clause which the purchaser may invoke with a supplier is as follows:

The Supplier shall not sub-contract any part of the Contract without the Purchaser's written consent. The restriction in this clause shall not apply to minor details nor for any part of which the makers are named in the Contract. The Supplier shall be responsible for all work done and Products or Services provided by all sub-contractors.

The final part of the clause above stated that: 'The Supplier shall be responsible for all work done and Goods or Services provided by all sub-contractors', which underlines the principle of privity of contract.

An exception to this rule is in the case of the creation of a collateral contract or collateral warranties/guarantees. A collateral contract arises when a statement that is not part of the main contract is nevertheless part of another contract related to the same subject matter. In English law, the leading case is *Shanklin Pier v Detel Products* (1951).

> Shanklin Pier made a contract with a main contractor to paint the pier. They specified that the main contractor should use paint to be purchased from Detel Products because Detel had assured Shanklin Pier that the paint would last seven to ten years. The main contractor used the paint but it only lasted three months.
>
> Shanklin Pier successfully sued the paint supplier, Detel Products, on the basis of their assurance that the paint would be suitable even though there was no written contract between the two parties. It was held that there was a collateral contract between them.

The same principle applies when a consumer buys goods and is given a manufacturer's guarantee. The contract is with the retailer, but the guarantee amounts to a collateral contract between the customer and manufacturer.

Collateral Guarantee

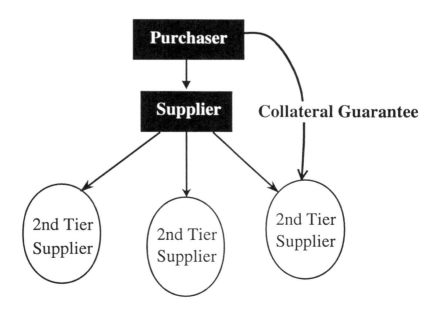

A collateral contract between a second tier supplier (or sub-contractor) can have the following advantages:

- Direct liability is created between the purchaser and the second tier supplier. The purchaser will not need to make a claim through the main supplier.
- The main supplier avoids liability due to the protection provided by the collateral guarantee. This reduces their risk and, potentially, the purchase price to be paid by the purchaser.
- The second tier supplier offering the guarantee stands to gain more credibility for his product offering, and so may gain marketing advantages over competitors.

Payment

The contract between the purchaser and supplier will normally state the payment terms applying in the contract. Here is an example of such a clause:

Unless other arrangements are agreed with the Purchaser, the Supplier will be paid within 30 days of a correctly rendered invoice. The Supplier's invoice should be addressed to the Finance Department and must quote the full Purchase Order number. The Purchaser will not be held liable for delays in payment caused by the Supplierís failure to comply with the invoicing instructions.

So, before progressing an invoice for payment, the purchaser needs to check that the details are in accordance with the purchase order or contract, and any delivery note.

On occasions, the purchase order-invoice-delivery note may not agree as there may be minor discrepancies. There could, for example, be a slight over or under delivery in terms of the quantity ordered. A system could be developed for carrying over minor discrepancies from one invoice to another, in order to avoid the administrative costs of amending the paperwork for the sake of a small amount of money.

Once the purchaser has confirmed that the order is complete, payment should be made in accordance with the payment terms agreed. Prompt payment may of course attract a discount from the price agreed.

Purchasing organisations often fail to comply with the contractual payment details as a way of improving cash flow. In the event of delayed payments to suppliers, the purchasing organisation has access to money which would otherwise have gone out of the business sooner to pay suppliers. Such a practice should be discouraged, since late payment to suppliers will only endanger supplier relationships.

Providing Information

The supplier will generally require information from the purchaser to be able to perform the delivery. It is important for such information to be provided to the supplier in a timely manner. Failure to do so can have a detrimental impact on the contractual delivery or completion date. Information that the purchaser may need to provide can include:

- Specifications
- Delivery details
- People involved
- Timescales of aspects of the work
- Quantity required
- Security regulations.

Many of these details will, of course, be included on the purchase order. In more complex contracts for either products or services however, the specifications of the work may not be agreed up-front in the contract and may evolve over the course of the programme. In such arrangements, it is vital for both parties to communicate the necessary information without unnecessary delay or interference. The following clauses may be useful from time to time:

The Supplier shall state the times by which they require the Purchaser to:
i.   Furnish any specifications or information
ii. Provide access to site
iii. Have completed any other work related to the Contract.

Similarly, the Purchaser may indicate key dates when information is required from the supplier.

In addition:
The Supplier shall submit to the Purchaser for approval such drawings, samples, or other information as may be necessary in the Contract, and the numbers of people involved in the Work

The Supplier shall be responsible for the detailed design of the Work to be supplied under the Contract and of the Works in accordance with the requirements of the Specification.

Designs for manufactured products will normally be submitted in the form of drawings. In cases where the supplier makes a mistake that causes additional expenses due to remedial work, the following clause could be incorporated in a contract:

> Not withstanding approval by the Purchaser of drawings, samples, patterns, models or information submitted by the Supplier, the Supplier shall be responsible for any errors, omissions or discrepancies unless they are due to incorrect drawings, samples, patterns, models or information supplied by the Purchaser.

The clause implies that the purchaser is not expected to be an expert in the supplier's business. The balance of risk therefore falls with the supplier.

Transfer of Ownership and Risk

It is important to ascertain exactly when the property of the work done passes from the seller to the buyer for the following reasons:

- if the goods are accidentally destroyed, it is necessary to know who bears the loss since risk normally passes with ownership;
- if either the seller or the buyer becomes bankrupt/liquidated, it is necessary to discover who owns the goods;
- the remedy of an unpaid seller against a buyer will depend on whether ownership has been transferred. If the property has passed to the buyer, the buyer can be sued for the price.

Passing of Property

> Risk normally passes when property passes

SOGA S18

Rule 1: Unconditional sale of specific goods property passes when the contract is made

Rule 2: Goods not in a deliverable state, property passes when put into a deliverable state

Rule 3: Conditional sale where the price needs to be ascertained passes when the act is done and the buyer given notice

Rule 4: Sale or return: when the buyer signifies approval or acceptance

Rule 5: Sale of unascertained or future goods, passes when the goods are in a delerable state and 'appropriated'

In English law, the rules relating to the transfer of ownership depend on whether the goods are classified as specific goods or unascertained goods and these rules are contained in the Sale of Goods Act 1979.

Specific goods: these are goods identified and agreed on at the time a contract is made (for example, purchasing a coat).

Unascertained goods: unascertained goods are those goods which are 'not identified' and agreed when the contract is made (for example, 10cwt of coal). It is impossible to identify which specific lumps of coal in the yard will make up the order. As soon as the coal is set aside to fulfil this order, the goods are said to be ascertained. Section 17 of the Sale of Goods Act (1979) states:

Where there is a contract for the sale of specific or unascertained goods the property (ownership) in them is transferred to the buyer at such time as the parties to the contract intend it to be transferred.

The passing of property is therefore a matter between the purchaser and supplier. A typical clause covering the passing of property may read as follows:

The Supplier will bear all risks of loss or damage to the Goods until they have been delivered and accepted by the Purchaser. Ownership will pass to the Purchaser on delivery or, if the Purchaser should make advance or stage payments, at the time such payment is made.

(Note that the purchaser may also require the supplier to mark the property as belonging to the purchaser).

Property (ownership) of the goods may often pass independently of payment to the supplier. As the clause above states: 'ownership will pass to the Purchaser on delivery...' Payment to the supplier may be some time later – even months later!

In order to protect the seller against non-payment in the event of the buyer becoming bankrupt, the seller can insist upon a 'reservation of title' clause stating that ownership will not pass until payment has been made. This will enable the seller to retrieve goods and resell them. These clauses are sometimes called 'Romalpa' clauses after the name of the case where they first gained prominence in the UK. If the clause works, and the purchasing company goes into receivership or liquidation, then the seller is able to recover the goods which the purchasing company still has and the proceeds of resale by the purchasing company. The seller will normally find such a procedure more advantageous than:

- proving in a liquidation for whatever they can get by way of dividend leaving the goods to be sold for the benefit of creditors generally, or
- in a receivership, leaving the goods with the receiver who may in law continue the company's business without paying its existing debts, including that of the seller.

A leading case in English law affecting the rights of both parties for the passing of property is provided by the Romalpa case: *Aluminium Industrie Vaassen BV v Romalpa Aluminium* (1976): AIV sold aluminium foil to Romalpa, the contractual conditions of sale being:

- that the ownership of the material to be delivered to AIV would only be transferred to the purchaser when they had met all that was owing to AIV, no matter on what grounds;
- that Romalpa should store the foil separately;
- that if the foil be used to make new objects, those objects should be stored separately and be owned by AIV as security for payment;
- that Romalpa could sell the new objects but so long as they had not discharged their debt they should hand over to AIV, if requested, the claims they had against purchasers from Romalpa.

Romalpa got into financial difficulties and was in debt for the sum of £200,000. The bank had a debenture secured over Romalpa's assets and appointed a receiver under that debenture. At the time of the receiver's appointment, Romalpa owed AIV £122,000 and AIV sought to recover foil valued at £50,000 and the cash proceeds of resold foil for £35,000. The proceeds had been kept separate by the receiver. The Court of Appeal held that the foil was recoverable and so were the proceeds of sale.

The Romalpa case has since be much criticised, and other cases have made different judgements. In *Borden (UK) Ltd v Scottish Timber Products Ltd* (1979), Borden (B) supplied resin to Scottish Timber (S) which S used in making chipboard. B incorporated the following clause in the contract:

Goods supplied by the company shall be at the purchaser's risk immediately on delivery to the purchaser or into custody on the purchaser's behalf (whichever is the sooner) and the purchaser should therefore be insured accordingly. Property will pass to the customer when (a) the goods subject to this contract, and (b) all other goods the subject of any other contract between the company and the customer which, at the time of payment under this contract, have been delivered to the customer but not paid for in full, have been paid in full.

S went into receivership and B sought to trace the resin into chipboard made from the resin and also to trace the proceeds of sale of chipboard made with the resin. The Court of Appeal decided that the resin had ceased to exist except as chipboard over which there was no contractual charge. There was no fiduciary or financial relationship; tracing was not available.

Variations

Variations to contract may be necessary because:

- The original specification may be inadequate
- A new innovation can be taken advantage of
- The purchaser may need to delete items due to a lack of funding
- The purchaser may need to react to changes in demand from their own customers
- People change their minds about their requirements

Variations should be avoided!

Variations

Peter Marsh in his book *Contracting for Engineering and Construction Projects* refers to variations to contract as being the cancer of contracting. The term 'variation' is commonly used to refer to any alteration of the specification whether by way of addition, modification or omission. Variations to contracts tend to result in increased costs and delays to the contract programme. It is in the purchaser's interests to minimise the number of variations.

Because variations can adversely affect the price paid to a contractor and the agreed completion date, there needs to be tight contractual control of any variations made to a contract. The purchaser should always include a clause covering variations to minimise the risks associated with cost and time. Let us consider the following clause, for example.

The purchaser shall have the right, before delivery, to send to the supplier an order amendment adding to or changing the goods or service. If the order amendment will cause a change to the price or delivery date, then the supplier must notify the purchaser without delay, calculating the new price and delivery date at the same level of cost and profitability as the original price. The supplier must allow 10 working days for the purchaser to authorise any new price and delivery date.

Default

All requirements of goods or services should have planned completion dates. So what are the implications when a supplier fails to complete a contract on the agreed contractual completion date? If we are to assume that the delay has been caused by the supplier, then the answer lies with what implied and express terms are prevailing in the contract. The following clauses could be used, for example:

The supplier shall provide a programme which will identify key dates of progress for the delivery of the product or service. The supplier will notify, without delay, if the progress falls behind or may fall behind any of these programmes.

And furthermore:

If the goods or services or any part of them are not delivered by the time or times specified in the contract, then the purchaser may by written notice cancel any undelivered balance of the good or service. The purchaser reserves the right to have the work performed by alternative means and any reasonable additional costs incurred shall be at the supplier's expense.

The question can be asked: 'what if there are no provisions in the contract to cover default (none delivery of the product or service)?' In English law, the courts have generally construed that where the time of delivery or completion is fixed by the contract, then failure to deliver or complete is a breach of a condition.

Liquidated Damages

It is implied by law that the supplier will be held liable for damages. In some circumstances, the purchaser and contractor foreseeing the possibility of a breach may attempt to assess in advance the damages payable in the contract. These are called liquidated damages. The definition of liquidated damages is: 'a genuine pre-estimate of probable loss'.

The use of liquidated damages creates a number of advantages. The amount of damages for any breach, such as a delay to the completion date, can be pre-agreed in the contract. If no such sum has been stated in the contract, then it can be a very time-consuming exercise in trying to agree the sum of money payable by the offending party. If the two parties fail to agree, then they may resort to litigation. Liquidated damages overcome this uncertainty, since both parties to the contract will know the extent of their financial liability in the event of a breach of contract. Here is an example of a liquidated damages clause:

> If the supplier fails to complete the work specified in the accordance with the contract, within the time for completion, or if no time be fixed, within a reasonable time, there shall be deducted from the contract price or paid to the purchaser by the supplier a sum of £X per week up to a maximum of 10 weeks lateness.

The liquidated damages clause refers to a sum of money (£X). This could equally be a percentage, for example 1% of the contract price per week to a maximum of 10%. What is important is that the damages specified are a genuine pre-estimate of probable loss.

If the amount specified is not a genuine pre-estimate, then the clause may be construed by the courts as being a penalty. A penalty clause is not binding on the parties and so the courts will not enforce the penalty but will award damages on the normal principles used in the assessment of damages. An extravagant sum which is specified in a liquidated damages clause will generally be construed as a penalty.

The difference between a penalty and liquidated damages was well stated by Lord Dunedin in the case of *Dunlop Pneumatic Tyre v New Garage Motor Co* in the House of Lords in 1915:

> The essence of a penalty is a payment of money stipulated as in terrorum of the offending party; the essence of liquidated damages is a genuine covenanted pre-estimate of damage... it will be held to be a penalty if the sum stipulated for is extravagant and unconscionable in amount in comparison with the greatest loss which could conceivably be proved to have followed from the breach.

Let us suppose that you have ordered a new vehicle which costs £20,000. You are to include a clause in the contract with the supplier to compensate you in the event of the vehicle being delayed. You are aware that the weekly hire charge for a similar vehicle is £300 per week. Which figure would be the most suitable to compensate you in the event of late delivery?

- 1% of the Contract Price per day;
- 1½ % of the Contract Price per week;
- ½% of the Contract price per week.

To answer this:

- 1% per day = £1,400 per week which is vastly in excess of the hire charge of £300 per week. Clearly a penalty and not enforceable.
- 1½% per week = £300 per week; the same as the weekly hire charge. These would be liquidated damages.
- ½% per week = £100 per week; £200 lower than the weekly hire charge. These would still be 'liquidated damages' as they are not a penalty sum.

Types of Claim

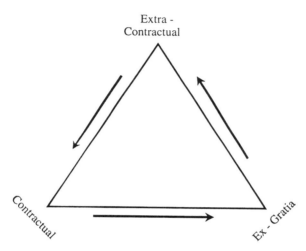

Claims

Normally, the amounts of money which a supplier can be owed by a purchaser are those sums included in the contract. Claims refer to additional monies sought by a supplier. In certain industries, such as construction, it can be argued that this practice is widespread to protect and, perhaps, improve the supplier's profitability.

There are various types of claim:

Extra-Contractual: these refer to claims not covered directly in a contract for additional expenses incurred by a supplier. The supplier may, for example, have quoted to supply a product or service at a fixed price, but then finds a situation where expenses have increased due to increased labour costs. In trying to pass these additional costs onto the purchaser by making a claim, then this would be an extra-contractual type of claim.

Contractual: these refer to sums of money which the supplier feels that they are entitled to in a contract. A variation made by the purchaser will invariably result in a 'contractual' claim by a supplier.

Ex-Gratia: an ex-gratia claim will normally refer to a request for payment on the grounds of 'fair play'. In the oil crisis of 1974, the costs of oil derivatives increased significantly, and the prices for many were re-negotiated across the board.

Dispute Resolution

A common feature of contracts management is the likelihood of disputes to arise between the purchaser and supplier. The vast majority of claims and disputes can be settled by amicable negotiation leading to an agreement.

Litigation: litigation is the term used to describe dispute resolution in the courts. In English law, cases between businesses will normally be heard in the High Court and such disputes are often heard by a single judge. Where either party wishes to challenge the judgement of the High Court, they may appeal to the Court of Appeal. If not satisfied with this judgement, they may seek to appeal to the House of Lords.

Litigation is an adversarial action under procedural rules established under a country's constitution, and will produce a legally binding decision. Litigation tends to be a time-consuming and a complex process.

Arbitration: arbitration resembles litigation, and many disputes between suppliers and purchasers dealing on an international scale are now settled by arbitration. If the parties to a contract are to settle a dispute by arbitration, then they will often refer to arbitration arrangements stated in the contract. A typical clause is as follows:

If at any time any question, dispute or difference shall arise between the purchaser and supplier in relation to the contract which cannot be settled amicably, either party shall as reasonably practicable give to the other notice of the question, dispute or difference. This shall be referred to the arbitration of a person to be agreed upon.

The parties to the contract may agree on an arbitrator at the outset of the contract. The name of a person or institution maybe included in the purchaser's invitation to tender documentation, as the choice of arbitrator forms part of the contractual agreement itself. The arbitrator should always be a suitably-qualified professional.

Adjudication: this differs to arbitration in that it is a process of expert determination. The expert is appointed by agreement between the parties, either generally or to decide a

DISPUTE RESOLUTION

LITIGATION

ARBITRATION

ADJUDICATION

NEGOTIATION

particular issue. Provided the expert keeps within the terms of the appointment and shows no bias, there is no restriction on the way a decision can be reached. It purports to be a quicker method in comparison to both arbitration and litigation. If the contract provides for the expert determination to be final and binding, a court will not interfere with the decision reached.

Progress Payments

Usually payment terms have a direct relationship to one or more of the following aspects:

- the value of the contract;
- the period over which the contract is to be performed;
- the extent of the contract which is to be performed on site;
- the cost influence to the seller of 'bought-out' items.

The term progress payments is used to describe payments which are made at prescribed stages during the progress of a contract. They are normally linked to work done and progress satisfactorily achieved as defined in the contract. The term advance payment is used to describe payments made to suppliers before the purchaser has received anything of value in return. An advance payment provides a supplier with working capital, to enable the commitments under the terms of a contract to be fulfilled.

Progress payments are commonly used for sizeable contracts. They save the supplier from having to borrow commercially to provide working capital and should, therefore, result in reduced contract prices. On the other hand a requirement for suppliers to use their own funds, or to borrow commercially, can increase their incentive to achieve on-time completion. If a supplier receives a high percentage of the contract price in payments for early stages, the incentive to complete the contract on time may be significantly reduced.

Where it is decided, in the light of these considerations, that progress payments would provide value for money, adequate contract conditions should be drawn up to protect the purchaser's position. Progress payments should be linked firmly to performance (in accordance with achievable milestones) linked to time. Wherever possible payment should, therefore, be tied to the achievement of performance milestones. There are obvious benefits to the use of progress payments:

- The contractor's cash flow is improved and this can be a factor used in post-tender negotiation to reduce total costs of the contract.
- The purchaser is attempting to pay only for work that has been done.
- The use of stage payments provides an incentive for the contractor to complete work and then receive payment. This helps to ensure timely performance of the contract.

Peter Marsh, a leading authority on contracting, comments that a number of contractual safeguards should be in place to reduce risk for both parties:

- Define precisely the events against which payments become due.
- Relate those events to the achievement of a particular objective.
- State the amount due at each stage or provide a mechanism by which the amount can be determined.
- Establish a time limit within which payment must be made.
- Provide the purchaser with contractual remedies to recover the value of payments made before completion should the contractor default and be unable to complete.

So, where the buyer has to concede partpayment of the price before delivery of the goods, care must be taken to attempt to safeguard the material value of such payments should the seller find himself in financial difficulties.

Retention Money

Typical in many works-type contracts is the use of retention money. This will often be used for contracts of a long duration (typically in excess of 12 months) and for high contract values. Let us take an example to understand the nature of retention money.

Contract Details

Contract Value	£200,000
Contract Programme	12 months
Progress Payments	10% with contract award
	25% Stage 1: Completion of Design
	30% Stage 2: Completion of production of materials
	35% Stage 3: Delivery to Field Operations
	5% Retension
Guarantee Period	12 months

The payments to the supplier would be

Progress Payment	Payment £	Less than 5% retention	Actual Payment to the Supplier
Contract award 10%	20,000	1,000	19,000
Stage 1 25%	50,000	2,500	47,500
Stage 2 30%	60,000	3,000	57,000
Stage 3 35%	70,000	3,500	66,500
Totals	**£200,000**	**£10,000**	**£190,000**

From the figures above, the supplier would be paid £190,000 in defined progress payments over the course of the contract programme as 5% of the contract price is held as retention. Retention monies are levied on a supplier as a contractual safeguard to ensure that the supplier's goods or services provided conform to the specification agreed in the contract.

In the example above, £10,000 is held as retention. The whole amount may be released at the end of the contract programme (12 months). In construction contracts, it is common to release half of the monies at the end of the contract programme (£5,000) and then the other half at the end of the guarantee period (a further 12 months).

Contract Pricing Arrangements

One of the most important considerations in the pre-contract stage of a contract is the choice of pricing method. When a contract is extended over a lengthy period of time, there is a wide variety of contract types which can be used as a pricing aid to the buyer. However, care must be taken by the purchaser in choosing the correct type for a particular situation and, in making the choice, all the relevant factors to the contract must be considered. The most important factors in making the choice are:

bility of price data;

on amongst sellers;

k involved.

to secure the 'right' price. This is generally interpreted as
...vices at a price which is fair and reasonable to both parties. Many
...influence the view of what is fair and reasonable, including:

- The supplier's position in the market;
- The strength of competition;
- The supplier's marketing skills;
- The supplier's costs.

These market factors will have a considerable impact on the prices charged by suppliers and can be heavily influenced by the supplier perceptions model which we will analyse in Chapter 6. To enable a comparison of the different pricing methods, we need to apply a common denominator of factors which can assess each method's advantages and disadvantages.

Level of Incentive

This refers to the degree to which the supplier will use resources efficiently, and therefore ensure timely outputs. This is an important concept to understand as there is always an element of risk to both parties of the contract.

Level of Contingency

This factor is closely related to the first. Contingency refers to the ability of the purchaser to obtain value for money in the contract price. Again, we will see exactly what this means when we compare the pricing methods open to us.

The Ease of Predictability

This an important consideration in the pre-contract stage as it is always advisable to have a good idea of how much contract is likely to cost!

Fixed Price

This refers to a non-variable price. It is fixed (cannot be changed) unless both the purchaser and the supplier agree to make changes. Under this arrangement, the supplier quotes a price for the supply of the product or service. Here is an example:

A purchasing organisation needed to implement a new computer system in their finance function. They wanted a new system to provide better cost control of the firm's production through implementing a budgeting system for all the departments throughout the company. In addition, they wanted a better system for managing administration such as invoicing and credit control and one that would be designed to meet their specific needs.

Three suppliers of such computer systems were contacted by the purchaser and asked to quote initially for carrying out an analysis of what type of system could be implemented. All suppliers would have to carry out systems analysis - which is the process of analysing how the purchasing organisation's finance department system currently operates before a solution could be proposed.

The first supplier estimated that it would take two systems analysts a total of 15 days each to conduct the systems analysis and then make a draft proposal for the design of the system. The supplier was able to quote a fixed price for the work as they calculated this by multiplying 30 days at their daily charge-out rate for such work at £800 per day. The fixed price quoted was therefore £24,000.

The fixed pricing method is most appropriate for work which can accurately be foreseen

Fixed Pricing

Definition:
A price that is non-variable and should only be varied by agreement

Advantages
- The purchaser knows their commitment before the contract starts
- The risk of under pricing is loaded onto the supplier
- Should be used for supplies of products or services that the supplier can estimate the level of resources required

and accurately measured. In this case, the supplier could make an estimate of the total resources required to complete the contract. The advantage of this method is that the buyer knows how much the contract should cost from the outset.

Another advantage is that no amendments to the contract price are allowed in the event of the supplier over or underestimating the resources required. There is a risk to the supplier, in our example, that the work may take longer than the 30 man-days quoted for. It may take 35, 40 days, or even longer! The supplier would still only receive the price agreed: £24,000.

Contract Price Adjustment

- Base Date For Cost Escalation

- Fixed Portion

- Labour / Materials Portions

- Labour / Materials Periods

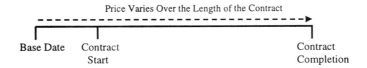

Price Varies Over the Length of the Contract

Base Date   Contract   Contract
            Start   Completion

Contract Price Adjustment

We have already seen that buyers would prefer to obtain fixed price bids to be able to know their commitment clearly before making any contract. Many sellers of goods and services, however, regard fixed pricing as an unacceptable commercial risk when the contract period is long, maybe a three-to-five year period. Consequently, suppliers may build in high risk margins to cover these contracts. The purchaser may end up paying high prices if a fixed price is insisted upon. Under these circumstances, suppliers will inevitably need to speculate on the increases of costs in terms of labour, materials and fixed costs over the contract period.

Variable pricing or contract price adjustment is an arrangement where the price can fluctuate over the length of the contract.

Contract price adjustment should be used when forecasting movements in cost is problematic. This is the case when suppliers have to forecast costs over a long period of time. Variable pricing can be used for commodities like agricultural crops as their prices fluctuate over short periods of time.

General Requirements for Operating Contract Price Adjustment

In making a contract on the basis of a variable price, the contract will almost inevitably end up costing a different sum to that quoted. But, we need to ensure that the supplier's price is controlled, otherwise the purchaser may end up paying a hefty price increase. One way to arrive at a reasonable price is to adjust the initial competitive quotes or offers in accordance with recognised indices. Indices track the changes in prices over time. Trade journals like the Chartered Institute of Purchasing and Supply Management's journal

Supply Management publish indices.

A formula can be used which links into a choice of index and generally works like this:

- The purchaser's requests for offers/ quotes should specify a date on which the offers should be based and should be compiled using the costs of labour, materials, etc. ruling on that date.
- Fixed portion: this is the percentage of the contract price which is to be assumed for the purpose of the formula is fixed. In our example the fixed portion is 5% of the quoted price.
- Labour and materials portions: there are two separate portions of the contract price which represent labour and materials. These will obviously vary according to the nature of the contract work being undertaken. A formula could, for example, assume that these are equal at 47.5% of the contract price. So 5% of the price will be fixed, plus 47.5% labour, plus 47.5% materials which then equals 100%. These labour and materials portions are then adjusted in accordance with cost movements recorded in the chosen indices.
- Labour and materials periods: cost movements of both labour and materials can be determined by comparison with the chosen indices over the length of the contract.

There is a formula for calculating contract price adjustment (the variation to a price).

$$P = P_o \left[a + \frac{bL}{L_o} + \frac{cM}{M_o} \right] - P_o$$

Where:

P = Price Increase/Decrease

a = Fixed Portion (eg. 0.05)

b = Labour Portion (eg. 0.475)

c = Materials Portion (eg. 0.475)

L = Average Labour Index During Labour Period

L_o = Labour Index at the Base Date of Offer

M = Materials Index at the end of the Materials Period

M_o = Material Index at the Base Date of the Offer

P_o = Initial Price

and:

Labour period = Final ⅔ Contract Period

Materials period = First ⅗ Contract Period

Let's look at how a variable pricing formula might work:

Using the following indices, try and attempt calculating the contract price Adjustment. Separate indices are stated below for both labour and materials. Assume the following:

The date that tender was compiled was at the end of April 199X.

The completion date of the contract was the end of September 199Y.

The contract commenced on 1 July 199X.

The tendered price was £100,000.

Indices:

Year	Month	Labour	Materials
199X	January	102.4	124.4
199X	February	104.6	124.9
199X	March	106.4	124.9
199X	April	105.6	125.5
199X	May	106.3	127.8
199X	June	107.7	129.6
199X	July	106.4	128.7
199X	August	109.8	131.5
199X	September	108.6	129.4
199X	October	110.4	129.4
199X	November	112.5	131.3
199X	December	115.7	137.0
199Y	January	112.0	132.0
199Y	February	113.1	132.0
199Y	March	113.1	133.7
199Y	April	113.6	135.8
199Y	May	113.3	136.4
199Y	June	115.1	133.7
199Y	July	116.4	135.1
199Y	August	117.8	134.8
199Y	September	118.6	135.1
199Y	October	119.4	135.4
199Y	November	120.5	136.1
199Y	December	121.7	142.6

The contract period is 15 months.

The labour period = final ⅔ of the contract period = the last 10 months of the contract December 199X to September 199Y

The materials period = first ⅗ of the contract period = the first 9 months of the Contract July 199X to March 199Y

Using the formula:

$$P = Po\left[a + \frac{bL}{Lo} + \frac{cM}{Mo}\right] - Po$$

$$P = 100,000 \times \left[0.05 + 0.475\frac{114.8}{105.6} + 0.475\frac{133.7}{125.5}\right] - 100,000$$

P = £7,241.84

And so the total price = £107,241.84
The amount of variation = £7,241.84

Cost Plus/ Cost Reimbursable Contracts

As the titles imply, the supplier is reimbursed for all his or her costs. Let us go back to our example mentioned earlier. The purchasing organisation needed to implement a new computer system in its finance function. It wanted a new system to provide better cost control of the firm's production through implementing a budgeting system for all the departments throughout the company.

One supplier quoted a fixed price of two systems analysts a total of £24,000 as it was estimated that two systems analysts would each take 15 days do the analysis. Another supplier was not prepared to quote a fixed price. He was unsure how long it might take from the purchaser's invitation to quote. They therefore quoted on a reimbursable day rate basis: £600 per day per analyst. If this supplier is awarded the contract, then they should carry out work to cover the requirement, and then submit records to demonstrate the days worked. There are significant dangers with this pricing method though!

The eventual cost of the contract will usually be very unclear at the pre-contract stage. At the outset of a cost plus contract, the purchaser has only a broad idea of the eventual financial commitment, despite safeguards which may be built into these types of contracts to avoid cost overruns. These safeguards may include:

- weekly or monthly financial reports of expenditure and performance;
- financial and performance progress meetings;
- 'open book' cost auditing on completion.

Incentive/ Target Cost Contracts

These type of contracts are used to provide incentives in situations where the risks are too great to enable fixed prices to be negotiated but not so great as to justify the use of cost plus contracts. The essential elements of a target cost incentive contract are as follows:

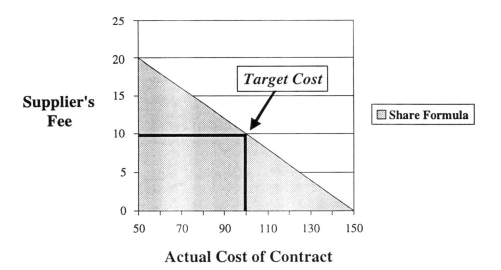

A **Target Cost:** this should be the best estimate of what the contract value should be. This can be determined by direct negotiation or sought through tenders, but is all agreed in the pre-contract stage.

A **Target Fee:** this is the amount of profit plus other overheads payable without adjustment if the costs come out at target cost.

A Share Formula: this determines how the excess cost (overrun) or savings (underrun) in relation to the target cost will be shared between the employer and the supplier.

Should the actual contract overrun or underrun, then the excess costs or savings are shared in accordance with a prearranged formula. The formula could be anything between 0/100 and 100/0: either the supplier or the purchaser will bear all the excess cost or reap all the savings. The general principle is that the supplier's fee will reduce if costs increase.

Let us assume that the target cost is £100K and the target fee as agreed as being £10K and the cost sharing formula is 80% risk to the purchaser and 20% risk to the supplier. The chart below illustrates the effect of the sharing arrangement on the amount of profit payable at any level of actual contract value between £50K and £150K.

When the actual contract costs are £50k, the supplier receives a higher fee – £20k, representing an incentive bonus of £10k in addition to the agreed target fee of £10k. Meanwhile, if the actual costs turn out to be higher than forecast, the supplier's fee is proportionately reduced. Should the actual contract cost be £150k, the supplier receives no fee.

Depending on the degree of confidence in the target cost estimate, limitations can be placed on the cost sharing arrangements. A maximum price may be set, for example. In a fixed price contract, the purchasing organisation has no share in the savings or excesses on the cost estimate and so the supplier takes on board the risk in the form of profits or losses for the eventual costs of the contract.

Alternatively, under an incentive/ target cost pricing mechanism, a maximum and minimum fee can be established as the graph below shows.

In a fixed fee contract, the purchaser will agree to pay all allowable costs plus a fixed sum of money to cover their fee. Under this method, the supplier's fee will be constant regardless of cost.

In addition to the use of incentives to control the prices paid to suppliers, incentive arrangements may be applied to other important factors involved in the performance of a contract. There are a number of steps to enable the processing of performance incentives:

- suitable performance measures need to be agreed;
- there should be a range of performance targets over which the incentive is required to operate;
- an arrangement needs to be put in place whereby the performance targets are agreed to thus providing incentives for the supplier to satisfy the purchaser's requirements.

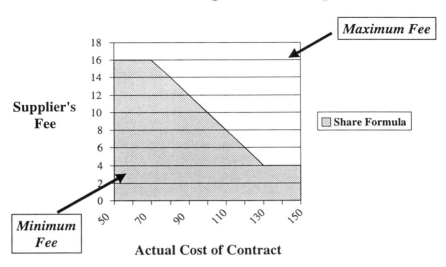

Network analysis helps the planning of major contracts. It shows the sequence of activities to complete a contract. We will now examine two particular methods which can be employed to monitor the progress of goods or services through the supply chain.

Gantt Charts

Gantt charts, invented by Thomas Gantt an American industrial Engineer (1861-1919), to monitor and control the maintenance of factory machines, are bar charts that graphically display the time relationship of the steps in a project. Gantt charts are a form of network analysis. Each step of a project is represented by a line placed on the chart in the time period when it is to be undertaken. When completed, the Gantt chart shows the flow of activities in sequence, as well as those that can be under way at the same time (parallel activities). To create a Gantt chart:

- list the steps required to complete a contract and estimate the time required for each;
- list the steps down the left side of the chart and time intervals along the top or bottom;
- draw a line across the chart for each step, starting at the planned beginning and ending on the completion date of that step;
- when your Gantt chart is finished, you will be able to see the minimum total time for the contract, proper sequences of steps and which can be under way at the same time.

Activity/Week	1	2	3	4	5	6
Receive Req	■					
Request Quotes		■	■			
Test Sampler			■	■		
Evaluate costs				■	■	
Adjudicate						■
Place Contract						

Critical Path Analysis (CPA)

A CPA chart or 'logic diagram' shows the sequence of activities to complete a project. Some activities can be paralleled, allowing jobs to be carried out simultaneously. By constructing the network, the projects 'critical path' is determined. The critical path is the longest timescale to complete the contract.

The CPA is represented by a series of arrows showing the activity and the timescale and a series of

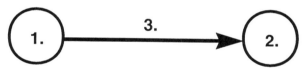

nodes(circles) representing the completion of one stage and the start of the next.

In the above example, 1. is the first activity, the line represents the time duration, in this case three weeks, and 2. represents the completion of the task and the commencement of task 2. Activities are by convention from left to right.

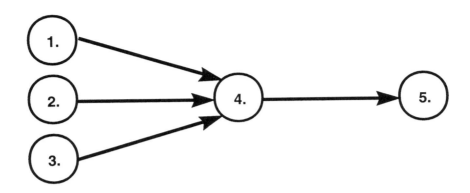

The activity leading to 5 cannot begin until all activities preceding 4 have been accomplished. 4 cannot be achieved until activities 1, 2 and 3 have been finished.

Some activities can be paralleled, allowing jobs to be carried out simultaneously. In the diagram below, activity 3 can be taking place at the same time as activity 4.

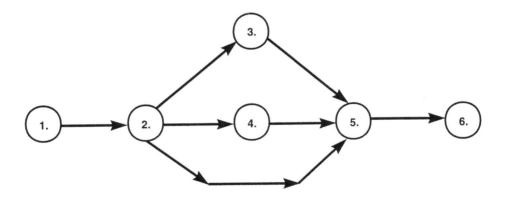

There are three phases:

Planning: the identification of activities and placing jobs into their logical and correct parallel and series sequences. Having drawn up a list of activities, the planner examines each to determine:

- what other work must be completed before the job can be started;
- what other work can be started as soon as the job is completed;
- what other work can be going on while the job is in progress.

Scheduling: the conversion of the plan into a feasible work schedule making optimum use of time, labour and equipment. From this analysis, it is possible to assign length of time to the various activities identified at the planning phase and to arrive at a total time for the project. The identification of the sequence which is critical to the performance of the project otherwise known as the critical path is made at this stage.

Controlling: the monitoring of progress against schedule. Actual performance can be compared with the schedule to show whether the overall project time will be achieved. A slippage in activities not on the critical path may turn out to be unimportant; a delay in critical activities may necessitate action to ensure adherence to the schedule, or rework a new schedule.

Expediting

One of the objectives of a purchasing department is to ensure completion of the contract on time. Expediting activities are frequently used to achieve this objective. (To expedite: 'to assist the progress of or hasten'. This definition suggests that the process is planned or pro-active).

It can be argued that expediting work does not add value to an organisation's activities or products in any way and a principle objective of many businesses should be to reduce the need to expedite work to zero. The approach to continuous improvement and the development of the 'partnership' philosophy of buyer-seller relationships can lead to significant improvements in this area.

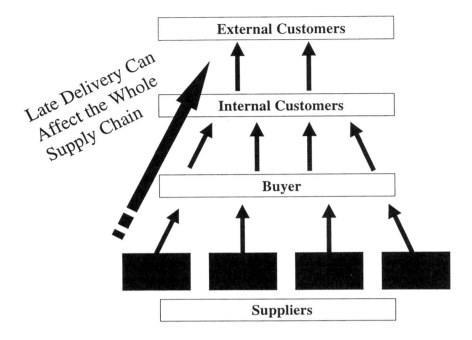

A more accurate description of expediting is 'downstream contract management' and this requires a good deal of skill and effort, as any contract management activity does.

As previously stated, the supply task is to deliver goods and services where and when they are wanted by the purchaser. Simply placing orders and leaving the rest to suppliers may not be sufficient to achieve this.

This process may be thought of as delivery assurance and delivery control in the same way we refer to quality assurance and quality control. Delivery assurance means making sure suppliers will meet very tight delivery schedules without expediting. Just In Time (JIT) systems rely heavily on this approach. Delivery control means setting up systems to indicate when orders are due and taking expediting action as needed.

It is a common practice for the expedition of work to be undertaken by the buyer, it being the natural responsibility of the buyer to work with suppliers. However, it is also the case that a separate expediting section exists within the purchasing department, with expediting activities being either at the direction of the relevant buyers or at the discretion of the expediting staff themselves, sometimes liaising with other user departments.

As an alternative, the expediting function may be attached to another department such as planning or production, the theory being that these people are more able to identify priorities. If the expediting function is not attached to the buying section, then it is of vital importance that robust lines of communications are in place between the buyer and expeditor, from initial sourcing enquiries and negotiations, through to placement of order.

The reasons for delays in supplier contract performance may be several, but typical problems may relate to:

- poor planning
- insufficient time
- tracking wrong goods/services
- selection of the wrong supplier/suppliers interest
- unrealistic timescales
- transport problems
- access to premises problems
- interpretation of quality
- stage payments

Further Reading

A D Allwright and R W Oliver *Buying Goods and Services: A Professional Guide to Contracting Including Model Conditions* Revised Edition CIPS (1997) provides a useful introduction to contractual terms.

P D V Marsh *Contracting for Engineering and Construction Projects* 4th Edition Gower Technical Publishing (1995) provides a more detailed approach to contract management, although the book is very much geared towards the construction industry.

chapter four
Quality Philosophies in Commercial Relationships

In chapters 2 and 3, we analysed the contractual aspects of forming relationships with suppliers. This chapter concentrates on the achievement of the supply of product or service quality from suppliers.

Definition of Quality

Quality conjures different meanings to different people. It is possible to think of examples of quality products or services which you may have recently purchased. What distinguished this particular product or service? Was it the fact that it has a luxurious image, such as a Mercedes or Aston Martin car; or was it that you bought something for what you considered to be value for money? There are many definitions:

Quality as 'Conformance to Specification'

Buyers can take the view that their role is to purchase goods or services which conform to specification. In many instances, the specification has been drafted by another business function.

Quality as 'Fitness for Purpose'

This definition of quality focuses on the performance in relation to the use of the product or service bought. A trend in purchasing management in recent years has been the increased use of performance-driven specifications which aim to identify the uses and applications of bought-out goods or services. The specifier will focus less on the make-up of the item, and more on its applications. The terminology of 'fitness for purpose' is an integral feature of buyer's statutory rights, since it is the essence of Section 14(3) of the Sale of Goods Act 1979.

Definition of Quality

Quality is Satisfying Customer's Expectations
Both Now *and* in the Future

Quality as 'Conformance to Requirements'

This definition of quality places the greatest emphasis on the role of the customer. Goods or services bought will need to satisfy the expectations of the customer. Organisational buyers therefore have the responsibility of identifying what the customers demands actually are. Their customers may not necessarily be the consumers as it is more likely to be an another internal business function. In this way, buyers will have internal customers, and it is they who provide the impetus to purchasing's dealings with suppliers.

The traditional means of controlling quality very much relied on detection of non-conforming products. Ideas on quality have evolved over time: definitions 20 to 30 years ago tended to highlight the role of the quality controller as the person responsible for checking the work done by others in the organisation. Statistical sampling techniques would be used to measure the errors of what had been produced. So quality controllers would be analysing whether the product or service conformed to its specification. Defective products could be separated from the conforming product. Acceptable quality levels would be set as 100% conformance was rarely expected.

More contemporary views of quality, however, demand a focus on the customer. We live in an age where 'the customer is king'. For many businesses, and what is becoming increasingly important for public sector organisations, finding a special way to focus on customer's needs and 'delighting the customer' is often the way that companies create competitive advantage.

The Costs of Quality

Philip Crosby argued that the costs of defective quality are varied. Few companies still actually have invested in systems to investigate the costs of defective quality. Studies have suggested that the cost of defective quality can be as high as 25% of total cost. The main categories of cost are:

Appraisal Costs: these include the costs of inspection processes of labour and equipment.

Prevention Costs: costs of personnel and the application of methods to prevent problems from occurring.

Failure Costs (internal): the costs of processing faulty goods/service, rectification areas, delays, scrap, overtime, additional resources to correct the problem.

Failure Costs (external): warranty costs and loss of reputation, sales because of delays, ultimately a complete loss of business due to the quality problems.

Quality Costs

Appraisal
Prevention
Failure Costs: Internal
Failure Costs: External

An example of these costs is provided by the following case study. These events happened to a division of a major food processing manufacturer in the Midlands during the mid-1980s.

The Costs of Quality: A Case History

The foods manufacturer had invested nearly £1 million in an extension to its existing premises. The new facility was designed for the manufacturing of salads, and the company had gained a commitment for orders from a major high street retailer. The production line technology was simple, as there were two production lines and operatives working on the line each had a specified role in the production process. The plastic tray containing the salad would pass down the production line, and the operatives would add ingredients to the tray, and so they were assembling the final product. Various ingredients were used according to the menu variation of the salad which was to be produced.

The manufacturer was totally dependent on the orders from one high street retailer. The pricing arrangements with the manufacturer guaranteed the firm a level of profit, although the margin was tight. It was in the manufacturer's interest to maximise sales volume to boost total profit. To ensure control of labour costs, the manufacturer had one production shift over a five day week. The production line ran quickly and the production operatives experienced real difficulties in performing their tasks. It was a regular occurrence for the food trays passing down the production line to mount up at a bottleneck. Bottlenecks were experienced by individual operators who performed the more difficult tasks, such as weighing a specific amount of salad ingredients before placement in the tray. The end result of this build up in work-in-progress on the line often had disastrous results, as some of the near completed salads would fall onto the floor! However, production quantities were of paramount importance and the company would not tolerate scrap. The contents would nearly always be scooped off the floor and a damage limitation exercise be carried out on the fallen trays.

One person was responsible for quality control. Her responsibility was to ensure that the salads complied with the exacting specifications laid down by the retail customer. These specifications were very precise as all ingredients had to be of specified weights and sizes. Hard boiled eggs of a specified size used for one of the menus, for example, had to be cut into quartiles with the yoke left fully intact and then placed in a particular spot on the salad tray. With the production line running at the pace necessary to maximise throughput, it was no wonder that the yokes would be displaced and that the eggs would end up in the wrong place on the tray. It is not surprising that there were many problems associated with the final product.

When the quality controller did detect problems, she would be ignored by the production managers. Their objectives were to produce the maximum volume at lowest cost. The company could not afford to halt production, and this was a rarity.

The retailer made frequent complaints to the manufacturer about the standards of the product. The company's answer was to blame the distribution company, which was a convenient excuse as this was a separate organisation. Frequent unannounced site visits were made by the buyers of the retail company but these had very limited impact since one of the office staff kept watch on arrivals at the car park! When a suspected buyer arrived, the order was given to slow the production line down and the workers told to look as though they were enjoying their work!

This pattern of events carried on for seven months, until the retail company decided to resource from another supplier. The manufacturer lost the orders and it took many months to find other buyers. By this time, the company had a damaged reputation and had lost an important customer in the process. Its financial performance once the contract had been terminated was disastrous. Relating this case to the costs of quality, we find the following:

Appraisal Cost: this category includes the costs of the quality controller and measuring equipment present in the production facility.

Prevention Costs: the costs incurred in this category are minimal as no efforts were made by the company to prevent problems from re-occurring.

Failure Costs (internal): these costs were considerable. The processing of faulty produce and individual operatives spent a significant amount of time rectifying output. There were delays caused to production resulting in overtime payment necessary on occasions.

Failure Costs (external): the retail company refused to pay in many instances for damaged stock. In addition, the manufacturer lost business from an important customer.

TASK

Does your organisation measure the costs of quality? If so which of the types of quality cost are measured?

It is argued that improving quality through a total quality programme (seen in more detail later in this chapter) actually reduces costs. Quality defects can produce higher costs. Purchasers need to work with suppliers to reduce the quantities of defects bought over time. This requires collaboration and a desire to tackle the causes of poor quality.

Costs of Quality

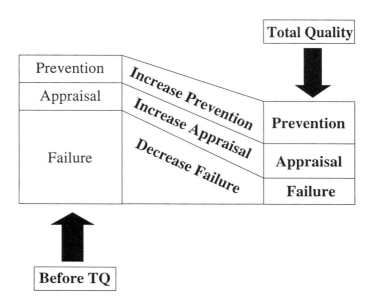

The Effects of Quality Defects

Increases Costs

- Delays in Inspection and Delivery

- Higher Safety Stocks Necessary Because of Defective Quality in the System

- Delays to Production

- Quality Problems May Not Be Noticed Until they Reach the End Customer

- Customers May Complain of Poor Quality

- People Become De-Motivated Because they Are Constantly Dealing with Problems

Quality Assurance

Quality assurance is defined by the International Organisation for Standardisation (ISO) as: 'All those planned and systematic activities implemented within the quality system and demonstrated as needed to provide adequate confidence that an entity will fulfil requirements for quality.'

This definition refers to the quality 'system' which consists of the organisation's structure, responsibilities, procedures, processes and resources for implementing quality. Essentially, quality assurance is a more complete management system concerned with defect prevention rather than detection. To ensure quality, therefore, organisations need a number of the following.

Structure

Organisations should have a structure in place where selected people have responsibilities for overseeing the management of quality. Often, there will be a senior manager appointed heading a specialist function, although in smaller organisations the manager will have other responsibilities.

Responsibilities

These should be defined not just at senior management level, but also for the ways in which each individual in the organisation has responsibilities for ensuring that contributions to the output produced conforms to customer requirements. In many instances, these aspects of quality management will warrant a section in the employee's job description.

Procedures

These are written statements of the processes used in the organisation to produce the product or service. Most organisations will have a quality manual, in which the key aspects of the means of achieving output and the responsibilities of individuals and departments are inscribed.

Processes

This refers to the means by which quality is produced. In a purchasing context, there should be processes in place which control the quality of bought out goods and services, such as, for example, the selection processes in place to source suitable suppliers.

Resources

These are the costs incurred for achieving quality output. These can include the appraisal and prevention costs outlined earlier but generally there are resource implications on the manpower and equipment necessary to achieve quality.

In forming a long-term commercial relationship, it will be important to know details of the supplier's quality assurance system. They should be able to demonstrate their structure showing who has responsibilities for achieving quality, their procedures, processes, and resources available for the contract.

A worldwide standard for quality assurance systems has now been established with BS EN ISO 9000. The standard was originally published by the British Standards Institute and, since its introduction in 1979, it has become the European and international standard for quality assurance systems. In the 1980s, there was a rapid expansion in the number of registered firms. The initials 'EN' stipulate the acceptance by the European Committee for Standardisation and 'ISO' refers to the International Organisation for Standardisation. Since its adoption as the international and European standard, it has now achieved worldwide recognition. BS EN ISO 9000 forms a general standard which assesses an organisation's quality. An organisation applying for ISO 9000 would need to demonstrate that they have the following:

- A quality manual which sets out the company's commitment to quality and how it addresses the standard.
- A quality procedure manual which sets out the formal procedures introduced to meet the requirements of the standard.
- Work instructions or operating procedures which cover how the organisation ensures compliance with the customer's requirements.

The procedures should cover the following activities in a business.

ISO 9000 Quality System

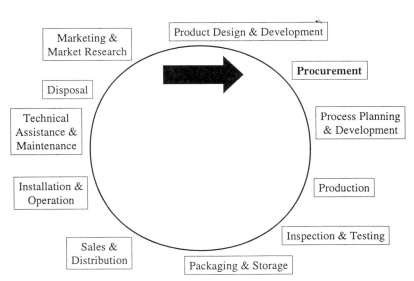

It is interesting to note that an organisation having accreditation to ISO 9000 should have procedures covering their procurement activities. The standard was first introduced by the British Standards Institute in 1979 as an attempt to standardise the requirements of organisation's quality standards. The objective of the standard was to provide organisations with the means of being able to supply their products or service at a stated level of quality. The system relies on organisations implementing and maintaining documentary procedures which demonstrate the organisations quality processes. These procedures affect a number of parts of the organisation and this point is illustrated in the diagram shown. There are many benefits to organisations for having the standard, including the following:

- Possession of the standard provides many organisations with improved marketing opportunities. Many organisations feature their possession of the standard in their promotional efforts, and this can improve their business prospects with both organisational buyers and consumers.
- Achievement of the standard does install a quality system, and many organisations may not have had such controls before seeking accreditation.
- The result of the standard is that the emphasis of the firms output is on meeting customers specifications and requirements.

However, the standard has been criticised and there are a number of concerns:

- Possession of the standard is not, in itself, a guarantee of quality product. Whilst the standard does focus on producing to customers' requirements, these requirements may be sub-standard.
- Firms may reduce their standards to ensure a better chance of success in achieving accreditation from the assessors.
- Consultants used to develop the necessary procedures can be a very expensive resource. Concerns have also been widely expressed about the expertise of the consultants since they may fail to understand the requirements of the business seeking accreditation. The result is that the procedures written may be difficult to operate to.
- The standard relies on written procedures and proof of adherence to these by means of a documentation system. This can result in a bureaucratic system heavily dependent on paperwork.
- The wording of the standard itself is geared towards manufacturing and can have little relevance to service sector organisations. Service organisations can experience difficulties in interpreting the terminology.
- Many organisations report that their main reason for obtaining certification was due to pressure exerted by purchasing organisations.

Total Quality

Total quality management (TQM) or as it is also referred to 'Total Quality Control' is arguably the most significant of management tools to affect organisations in the 1980s and 1990s. As we have all ready discussed, originally quality was achieved by inspection, the process of sorting the defects from conforming product. Quality assurance systems then developed placing greater emphasis on quality systems and controls which prevent problems from occurring. According to Nigel Slack and his co-authors from Warwick University TQM is regarded as being concerned with following:

- meeting the needs and expectations of the customer;
- covering all parts of the organisation;
- including every person within the organisation;
- examining all costs which are related to quality;
- achieving right-first-time production of goods or services;
- developing the systems and procedures which support quality and improvement.

What distinguishes total quality from quality assurance is the harnessing of individual commitment to continuous improvement. To achieve this ideal, TQM is a philosophy which relies on the achievement of all employees in the organisation recognising their role in contributing to quality.

Customer-Supplier Relationships

An important feature of total quality is the chain of customer and supplier relationships. For a total quality programme to be successful, there needs to be an organisational culture where everyone in the organisation recognises his or her roles and responsibilities within these chains. The organisation consists of micro operations, and each of these operations will have internal customers and suppliers. Consider, for example, the role of the procurement department. Whilst it is responsible for the effective management of external resources, it needs to provide an error-free service to its customers. The customers will be micro operations (other business functions) requiring a number of aspects of performance from the purchasing department. For example:

- advice on specifications;
- information about supply markets;
- details of likely costs, lead times, etc;
- purchases of goods and services which achieve VFM;
- quick responses to queries, etc.

For the purchasing department to provide an error-free service, it needs to understand what its customers actually require. In addition, the procurement department may need information and other services from other functions. For example, it may be dependent on the finance department for information regarding budgets, analysis of costings or payment of suppliers. In this way, the finance department may act as an internal supplier of the procurement department. The finance department will therefore, in turn, need to understand procurement's requirements.

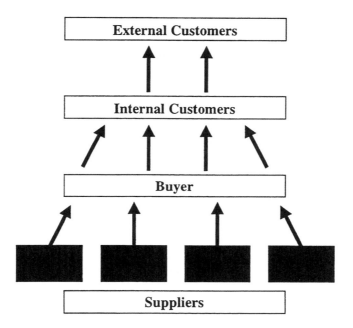

External suppliers will inevitably impact on the ability of the organisation to satisfy its external customers too. The supply chain will link suppliers' performance through to the achievement of cost, quality and delivery to the organisation's customers. In turn, the external customer may have other customers in the supply chain. The micro operations of all parts of the supply chain contribute to the quality of the product or service provided, and can be responsible for the creation of defects to the product or service. These defects may show up later in the supply chain. Consider a faulty part produced by a supplier which is assembled by a car manufacturer. The error may not actually be detected until the customer has used the car for some months after taking delivery. The defect would then need to be traced back to the supplier at fault, and the supplier may be located some way back in the supply chain as it may not necessarily be a first tier supplier to the car manufacturer. In this way, it is important for all those involved in the supply chain to produce 'defect free' products and services required by their customers.

Continuous Improvement

Total quality stresses the role of the individual in achieving quality output. Each person in an individual operation has a responsibility to produce output which is free from defects. In addition, each member of staff also the ability to improve quality and individuals can do much to avoid errors. Consider, for example, the operative working on the production line, the bank clerk serving customers, or the nurse attending to patients; each of these people can be able to make effective contributions to the production of the product or service. If all individuals understand their roles in achieving quality, then significant improvements can be made if all employees contribute to the improvement of the processes involved in making the product or service. The organisation will be able to make small, incremental steps to improving quality if the contributions made by individuals can be effectively implemented. The Japanese term quality improvement is 'kaizen'. Central to this philosophy is the impetus of the efforts made to improve quality.

Individuals, therefore, need to be encouraged to generate ideas which can improve the performance of the organisation. People usually have a wealth of experience in the tasks demanded of their particular roles. Management need to encourage employees through the implementation of an employee empowerment programme.

The Quality 'Gurus'

There are a number of very influential writers on quality management. These writers are referred to as the 'quality gurus' because of the profound effect of their teachings on the conduct of businesses. Each of these writers has prescribed tools to achieve quality. Much of the transformation in highlighting the importance of quality is credited to the work of three American quality gurus in the immediate postwar period, namely, Edwards Deming, Joseph Juran and Kaoru Ishikawa.

W Edwards Deming

The Americans were themselves effectively responsible for making possible the miraculous turnaround of Japanese industry and for putting Japan on the road to quality leadership. Much of this transformation was associated with the introduction of statistical quality control into Japan by the US Army over the period 1946 to 1950 and the visits by three key American Quality Gurus. The first of these is W Edwards Deming.

After the Second World War, Deming was sent to Japan as an advisor to the Japanese government. He became involved with the Union of Japanese Scientists and Engineers (JUSE). In the early 1950s he lectured to engineers and senior managers. He was honoured by the Japanese for his teachings, but it was not until the late 1970s that Deming started to make an impact in the West.

According to Deming, there are two sources of variability. Firstly, there are special causes of variation in a product, process or service and these prevent its performance from remaining constant in a statistical sense. Deming argued that these causes are often easily assignable: changes of operator, shift, or procedure, for example. These special causes can be identified and problems can be solved by local operators. On the other hand, there can be common causes which remain once the special causes have been eliminated. They are due to the design, or the operation of the process or system. Only management action can eliminate these common causes.

The underlying philosophies of his teachings were firstly, his 'chain reaction' which he says was on the blackboard of every meeting with top management in Japan from 1950 onwards. Secondly, Deming encouraged the Japanese to adopt a systematic approach to problem solving, which became known as the Deming Wheel or PDCA (Plan, Do, Check, Action) cycle. The cycle starts with the planning stage which examines the current method or the problem area being studied. This stage will involve analysing data to enable the formulation of a plan of action which can produce improvements to the task in question.

Deming's PDCA

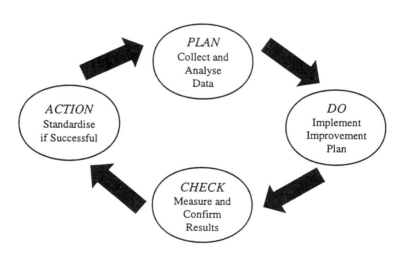

The second stage of the Deming Wheel refers to the 'Do' or implementation stage. The stage may also involve a mini-PDCA cycle to achieve successful implementation. The 'Check' stage is where the newly implemented solution is evaluated to see whether it has resulted in the expected improvement. Finally, there is the 'Act' stage during which the change is standardised if successful. Like other authors, Deming highlights the importance of the customer. In his book *Out of the Crisis* he writes:

It will not suffice to have customers that are merely satisfied. An unhappy customer will switch. Unfortunately, a satisfied customer may also switch, on the theory that he or she could not lose much, and might gain. Profit in business comes from repeat customers, customers that boast about your product and service, and that brings friends with them.

Deming also spoke of the need to 'stay ahead' of the customer. The customer, he argued, does not know what he will need one, three or five years hence. If potential suppliers wait until then to find out, they will hardly be ready to serve them.

In order to help people understand and put into action his teachings, Deming produced a list of '14 Points for Management' to help Western organisations complete the necessary transformation needed to enable them to compete against the Japanese. These points do not in themselves constitute the whole of the Deming philosophy, though they are important aspects of it.

Deming's 14 Points For Management

1. Create Constancy of Purpose to improve product and service. Organisations need to allocate resources for long-term needs rather than short-term profitability with plans to become more competitive. As Deming argues:

> This can only be accomplished by management taking the trouble to understand deeply the new (to them) philosophy, and then setting a good example through their own consistency of purpose constantly filtering down through the organisation to feed and nurture a consistency of purpose throughout.

2. Adopt the New Philosophy for the new economic age created by Japan; Western management must awake to the challenge, learn their responsibilities, and take on leadership for the change. Transformation of the Western management style is necessary to halt the continued decline of industry.

> If you do not accept fact that we are talking about this radical a change, then it will not happen. In any case, it will not happen overnight. But there must be a constant, consistent movement in the right direction: every day you need to move closer to the philosophy of ever-improving quality of all systems, processes, and activities within the company.

3. Cease Dependence on Inspection: to achieve quality, eliminate the need for mass inspection by building quality into the product/service. Statistical evidence of built-in manufacturing and purchasing is essential to achieve this. Deming advocated the regular recording of measurements of a process through statistical process control, which is analysed later in this chapter.

4. End Awarding Business on the Basis of Price; instead minimise total costs and move towards single suppliers for items. This is a particularly far-reaching point for the procurement department. Deming advocates moving towards a single supplier for any one item, on a long-term relationship based on loyalty and trust. The aim should be to minimise total cost, not merely initial cost. So he argued that 'Purchasing managers have a new job, and must learn it.'

5. Improve Constantly the systems of planning, production and service to improve quality and productivity, and thus to constantly decrease costs. Managers need to continually work on the system to improve processes, and also encourage workers to contribute to the efforts of continuous improvement.

6. Institute Training on the Job: Deming calls for the use of training and retraining on the job for all, including management. The emphasis should be on making better use of every employee to keep up with changes in materials, methods, product design, machinery, techniques and service.

7. Institute Leadership aimed at helping people do a better job. Management therefore needs to take immediate action on reports of defects and conditions detrimental to the achievement of quality. He talks of the existence of a vicious circle experienced at the workplace where conditions force a worker to do a bad job. The worker loses interest in the work, which results in poorer work, which then lessens the worker's interest, and so on.

8. Drive Out Fear so that everyone may work effectively for the company. As Deming argues:

> Anyone working in fear of their superiors cannot be working in true co-operation with these superiors...this will never result in much progress. Successful joint working relationships achieve so much more than isolated individual efforts – but these will not do so unless nourished by mutual trust, confidence and respect Those working in fear try to withdraw from the attention of those of whom they are afraid.

In addition, Deming argues that it is just as important to break down barriers between departments as to break down the barriers between manager and subordinate. In an environment which is characterised by fear, managers will be fed with information which they want to hear. In so doing, they then lose touch with reality. Mistakes and errors are buried impairing the ability of he organisation to improve quality.

9. Break Down Barriers Between Departments: research, design, procurement and operations must work together to foresee problems in production and in use by the customer. Teams should therefore be created to tackle and prevent problems from occurring. Organisations need to operate cross-functionally.

10. Eliminate Slogans, Exhortations and Numerical Targets asking the workforce for zero defects and new levels of productivity; these only help to create adversarial relationships. Most problems lie in the system and so lie beyond the power of the work-force to rectify. Deming calls for reasonable requests to be made of managers, colleagues and subordinates. This, he argues, is far more likely to achieve better than expected results.

11. Eliminate Work Standards by Numerical Quotas and Management by Numbers. Deming argues that it is a dangerous approach to focus on achieving arbitrary numerical targets, as hitting the targets becomes more important than satisfying the customer. A target set beyond the capability of the system can only be reached by improving the system or by 'beating the system'.

12. Remove Barriers that Rob People of Their Right to Pride of Workmanship. This is one of Deming's more contentious points, as he advocates the abolition of the ranking of people, teams, plants, divisions with reward and punishment.

13. Institute a Vigorous Education and Self-Improvement Programme for Everyone. The organisation therefore needs people who are continually improving through education. People improve through acquiring knowledge by contributing to society and the organisation.

14. The Transformation is Everyone's Job. Management's obligations are to implement these points to put everyone in the organisation to work to accomplish the transformation. Managers also have to accept what they have to learn, and then learn it. Deming concludes by arguing that: 'The only survivors will be companies with constancy of purpose for quality, productivity, and service.'

Deming's Contributions to Purchasing Management

Traditional texts on purchasing management underline the importance of the achievement of the five rights by purchasing personnel. These are: the right price, the right quantity, the right time, the right quality and the right place. Organisations have a tendency to choose suppliers on the basis of the lowest price. It is often a standard internal procedure which requires personnel having the responsibility for obtaining outside supplies to obtain a number of quotations, usually three, and then to select on the basis of price, all things being equal.

As has all ready been stated, the fourth of Deming's 14 points for management encourages every organisation to 'end the practice of awarding business on price tag alone. Instead move towards a single supplier to reduce variation and minimise total cost.' Price is therefore only one variable in assessing the total cost of supply. This concept is summed up in the following quotation: "If you had, say, six suppliers, all pretty much the same as each other, would you buy on the lowest price? Yes of course you would; you'd be a fool not to. But that's not this world".

To maximise profit, therefore, an organisation should not just consider price but total cost: purchase price plus cost of use. The motivation behind Deming's concept is simple: to improve quality and reduce total costs, thus ensuring competitiveness and profitability in the long term.

Deming therefore argues that it is vital to recognise and know the total cost of products and services which are bought from external suppliers. In the case of products, in addition to the actual purchase price, costs are incurred from administration, maintenance, service, delays, downtime, scrap, rework and warranty claims.

Joseph M Juran

Joseph Juran was also invited to Japan in the early 1950s by the Union of Japanese Scientists and Engineers (JUSE) and he conducted seminars for Japanese business people at this time. His teachings focused on the need to set targets for improvement and emphasised that quality control should be conducted as an integral feature of management control. So, quality does not just happen – it needs to be planned for by all aspects of an organisation.

Juran argued that quality planning needs to identify customers and their needs. His 'Quality Planning Road Map' consists of the following steps:

- Identify who are the customers
- Determine the needs of the customers
- Translate those needs into our language
- Develop a product/ service that can respond to those needs
- Optimise the product features so as to meet our needs as well as customer needs
- Develop a process which is able to produce the product/ service
- Optimise the process
- Prove that the process can produce the product/ service under operating conditions
- Transfer the process to operations.

Juran's teachings therefore emphasise the roles of both internal and external customers, so that all in an organisation focus on the needs of the customer and argue that the majority of quality problems are the fault of poor management, rather than poor workmanship on the shop-floor.

In addition, Juran was critical of senior managers: 'Their instinctive belief is that upper managers already know what needs to be done, and that training is for others – the workforce, the supervision, the engineers. It is time to re- examine this belief'.

Tom Peters

Another American author who became famous for his teachings is Tom Peters. His first book, written with Bob Waterman, *In Search of Excellence,* was published in 1982 and examined the common features of excellent performance within 43 American companies. It was a worldwide best seller and although the research of the book has been criticised, it still provides today a stimulating account of the ways that organisations can improve. Many of the principles outlined by Peters and Waterman were implemented by organisations.

Tom Peters
Stressed the Importance of

Care of Customers

Leadership
Management by
Wandering
About (MBWA)

People

Constant
Innovation

In Peters' second book, *A Passion for Excellence,* he identified leadership as being central to the quality improvement process. The leader has a responsibility to:

- listen to subordinates, which suggests a caring approach;
- teach: whereby values should be transmitted face to face;
- facilitate so that managers are able to provide on-the-spot help.

The basis for leadership is 'management by wandering about' as this enables the leader to keep in contact with customers, innovation and people. These, he cites, are the three key areas in the pursuit of 'excellence'. Tom Peters also describes 12 attributes, or traits of a quality revolution. These are:

Management Obsession with Quality: this point highlights the importance of practical action to back up the emotional commitment to quality.

Passionate Systems: he argues that failure is invariably due to passion without a system, or a system without passion. Systems are as important as having an ideology.

Measurement of Quality: this needs to be carried out throughout the improvement programme, and should be publicised and adhered to by all of the participants.

Quality Is Rewarded: there needs to be a compensation scheme to reward quality improvement. This helps to improve the prospects of achieving an early breakthrough in the improvement process.

Everyone Is Trained for Quality: each person in the company should receive extensive training in quality. Particularly important is cause and effect analysis, statistical process control and team interaction.

Multi-Functional Teams: quality circles or cross-functional teams need to be introduced.

Small Is Beautiful: all small improvements are fundamental to the quality improvement effort.

Create Endless 'Hawthorne' Effects: these refer to experiments used on work teams. The Hawthorne studies conducted by General Electric found that productivity improved when people participated in experiments.

Parallel Organisation Structure Devoted to Quality Improvement: this refers to the creation of quality teams who shadow the work of others in the organisation searching for possible improvements.

Everyone Is Involved: Peters emphasises the role of suppliers, as well as customers, distributors and other groupings linked to the organisation.

When Quality Goes Up, Costs Go Down: he argues that quality improvement is a source of cost reduction.

Quality Improvement Is a Never-Ending Journey: 'Each day, each product or service is getting relatively better or worse, but never stands still'.

Problems Associated with Implementing Total Quality

According to research conducted by Warwick University in 1996, 65% of UK private sector manufacturing firms had implemented total quality. The sample for the research was 988 different firms. Whilst total quality appears to be the solution to improving corporate performance, many organisations have suffered from a high level of disappointment and failure to achieve the dramatic gains promised by total quality. A study published in 1992 of 100 UK firms by the management consultants AT Kearney suggested that as many as 80% of programmes fail to produce any tangible benefit. In 1993, the American-based consultancy firm, Arthur D Little carried out a survey of 500 US firms, and only one third of the sample felt that total quality was having a significant effect on their competitiveness.

According to Slack et al (1995), even total quality programmes which are successfully implemented do not guarantee to bring long-term improvement and may lose impetus over time. Slack describes this phenomenon as 'quality droop.'

A feature of this model is that organisations typically make attempts to re-introduce quality programmes when problems occur with the existing scheme. According to research by Bessant, Levy, Sang and Lamming, many total quality programmes have resulted in 'partial total quality'.

Success of Total Quality Programmes

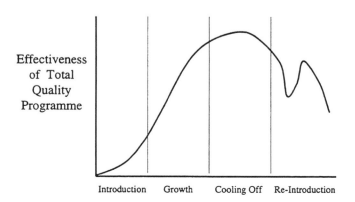

Characteristic	Partial Total Quality
Framework	Local rather than organisation-wide
	Total quality is a short-term 'fashion' rather than a long-term development
	There is little strategic planning of TQ
Infrastructure	TQ implemented without organisational change
	Little training given
	Over reliance on single tools like 'quality circles'
Culture	Espoused change in values not supported by
	actual behaviour
	Organisational culture no different with TQ

The characteristics of partial total quality can be compared with total quality:

Characteristic	Total Quality Management
Framework	Clear strategic framework and a shared and communicated vision
	TQ a long-term development with real commitment to continuous improvement
Infrastructure	TQ implemented without organisational change
	Significant organisational rethinking
	High investment in training reflecting the shift in view of 'human resources'
	Flexible use of a broad range of tools
	task forces, improvement teams, Deming Wheels
Culture	Change in behaviour to reflect the change to total quality

(Source: Adapted from 'Managing Successful Total Quality Relationships in the Supply Chain' Bessant, Levy, Sang and Lamming, *European Journal of Purchasing and Supply Management* Vol1 Number1 (1994)

Further Reading

Bessant, Levy, Sang and Lamming Managing Successful 'Total Quality Relationships in the Supply Chain' *European Journal of Purchasing and Supply Management.* Vol1 Number1 (1994)

Crosby *Quality is Free* McGraw Hill (1979)

Deming *Out of the Crisis* Cambridge University Press (1988)

Juran *Juran on Planning for Quality* The Free Press (1988)

Peters and Waterman *In Search of Excellence* Harper and Row (1982)

Peters et al *A Passion for Excellence* New York, Random House Inc (1985)

Slack, Chambers, Harland, Harrison and Johnston *Operations Management* Pitman Publishing (1995)

chapter five
Managing Internal Customers

Purchasing's Role in Managing Quality

The previous chapter identified different approaches to managing quality. The models and ideas produced by the quality gurus like W Edwards Deming and Joseph Juran have had a significant impact on the operations of organisations. This chapter will firstly concentrate on the means of satisfying internal customers to help enable produce a quality output.

We have already identified that purchasing has a number of internal customers. As we saw in the last chapter, central to the achievement of quality is the identification of customer requirements, producing an error-free service which satisfies, if not exceeds, these needs. Purchasing clearly needs to focus attention on how best to satisfy customers. Central to the satisfaction of customers will be:

- the recognition of customer requirements;
- the effective implementation of the purchasing cycle;
- an awareness of the nature of the product or service purchased.

In the previous chapter, Joseph Juran's work on planning for total quality provides a methodology which enables purchasers to identify customer requirements.

- Identify who are the customers
- Determine the needs of the customers
- Translate those needs into our language
- Develop a product/ service that can respond to those needs
- Optimise the product features to meet our needs as well as customer needs
- Develop a process which is able to produce the product/ service
- Optimise the process
- Prove that the process can produce the product/ service under operating conditions
- Transfer the process to operations.

Purchasing has an 'internal interface' dealing with both internal customers and suppliers. The 'external interface' of the department is mainly concerned with the selection and motivation of suppliers required to satisfy the purchasing organisation's requirements.

External Interface

Supplier Management

Purchasing's Role

Internal Interface

Satisfying Customers

The Internal Interface

Much has already been stated about customer satisfaction. Purchasing needs to identify the requirements of customers. Typically customers may demand:

- Advice on specifications
- Information about supply markets
- Details of likely costs, lead times, etc
- Purchases of goods and services which achieve VFM
- Quick responses to queries, etc.

Different customers may have different requirements and require different purchasing skills. Consider, for example, the buyer who is responsible for purchasing materials and components for a design department. The emphasis here may be on researching possible suppliers and forming collaborative development projects. On the other hand, there may be less emphasis on supply market research for the buyer responsible for buying large volume components for a manufacturing concern.

In addition, of critical importance to the purchaser's ability to satisfy the customer is the understanding of the characteristics of the product or service required. The traditional selection criteria of lowest price does not necessarily guarantee customer satisfaction.

The user of the purchase requirement is unlikely to obtain the product or service required. A low price can, of course, lead to deficiencies elsewhere of the purchase, such as technical defects, poor service or delivery.

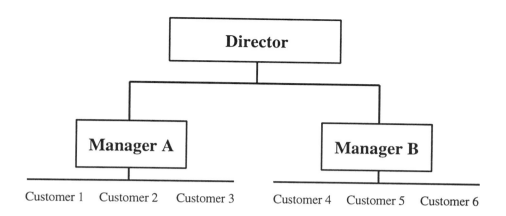

A typical structure of sales and marketing functions is specialised on the basis of target customer groups. In the diagram above, the two senior managers reporting to the director are responsible for different customers. The two sets of customers may be operating in two different sectors. Many sales and marketing functions have implemented a structure of 'account managers' where the customers' interests are the focus of the firm's structure.

Research by Marion Kempeners advocates the adoption by purchasing departments of an account management structure. A similar structure can therefore be implemented by larger purchasing sections, where individual buyers may be allocated to form relationships with particular customers. Their main responsibility will be to ensure that the customer is provided with help and information, as well as the actual purchases required.

There can be a variety of different structures implemented by purchasing sections, and these will be discussed in greater detail in Chapter 6, Structure and Strategy.

Once purchasing has identified its internal customers and developed services which will satisfy customers, these services need to be brought to the customers' attention through a marketing plan. This is particularly important for larger purchasing sections and can help improve communication links with other business functions. A marketing plan stresses the four Ps:

- Price
- Product
- Place
- Promotion

Price

Deming refers to the importance of buying on the basis of lowest overall cost rather than purely on price. The purchasing function clearly needs to provide customers with cost-effective products and services sourced from suppliers. Customers should be informed of the cost benefits of the acquisitions. This can be done through providing a short report which highlights the life-cycle costing exercise or total acquisition costs. A life-cycle costing exercise will take into account the running costs and maintenance of products purchased. Purchasing need to demonstrate cost savings to persuade internal customers of the added value provided by the function.

Product

The product refers to the actual goods or service that the purchaser buys. In addition to the actual purchase, the purchaser provides a service information, help, advice as well as completion of the contract.

Place

The purchaser also needs to recognise the customer's requirements in terms of the location for the purchase. This can be a very important decision and affects the 'contract strategy'. The purchaser may be able to aggregate requirements together for different locations or customers. In addition, logistics support may also need to be arranged to enable suppliers to provide the products/ services where required.

Promotion

Finally, purchasing needs to promote its services. This can be done through distributing a pamphlet which outlines the services provided and the people involved. Some purchasing departments publish a regular newsletter which is sent to internal customers. The department may also have a mission statement and details of goals and objectives. These need to be communicated to the internal customers.

TASK

Does your department promote itself?

Managing Change

The purchasing manager will generally be involved in managing changes. The changes could be geared towards improving relationships with internal customers, or, managing improvement through the supply chain. However, change breeds mistrust and so the purchaser will invariably meet considerable resistance to his or her initiatives.

A simple model for charting change was developed by Kurt Lewin. He suggests that we can look at any situation as being held in balance, or equilibrium, between the forces which are driving it or seeking to change it, and the forces that are restraining it. In Lewin's view, if nothing is happening it is because the forces restraining or inhibiting any change are equal to any forces which are driving change (the pressures for change). As a result, the situation remains in a state of equilibrium – that is, nothing happens.

Kurt Lewin: Force Field Analysis

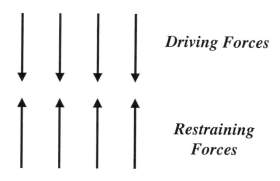

Driving Forces

Restraining Forces

Stages:

(1) Unfreezing

(2) Changing

(3) Refreezing

Typical Restraining Forces:

(1) Threats of Redundancy

(2) Threats to Status and Power

(3) Fear of the Unknown

(4) Lack of Belief in Ability to Learn New Ways

(5) Established Routines Will Be Distorted

The most significant barrier to the effective implementation of any change is resistance. Consider, for example, any restructuring that your department may have undergone. Within the organisation, there are driving forces reinforcing the need to change (to improve efficiency/ effectiveness/ get closer to internal customers, etc) and restraining forces resisting that change.

There can be many reasons for resisting change. According to research carried out by Kotter and Schlesinger in 1979, the main reasons are as follows:

Parochial Self-Interest: it is often human nature to put one's own interests before those of the organisation or the department.

Misunderstanding: misunderstandings can often occur in the implementation of change as a result of people failing to understand the implications of the change, particularly when the objectives have not been fully communicated. It occurs more frequently when there is a lack of trust in senior management.

Low Tolerance for Change: some people fear that they will not have the ability to learn new skills or work behaviour. This resistance to change is most common when new technology is introduced. For example, when ICL recently redesigned the jobs of a number of its employees, there was some fear that there would be redundancies. In fact, there were none. The purchasing manager will clearly need to overcome resistance to change. There are various ways of dealing with such resistance.

Education and Communication: communication of the objectives of a project will usually help people to understand the need for and the logic of a change.

Participation and Involvement: if the initiators involve the potential resistors in some aspect of the design and implementation of the change, they can often forestall resistance.

Negotiation and Agreement: another way to deal with resistance is to offer incentives to active or potential resistors.

Coercion: the most risky strategy for project managers is to deal with the resistance coercively. Here, they force people to accept a change by issuing threats.

The Stages of Change

Lewin identified three stages in the implementation of a change or innovation.

- unfreezing
- changing
- refreezing

Stage 1 Unfreezing: the first stage, when the project manager is trying to get everyone to adopt and implement the change is the most crucial. At this stage, it is likely that the greatest resistance is likely to be encountered. Ways in which the resistance might be overcome have been identified.

Stage 2 Changing: it is at this second stage that the change is implemented. In 1985, Alexander led a survey of 93 private sector companies to determine which implementation problems occurred most frequently. The most common problems were:

- implementation often took much longer than anticipated;
- major problems often surfaced during implementation that had not been identified earlier;
- coordination of activities was often not effective enough;
- training for employees was often inadequate;
- uncontrollable factors from outside the organisation had an adverse effect on implementation.

Stage 3 Refreezing: at this stage, the project manager needs to consolidate the change and ensure that a new balance or equilibrium is established. New resistances can often appear and so the manager needs to monitor the change and take action as the need arises.

Internal Customer/Purchaser/ Supplier Relationships

Purchasing managers in setting up agreements with suppliers will be performing a contract management role. There are typically three parties involved in commercial relationships formed with external suppliers:

Internal Customers

Users needs (internal customers) must, ultimately, drive the contract manager and supplier. This is not to say that internal customers should be given all that they ask for. There are three approaches which can be taken by the purchasing or contract manager:

Ask Customers What they Want: the contract manager therefore becomes a follower with few risks of upsetting the customer. However, what the internal customer may want may not be in keeping with the needs of the business. Consider the purchasing manager setting up a contract for business travel. A significant number of customers would generally want to travel first or executive class each journey because of the added comfort of such a service in comparison to travelling by standard class. The danger of asking customers what they would like is that the product or service required may be a 'gold plated' one and excessively over-specified.

Customer Care

Purchasing Functions Can Have 3 Approaches:

• Ask Customers What they Want

• Push Customers in Directions they Do Not Want to Go

• Lead Customers Where they Need to Go Before the Customers Know it

Push Customers in Directions they Do not Want to Go: an alternative approach to the managing of internal customers is to force purchasing intiatives on the customer. This appraoch would fuel the greatest resistance to change from the customers, and they may try and avoid the contract and perhaps use other means of obtaining their requirements!

Lead Customers where they Need to Go before they Know It: this is achieved by an insight of customer needs and aspirations and should be the standard the contracts manager aims for. This comes from an analysis and understanding of the supply market and matching the abilities of supplier to the business requirements for the contract in question. This requires effective internal marketing to the internal customer.

The relationship building starts with forming relationships with internal customers!

To form a productive relationship, purchasers should:

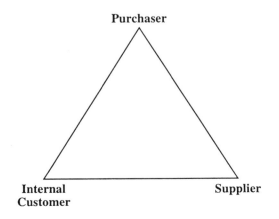

Purchaser

Internal Customer   Supplier

- Devise a strategy for managing the relationship with the internal customer, and specify respective roles in terms of contract monitoring and control. This is likely to vary from daily/ weekly contact to the less frequent involvement needed for well managed contracts.
- Try to be non-adversarial and create a win-win relationship with both the internal customer and the supplier. This can help achieve best results.
- Aim for continuous dialogue and, where appropriate, a joint and mutually beneficial approach to problem solving.
- Keep the supplier up-to-date with internal organisational changes within the purchasing organisation that could have an impact on the supply contract.

The purchasing manager should also act as a coach and leader of others in the organisation to help sustain the right relationship with the supplier. In reviewing the contract, the main aim will be to determine the extent to which requirements were met. Points to consider may include:

- achievement of objectives/ reasons for under-performance;
- costs versus budget;
- effectiveness of the relationship/ liaison between the supplier, internal customers and the contract manager;
- initiative/ responsiveness of the supplier;
- planning/ control provided by the supplier;
- internal customer satisfaction level;
- extent of the achievement of value for money.

To attempt to make a decision that will gain the trust of others we can use a model to help. The purchasing manager may need to get the participation of those involved in the decision, rather than making it autonomously. Victor Vroom advocates a useful decision tree model to provide guidance to the purchasing manager on how to best make such decisions. Vroom argued that the right choice of participation in the decision depends on answering seven different questions. The different ways of making decisions are:

- A1: solve the problem or make the decision yourself, using information available to you at that time.
- A2: obtain the necessary information others involved, then decide on the problem/ decision yourself.
- C1: share the problem with relevant people individually, getting their ideas and suggestions. Then make the decision.
- C2: share the problem with other people as a group, usually in a meeting, then you make the decision.

- G2: share the problem with the others as a group. Together, you generate and evaluate alternatives and attempt to reach agreement on a solution. Your role is much like that of a chairman. You do not try to influence the group to adopt 'your' solution, and you are willing to accept and implement any solution which has the support of the entire group.

Trust needs to be gained with suppliers too. A lack of trust will generally lead to an adversarial type of relationship. This can be damaging as the purchasing organisation and seller will be in conflict with one another.

Trust Can Be Gained By:

> • **Being fair and honest**
>
> • **Never trying to deceive the supplier**
>
> • **Communicating on a regular basis**
>
> • **Giving feedback when the supplier has not succeeded in a tender bid**

Suppliers also need to be motivated to provide the products and services required by the purchasing organisation. To motivate suppliers, the purchasing manager needs to understand how to lead members of his or her team, as well as suppliers.

Charles Handy in *Understanding Organisations* defines leadership as 'the ability to influence the behaviour of other people in a certain direction.' Handy, in his chapter on leadership, comments that these analyses of traits rest on the assumption that the individual is more important than the situation. Most studies of personality traits that are akin to leadership qualities single out the following traits:

- intelligence – generally above average but not of genius level;
- initiative – independence and inventiveness;
- self-assurance – self-confidence, reasonably high self-ratings on competence and aspiration levels, and on perceived status within society;
- a 'helicopter' factor – the ability to rise above the particulars of a situation and perceive it in its relationship to the overall environment.

Effective leadership has a consequential affect on motivating others to achieve effective performance. Motivation theories also help to provide guidance to purchasing managers. Frederick Herzberg's theory was developed from an interview investigation of 203 accountants and engineers. They were asked what job events had occurred in their work that had led to extreme satisfaction or extreme dissatisfaction on their part. The responses were broken down into positive job events (leading to satisfaction) and negative job events (leading to dissatisfaction).

In positive experiences, intrinsic sources such as achievement, recognition, the work itself, responsibility and advancement were mentioned frequently. In negative experiences, extrinsic sources such as company administration, supervision, relationships with others, status and security were frequently mentioned. Herzberg argued that the factors which provide satisfaction to people's work are different from the factors which provide dissatisfaction. The dissatisfying factors are called 'hygiene' factors and those that produce satisfaction are called 'motivators'. It is interesting that money is a hygiene factor, as it is an aspect of work that people tend to feel dissatisfied with.

Motivation: Herzberg's Dual Factor Theory

Motivators:	*Hygienes:*
Achievement	Company Policy & Administration
Recognition	Supervision
Work Itself	Interpersonal Relations
Responsibility	Money
Advancement	Status
	Security

Herzberg's theory is a useful one. Suppliers are organisations but organisations obviously consist of people. Suppliers can therefore be given a sense of:

- achievement – by congratulating them on their performance;
- recognition – by giving awards or prizes, for example, to the best performing suppliers;
- the work itself – by asking suppliers to provide creative solutions to the purchaser's requirements;
- responsibility – by empowering the suppliers to take on greater responsibilities;
- advancement – by rewarding good performance with further business.

Purchasing Managers Need to Motivate:

Suppliers:

They Need to Be Encouraged to Provide the Right Product/ Service at the Right Time, Place, Quality and Cost

Other Procurement Staff:

The Manager May Be Responsible for Other Members of Staff

Internal Customers:

Need to Comply with Procedures and Purchasing Policies

Themselves!

To Help Create Improvements to Bought-out Products and Services

Measuring Performance

Purchasing needs measures of performance to assess whether the services provided to internal customers are being given correctly. Some commonly used measures of performance are:

Area	Measure
Quality	Percentage of rejects in goods received
	Percentage of parts rejected in production
	Warranty claims from customers
	Number of problems experienced with supplier
Quantity	Percentage of stock which has not moved over a specified period
	Number of stockouts
	Number of small value orders
	Number of emergency orders
	Comparison of stock with target stock
Timing	Suppliers' actual delivery performance against promised
	Time taken to process requisitions
	Time taken with remedial actions required
	Completion times of aspects of the contract
Price	Prices paid against standard
	Prices paid for key items compared with market benchmarks
	Prices paid against budget
	Price at the time of use against price at the time of purchase
Operational Costs	Costs of processing an order
	Progressing costs as a percentage of total
	Operational costs (accommodation, people, telephone/fax/cars/ transport, etc)

TASK

Does your department use measures of performance?

Does it measure customer satisfaction?

Coordination with internal customers can be difficult to appraise. Measures which have been used include:

- the number of complaints from other departmental managers;
- periodic customer-satisfaction surveys through questionnaire surveys;
- time taken to process requisitions/ contracts;
- time taken to deal with queries from customers;

The External Interface

Negotiation with Suppliers

Purchasing's customers will usually expect the department's buyers to be competent at negotiation. Purchasers need to work with suppliers to:

- reduce total costs;
- achieve reliability in terms of delivery times for products and completion times for services;
- achieve zero defects.

Negotiation of the requirements with the supplier is an important stage of the purchasing cycle. The buyer needs to obtain the supplier's agreement and commitment to producing a quality product or service. However, there may be a mis-match between the buyer's requirements and the supplier's quotation or, for that matter, their view of the purchaser's needs. The two parties may need to conduct negotiation. It can be helpful to break the negotiation process down into various phases and it is useful to think of the negotiation process as consisting of five phases.

The Stages of Negotiation

Preparation:	Meeting:	Bargaining:
Collation of Information On: • The Supplier • The Supply Market • The Purchaser's Own Organisation • The People Involved • The Product/ Service to Be Supplied • SWOT Set Objectives	Explore Interests Find Out their Needs Use Questions Questions	Use the Information Trade Concessions Package Variables

Phase 1: Preparation

It can be argued that the preparation stage is one of the most important. If it is carried out thoroughly, then this will help the negotiation process. Brian Farrington, a foremost purchasing consultant, has traditionally argued that for each hour of contact negotiation there should have been six hours spent preparing for this. In important negotiations for high spend, critical items, this may certainly be an effective use of time. However, for less significant purchases, this could be regarded as superfluous effort. Information needs to be gathered on a variety of different aspects of the purchase:

The Supplier: information about the supplier's performance can, of course, be extremely useful when planning for the negotiation. If the purchasing organisation records the supplier's performance through a vendor rating system, then this information may be made available. It is, perhaps, useful for the purchaser to be objective about such information, since many of the supply problems may have actually been caused by the purchasing organisation.

The Supply Market: many industrial markets are oligopolistic, whereby the market is dominated by a few suppliers. Under such conditions, the suppliers involved may have substantial power. The buyer needs to recognise the limitations of his purchase decision, and appreciate the relative importance of the purchase to the supplier's business. This aspect is discussed in greater detail in Chapter 6, 'Structure and Strategy'.

The purchaser may be able to consider opportunities to expand the supply market, by redeveloping the purchase or persuading different suppliers to supply the requirement. This can be a particularly effective policy when dealing with a monopoly supplier.

Another important consideration is the current and forecast level of demand and supply, for both the purchaser's requirements and also in the market as a whole. The seasonality and cyclical behaviour of certain markets can inevitably have an impact on prices and lead times.

Purchaser's Own Organisation: the buyer needs to be aware of aspects of the purchasing organisation's performance. As has already been mentioned, the purchaser may have been responsible for problems experienced by the supplier due to poor planning or variations to requirements. Developments in the purchaser's own financial performance can also have an impact on the motivation of the purchaser to improve aspects of the supplier's performance. There may be other commercial and technical characteristics of the purchasing organisation which may have a bearing on the purchase.

The People Involved: the buyers also need to prepare for the people who are likely to be involved in the negotiation, internally and externally. Effective team management can be difficult to achieve because of different priorities which different people in the organisation may hold. Traditional purchase behaviour is characterised by the buyer wanting the purchase at the lowest price, whereas users are more concerned with quality and service aspects of the purchase.

The Requirements of the Actual Purchase: the features and characteristics of the purchase requirement also need to be understood. With the increased use of performance specifications, suppliers are now being increasingly encouraged to provide solutions to the requirements set by purchasing organisations. The buyer's role has to be one of understanding the use of the product or service purchased, as well as being familiar with the basics of the technical details of suppliers' proposals.

Other features may also need to be prepared. The buyer may find it useful to build up a SWOT (Strengths, Weaknesses, Opportunities and Threats) analysis. This is a useful tool which can be committed to writing and distributed to the other members of the negotiation team before any meeting.

The next important element of the preparation stage is to set objectives for the negotiation. Objectives should be quantifiable measures of performance. An estimation needs to made of the objectives which could be achieved in the negotiation, and these objectives should focus on the variables of the purchase decision, such as price, delivery/completion, elements of the service, payment and other commercial terms, the specification and so forth. It can be useful to generate three levels of objectives: the L I M approach.

- objectives which the purchaser would *like* to achieve – these would represent the ideal package;
- objectives which the purchaser *intends* to achieve – these represent the most realistically achievable outcomes which the purchaser could expect;
- objectives which represent the *minimum* acceptable – the so called 'walkaway' position.

These three sets of objectives should be:

- measurable: the performance criteria set can be evaluated through quantifiable data;
- achievable: the outcomes should be attainable as unrealistic objectives may de-motivate behaviour;
- stretching: whilst the objectives set should be achievable, they should also be ambitious.

Phase 2: Meeting

The second phase assumes that the preparations for the negotiation have been completed and that the parties to the negotiation process meet to discuss the requirement. Each of the parties involved needs to understand the interests of the other party otherwise there could be a misunderstanding of each others requirements. This is illustrated in the diagram.

To establish the interests of the other party, negotiators should concentrate on asking effective questions to clarify the position and details of the purchase decision. In addition, answers to these questions need to be understood, and this highlights the benefit of effective listening skills.

At this stage, the parties may test assumptions, exchange information, explore interests and practice being noncommittal about their proposals and their explanations.

Phase 3: Bargaining

The bargaining stage occurs when the participants attempt to persuade the other parties to change their position. Paul Steele, a leading purchasing management consultant, identifies five methods of persuasion.

Methods of Persuasion

- Logic

- Bargain

- Emotion

- Threat

- Compromise

Logical Persuasion: this refers to the use of rational arguments to drive the other party to change position. Steele views that the constraint on the use of logic is that humans are essentially irrational. Therefore, the parties may not share a common perception of what is logical.

Emotion: logical argument may not be able to convince the other party. The arousal of emotions can be an effective tactic, as the purchaser may for example use arguments that play on the suppliers' conscience. The drawback to the use of influencing the other party by emotion is, it is argued, that it may not be effective in all circumstances. The use of emotion may, to a certain extent, invade on the privacy of the other party, for example.

Threat: logical persuasion may have little effect. This could result in a sense of frustration, which may then lead to threats being made to influence the other party. Should the threat be backed by power, then this improves the negotiating position. According to Charles Handy, there are a number of sources of power:

- physical power and its use in dealings with suppliers should, perhaps, be kept to a minimum!!
- resource or reward power which, in a purchaser/supplier relationship, can be related to the ability of the purchaser to award future contracts;
- position power, which may also be called 'legal' or 'legitimate power': this is the power that comes as a result of the role or the position in the organisation, which was discussed in Chapter 1;
- expert power which refers to the authority that is vested in someone because of their acknowledged expertise;
- personal or charismatic power which is the degree of popularity of the individua: this can be enhanced by position or expert status;
- negative power which is the ability to stop things from happening, such as the buyer who refuses to place a contract with a supplier

If power is used, the general consensus is that it should be used with care. The use of power is seldom one-sided as the receiver will often try and achieve parity at some point in the future. The supplier's power may change over time, particularly when their economic position improves.

Bargaining: this refers to the exchange of concessions to achieve agreement. The supplier may, for example, be encouraged to improve lead time and delivery reliability in return for a concession given by the purchaser over payment terms. Bargaining is an essential element of most negotiations and it is important for the buyer to draw up a list of possible concessions which could be traded in the negotiation. These concessions should be costed as this information is essential if one is to evaluate the total cost of acquisition.

Compromise: this refers to the practice of 'splitting the difference', which is a commonly used method of gaining movement from the other party. This tactic will generally favour the negotiator who sets his or her objectives at the highest level, and should only be used when bridging a gap if there is a disagreement over a small difference in positions.

The Stages of Negotiation

Agreement	*Post-Evaluation*
Establish the New Position	Which Objectives Were Achieved?
Summarise	How Were they Achieved?
Ensure that the Agreement is Correctly Interpreted	What Prevented Certain Objectives from Being Agreed?

Phase 4: Agreement

The penultimate phase of the negotiation process is the agreement phase. The details of the negotiation are concluded and often an agreement will be signed by both parties for the terms of the purchase. It is important that the parties interpret agreement in the same way. It is a useful ploy to summarise what has been agreed, to prevent any confusion once the process has been completed and the contract is underway.

Phase 5: Post Agreement

Post-agreement analysis should be an essential part of the negotiation process. On many occasions it is not done. The purpose of this vital stage is to analyse whether the objectives were achieved and, if any objectives were not secured, the reasons for this. Any number of reasons could explain why there was a failure, and it is always important to analyse the objectives that were set in the first place. Perhaps the most important issue for the individual involved in the negotiation is to analyse the lessons that could be learnt from the experience. Successful negotiators are more likely to be aware of their mistakes and to be self-critical of their performance, whilst still retaining the necessary degree of confidence to influence other people.

Post-Tender Negotiation

Post-tender negotiation refers to the practice of seeking clarification and improvements to the offers made by supplier organisations. The Chartered Institute of Purchasing and Supply provides the following definition:

> Negotiation after receipt of formal tenders and before the letting of contracts with the supplier submitting the lowest acceptable tender with a view to obtaining an improvement in price, delivery or content, in circumstances which do not put other tenderers at a disadvantage or affect adversely their confidence or trust in the competitive tendering system.

The traditional tendering system does not facilitate the extensive use of negotiation. Purchase decisions would primarily be based on awarding contracts to the lowest bidder. Post-tender negotiation therefore provides the means of eradicating any misunderstandings before the contract is placed, and also can be used to secure improvements to offers produced by suppliers. The Chartered Institute of Purchasing and Supply provides guidance on the use of post-tender negotiation in which the following criteria and controls should be considered:

- The value of the contract, potential for savings, and the cost to the buyer of conducting PTN against the likely saving in price.
- Is there time to conduct PTN without delaying the completion date of contract?
- What effect will it have on the future supply position?
- Is the contract affected by EC directives which require equality of treatment of potential suppliers? (See Chapter 9).
- Is it or would it be considered ethical?

Controls to be implemented may include the following:

- Who will authorise PTN in particular cases and how will that person relate to the person authorised to award the contract?
- Who will take part in and who will lead the negotiations?
- Who will award the contract? What documentation is needed to record events before, during, and after PTN and does this provide a satisfactory audit trail?
- How will the conduct and results of PTN be reviewed and by whom?

The Central Unit on Purchasing, the Treasury Department which provides advice to central government purchasing organisations, has also issued guidance on the use of PTN, pointing out that it is not unethical for buyers to challenge the prices tendered. The CUP has stated that post-tender negotiations can apply to almost any order or contract although care must be taken to ensure that the cost of negotiation does not outweigh any savings. In particular, post-tender negotiation (PTN) are recommended for:

- all orders potentially worth £100,000 or over;
- where the final bid evaluation does not present overwhelming evidence for one tenderer;
- where there is doubt regarding quality or performance or where clarification of terms and conditions is required;
- all supply agreements made for a period of 12 months or longer.

In terms of direct price negotiation, the Central Unit on Purchasing also identifies eight common areas for direct price negotiation as follows:

- where single tender action has been authorised;
- where it is known or suspected that pricefixing cartel-type arrangements are in operation;
- where tender prices appear grossly inflated over known market rates or reliable estimates or the price paid for identical or similar goods;
- where, despite competitive tendering, a particular supplier is consistently successful in obtaining the contract (some degree of care should be exercised here as this may be due to the fact that the supplier is superior to its competitors, although CUP's advice is to take a periodic check on its costings);
- where the enquiry is based on a functional or developmental specification rather than a detailed specification;
- where the purchaser needs to justify selections by testing the market;
- where the quantity to be ordered justifies splitting requirements between more than one supplier;
- to evaluate whether market conditions are in the buyer's favour.

Contract Award

Once the negotiation process has been completed, the next stage of the purchasing cycle is the selection of the most appropriate supplier. A contract should be issued which provides details of the specification and contractual terms which have been agreed. As we saw in Chapter 2, acceptance must be total and unqualified, otherwise it is not an acceptance but a counter offer which the other party in turn can either accept or reject. Similarly, acceptance must be communicated to the offeror unless the offeror when making the offer stipulated that a certain course of conduct would create sufficient acceptance. However, a negative instruction from the offeror is insufficient to make a contract; silence cannot constitute acceptance.

A Comparison Between Buying Products and Services

Purchasing departments have not traditionally had a great involvement in the management of commercial relationships for services bought externally. The choice of auditors, marketing agencies, lawyers and management consultants has been very much the perogative of senior and executive management. It is vital that the buyer fully appreciates the differences between service and product procurement to be able to provide value-added benefits to internal customers.

Chapter 2 identified differences in legislation through the Sale of Goods Act and the Supply of Goods and Services Act. Goods bought often have a service element too. Consider the following aspects of a purchase, for example:

- The ability of a supplier to react quickly to quoting for the buyer's requirement.
- The delivery of the goods to the necessary location.
- Correct invoicing.
- Efficient after-sales service.

It is important for the purchaser to recognise these requirements as well as the physical characteristics and prices of the goods purchased.

Major differences exist between the procurement of services and the procurement of products. Most products are delivered to the buyer, but the customer often performs the service on the buyer's premises. The table below highlights some of the differences:

SERVICE	PRODUCT
Intangible	Tangible
Not held in stock	Can be held in stock
Often performed at the purchaser's premises	Is delivered
Change of personnel can vary the quality	Output consistent
Standards can be difficult to establish and measure	Standards can be established and tests done to check conformance

Let us explain these terms in a little more detail.

Intangible Services

Services are usually intangible. You cannot for example touch consultancy advice or a haircut (but you can often see the results of these services). On the other hand, products can be measured, weighed, tested and inspected to evaluate whether they conform to requirements.

Services, are more difficult to measure. We need to distinguish the 'deliverables' of the service. Remember that most services have some form of output which can be assessed. For example, when we eat out we typically think of the restaurant as providing a service. The service element is certainly a significant to the transaction and we are usually very unsure, as customers, whether or not to leave a tip for the service. The deliverables are of course the meal. The same principle can be applied to any service contract.

There is a danger of seeing the procurement of goods or products and the procurement of services as two different things. However, analysis of a particular service should reveal that there is normally the combination of both goods and a service.

For the effective management of contracts, the buyer needs to distinguish what the outputs or deliverables are from any agreement. There is always a mixture of a product and an element of service with any arrangement with a supplier. An engineering manufacturer may provide delivered product, but the service element is the way in which they may deal with queries, correct administration (such as invoicing, etc.) and contributions made to reducing costs of supply. At the other end of the spectrum, a contract for consultancy has a goods element, since the supplier may be required to produce reports. These would be the deliverables in the supply contract.

Tangibility of Supply

Chemical Producer

Construction Sub-Contractor

Light Engineering Manufacturer

Travel Agency

Computer System

Marketing Agency

Consultancy

Security

◀ ■■■■■■■■■■■■■■■■■■■■■■■■■■■■■■■■■ ▶

Pure Product   *Pure Service*

Storage

By their nature, services cannot be stored. This means that they must be provided at a time which exactly coincides with a need. It is not possible for the services supplier to stockpile the service. Take for example, accommodation at a hotel: whilst there are a number of rooms available, the supply of rooms is a relatively fixed variable.

Place

Products tend to be manufactured at a supplier's plant and subsequently transported via the supply chain to the different customers involved. A service, however, will typically be performed at the purchaser's premises. Take for example, contracts which may be made with suppliers for the kinds of services which help keep the building functioning (facilities management). There may be cleaning, building maintenance, security and catering. All of these services would be performed at the purchaser's premises.

Role of People

Services tend to be done by people. The content of the work depends on their inputs and care for the customer (the purchaser). The quality of goods on the other hand is reasonably evident. In services though, the customer judges not only the outcome of the service, but also the way in which it was produced.

Continuous Improvement and Benchmarking

The definition of quality, 'meeting customer requirements' in customer/ supplier relationships, is fundamental to the achievement of business requirements. However, business requirements never stay constant: competition is always there. Organisations need to be constantly improving their service to customers and developing new products and services to capture market share.

The Japanese call continuous improvement 'Kaizen'. It is the attitude of not being satisfied with meeting requirements once, but improving all the time. The focus on the supply chain therefore needs to be on both reducing cost, improving quality and improving time to market.

Another way of measuring efficiency is by comparing data with best practice. This process is called benchmarking, as it provides a means by which a firm can compare itself to the best in the market. The process builds on Kaizen (continuous improvement). The goal of benchmarking is to build on the success of others to improve future performance. By benchmarking on a continuing basis, the organisation is researching current best practice and the objective is to put improvements into action. Benchmarking is analysed in Chapter 8.

References/ Further Study

Handy *Understanding Organisations* Penguin Business Library

Herzberg *Work and the Nature of Man* World Publishing Co (1966)

HM Treasury, Central Unit on Purchasing *CUP;* Guidance Numbers 1 (Post Tender Negotiation) and 19 (PTN Update)

Juran *Juran on Planning for Quality* The Free Press (1988)

Marion Kempeners *Account Management for Purchasing Management: A Way to Manage Relationships with Key Suppliers* IPSERA Conference Paper (1996)

Kotter and Schlesinger 'Choosing Strategies for Change' *Harvard Business Review* (March/ April) (1979)

Lewin *Field Theory in Social Research* Harper (1951)

chapter six
Structure and Strategy

Purchasing Structure

The authors, Hay and Williamson in *The Strategy Handbook* (1991) state that organisations have an internal design or structure. This comprises of:

■ the definition and allocation of specific tasks;
■ the grouping of similar tasks into functional departments such as purchasing, for example;
■ the creation of systems that facilitate the co-ordination of activities between and within departments;
■ the allocation of responsibilities within a department along the basis of a hierarchy;
■ the distribution of formal authority throughout the organisation.

The structure of an organisation, therefore, includes the linking mechanisms between the different roles within the organisation, and the co-ordinating structures of the organisation. Charles Handy in *Understanding Organisations* refers to the structure as being the skeleton of the organisation. An effective organisation should have an appropriate structure and culture, which will depend on a number of forces such as the technology, the market, the size of the organisation, and its customer base.

According to the authors Johnson and Scholes in *Exploring Corporate Strategy Text and Cases*: 'Managers asked to describe their organisations usually respond by drawing an organisation chart, in an attempt to map out its structure.' There are a number of structural types:

The Simple Structure

A simple structure could really be thought of as no formal structure at all. It is the type of organisation, common in many small businesses, where managerial responsibilities for operations, purchasing, personnel, design, etc. are shared between those involved in the firm. In such organisations, there will rarely be a specialist buyer. It is likely that the managing director will make the key decisions concerned with the procurement of goods and services.

The organisation will be able to operate effectively up to a certain size of operation, beyond which it becomes too cumbersome for one person to control.

The Functional Structure

A functional structure is based on the primary tasks (operations, purchasing, personnel, design, etc). Providing the firm is not too large, it enables the chief executive to keep directly in touch with the various aspects of the business because of the vertical flow of information and short lines of communication. According to Johnson and Scholes: 'In functional structures, job roles are likely to be clearly understood and easy to define because they are based on the tasks that the organisation has to carry out.'

The main disadvantage of such a structure, common in traditional organisations, is that there is a lack of both market and product focus. The organisation is, of course, focussed on its internal functions. A result might be that such organisations fail to adapt to changing competitive situations. A further problem is encountered when cooperation is needed between the different functions, such as the launch of a new product or service. The structure will require communication to be referred vertically upwards causing problems with cooperation between different functions. This structure is shown as follows:

Simple Functional Structure

Avantages	Disadvantages
Managing director in touch with operational decision making	Senior managers overburdened with routine matters
Simple, understandable structure	No market/ product focus
Clear definition of responsibilities	Little strategic focus
Encourages specialisation at senior/ middle management levels	Co-ordination becomes difficult

It will be unlikely for the organisation to have a senior purchasing manager. Purchasing responsibilities are likely to be undertaken by a number of people in the organisation. It is generally the case that the operations manager will make decisions over the procurement of bought out supplies necessary for the process technologies deployed by the organisation. The design or development team may make decisions over sources for new products or services which the organisation may be planning to introduce to the market. Finance on the other hand may make decisions over leased equipment and services necessary for the functioning of the organisation such as external services and IT-related spends.

The Multi-Divisional Structure

According to Johnson and Scholes:

> The main characteristic of a multi divisional structure is (that the organisation is) subdivided into units which are responsible for defined markets, service/ product areas. These divisions may be formed on the basis of products: other bases for divisionalisation are geographical areas, or the processes of the enterprise. For example, a vertically integrated company might have manufacturing, wholesaling and retail divisions.

The most popular structure now adopted in industrial organisations is the multi-divisional structure. The main advantage of the structure is that each division is able to concentrate on the customer requirements associated with that division. In larger organisations, a key characteristic is the diversity of the product and service range. It therefore makes sense to separate the organisation into different divisions, each being able to concentrate on dealing with its own problems and developing products and services which serve the needs of their market. In Chapters 4 and 5, we highlighted the point that having a customer focus is an important ingredient of total quality. This need to focus on customer requirements can also be replicated in an organisational context, since the different divisions of a company can reflect the organisation's customer base, so that different divisions – whether by geography or by product – are focused on its customers.

TASK

Is your organisation's structure customer-focussed? What are the advantages of being customer focussed?

This structure helps overcome a number of disadvantages of the functional structure, as each business area or division is better able to concentrate on the particular aspects of its market.

Multi-Divisional Structure

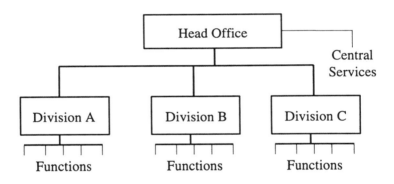

Advantages	Disadvantages
Allows concentration on a particular business	Confusion over centralised and decentralised responsibilities
Can enable greater customer focus	Conflict between centralised and decentralised functions and between different functions
Organisation can add or divest business units	Co-ordination of different business units can be difficult

The divisional structure highlights the debate over which functions should be placed within the central service functions, and which should be placed within the divisions. The purchasing function is one that will be at the crux of such a debate. This is an issue which will be addressed in this chapter.

The Matrix Structure

A matrix structure is a combination of different structures, and can take the form of different product or services units, geography and customers operating simultaneously. Very simply, the matrix structure is shown in the diagram.

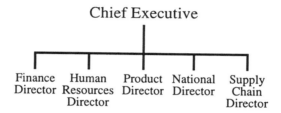

Matrix Structure

Chief Executive

| Finance Director | Human Resources Director | Product Director | National Director | Supply Chain Director |

Geographical Areas

	South	Midlands	North	Export
Product Group 1				
Product Group 2				
Product Group 3				

Business Units

Reporting to the chief executive are the directors for finance, human resources and the supply chain. The supply-chain director would be responsible for internal logistics, purchases, and operations. Many organisations will have a director for operations, but in this case the role of the supply chain has been emphasised.

In the diagram showing the matrix structure, the other directors represent the areas and different product groups of the organisations operations. This will enable the organisation to concentrate on its customers by having the geographical focus, and on its core product groupings.

Rather than having a matrix structure based on geography and product groupings, the structure could be based on trade sectors (which may represent both types of customer and product groupings) and, in addition, the normal functions of the organisation, human resource management, finance, operations, etc. With such a structure, the organisation will not have a need for corporate functions separate to the matrix, as these will be an integral part of it. Perhaps an important aspect for the organisation's structure is the integration of value chain activities identified by Michael Porter.

Value Chain Activities

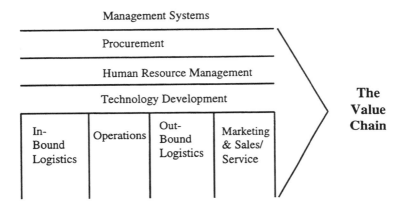

Management Systems			
Procurement			
Human Resource Management			
Technology Development			
In-Bound Logistics	Operations	Out-Bound Logistics	Marketing & Sales/ Service

The Value Chain

Advantages

Different aspects of the organisation's operations are integrated into the structure

Structure improves communication links between people involved

Organisation can concentrate on key aspects of the business

Disadvantages

Decision making can be slow due to the complexity of the structure

Responsibilities can become unclear because of the number of people involved

The structure can be overly bureaucratic

Task Forces

There can be hybrid structures which are combinations of those already identified. Intermediate structures often develop when the organisation persues activities outside the responsibility of any one function or business division. Consider, for example, the organisation which is seeking to implement electronic data interchange. Whilst this can represent a major development for the procurement function, it can have repercussions in other parts of the business, for example in marketing, finance and operations. Peters and Waterman in their book, *In Search of Excellence* highlighted the importance of project teams or task forces. They also argue that organisations should maintain a simple or lean form of structure which is easy to understand. This helps avoid bureaucracy and assists communication.

Henry Mintzberg argues that there is a new form of structure developing in those organisations which experience complex and dynamic environments. They can be characterised as having little formal structure at all, as the organisation is seen to consist of specialists working together to solve issues. They have few bureaucratic procedures, and there is little use of job descriptions and normal organisational bureaucracy. This form of organisation is referred to as adhocracy (Henry Mintzberg *The Structuring of Organisations*).

Centralised/ Decentralised Procurement

In the matrix and multi-divisional structures, procurement may be placed as a centralised service function serving the requirements of the business units. There has been a long debate over the relative advantages and disadvantages of centralised control on procurement. Larger organisations with well established purchasing departments have most probably been party to restructuring at one time to a centralised approach, and then to reverse this structure years later to adopt a decentralised structure where responsibility for procurement is passed back to the business units. Years later, the organisation may then readopt a centralised approach because of the drawbacks of the decentralised approach!

TASK

Is procurement from outside suppliers centralised or decentralised in your organisation?

What are the shortcomings of this structure in terms of the effects on operational buying?

Complete decentralisation does imply the winding up of the central buying department. Each division would then have responsibility for forming commercial relationships.

Complete centralisation infers that all key decisions would be made by the central head office procurement personnel, and so routine or clerical tasks such as scheduling requirements may then be devolved to the individual site or division. According to Kenneth Lysons in his book *Purchasing,* there are three possibilities for the location of purchasing within the organisation's structure:

- Purchasing may be completely centralised at the head office or a particular plant.
- Purchasing may be completely decentralised, i.e each plant will undertake its own purchasing.
- A combination of centralisation and decentralisation may apply.

Advantages of Centralised Procurement

Control from the centre means that suppliers will be contacted by only one person. This in turn will help to establish economies of scale in negotiating agreements with suppliers. Higher quantities will help achieve savings in cost, particularly in price for the purchasing organisation. A centralised procurement function can standardise processes associated with purchasing goods and services, such as:

- Policies and procedures
- Contractual terms
- Lists of suppliers
- Improvements in technology, such as IT systems and Electronic Data Interchange.

A centralised function helps accumulate expertise. Buyers become experts in their own fields, such as inflation technology, energy, stationery and consumables, products, services, etc. A centralised department also enables the retention of information on suppliers in one key location. Knowledge is power! A centralised purchasing authority enables purchasing research on supply market conditions. Staff training and development can be readily standardised and improved.

Whilst there are many advantages to centralised procurement, there are also many drawbacks.

Disadvantages of Centralised Procurement

A centralised function can be a very inflexible one. Part of any purchasing department's mission should be to satisfy its internal customers. This can be very difficult when the centralised department becomes remote from its customers. Communications are difficult and relationships suffer. The result is the internal customers distrust of the buyers and the buyers distrust of the internal customers!

Purchasing often misinterpret the internal customers' requirements. The end result is that goods or services are bought which do not satisfy the customer's requirements. Problems in the field are not actually seen by procurement and they can remain blissfully unaware of the chaos caused by their individualistic decisions. Little notice may be taken of local needs and requirements.

The whole system becomes a very bureaucratic one that may be logistically very expensive. Total centralised control means that small-value items will need to be purchased through the central procurement department. In large organisations, the supply chain which may result can be an overly complex one. The small-value goods may be delivered not direct to the user, but to a centralised warehouse facility and then subsequently sent to a regional stores centre before being shipped to the customer. Whilst this may seem rather excessive, it is still a reality in many centrally co-ordinated organisations. The end result is that users can wait for a long time to receive their requirements.

Users find ways to by-pass the procurement function because of the long periods usually taken by the function to set up individual purchases and mis-interpretation of customers' requirements. Requirements can, for example, be fragmented into small lots, to enable procurement within delegated authority levels.

Purchase Portfolio Analysis

The advantages and disadvantages of centralised procurement do not in themselves point to any easy answers. A tool which can be used to help determine which decisions can be best made at a local level and which should be made by the centralised department is purchase portfolio analysis.

The technique uses a matrix which analyses the supply base according to supplier risk factors: risk relates to exposure to supply failure and supply market complexity. This will be low in competitive markets for standardised products and services and high for specialised products and services unique to the purchasing organisation where there is a limited choice of available suppliers.

Equally, the impact on profit or budget on the purchasing organisation can be high or low. The technique was first advocated by Peter Kraljic in 1983 in 'Purchasing Must Become Supply Management' published in the *Harvard Business Review*. There are now a number of derivatives of the portfolio technique, with some authors highlighting expenditure on the x axis.

Purchase Portfolio Analysis

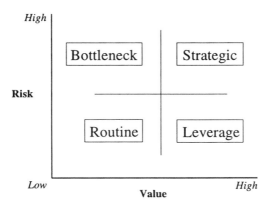

Let us analyse each of these quadrants.

Non-Critical Items

These items are usually

- low in value;
- numerous in volume;
- have a wide choice of suppliers;
- administratively time consuming;

TASK

Think of some examples of goods and services which could be categorised 'non-critical'.

The advice to purchasing organisations for these items is that they should be administered efficiently. For example, arrangements can be made with suppliers by the purchasing function to buy certain items from selected suppliers using corporate purchasing cards (charge card purchasing) thus saving the purchasing department the time taken to place orders. A more detailed analysis of the potential of corporate purchasing cards is included in Chapter 10.

Bottleneck Items

Bottleneck items will usually have similarities to non-critical items: the key difference is the greater risk of non-availability and, hence, shortage of supply. The leverage, or negotiating strength, of the purchaser is limited because of the high degree of strength of suppliers.

The advice to purchasing organisations is to try and ensure supply. This can be carried out by adopting a long-term partnership strategy incorporating targets for performance (see Chapter 7) or alternatively, by adopting a multiple-sourcing strategy to minimise the risk of placing too much business with any one supplier.

Leverage Items

Leverage items are those where significant buying power is exercised in favourable market conditions. The purchasing organisation should be exploiting its position, as the supplier market will be competitive and the because the buying organisation's spend will be one that puts them in a more powerful position with suppliers. The choice of strategy to maximise the buyer's position could be a long-term contract resulting from competitive tender.

Strategic Items

Strategic items will be high spend and on goods or services which have few suppliers. A balance can exist between the power of the two parties, and the two companies may in fact be dependent on each other. Much will depend on the size of the two organisations. Again, the choice of supplier strategy can be to pursue a long-term partnership agreement (see Chapter 7). This can be difficult if the buying organisation is dealing with a more powerful supplier.

The highest number of suppliers will usually fall in the non-critical quadrant. An organisation can typically have up to 80% of its suppliers falling into this category in accordance with ABC or Pareto analysis. This practical tool is derived from a nineteenth-century Italian economist who observed that a minority of the population owned the majority of its wealth. Under Pareto Analysis, there are three categories of product or service bought by the organisation. The diagram illustrates that category A items, whilst small in number, account for a significant amount of spend.

Category C items of expenditure can be considered to be a nuisance. In the case of a highly-centralised procurement section, the procurement process for these items will be time-consuming and the potential for adding value is limited.

A simplified version of ABC or Pareto analysis is the 80/20 rule. In approximate terms, 20% of the number of products/ services bought will account for 80% of the purchaser's spend. This simple rule can apply to other aspects of procurement too:

Pareto Analysis

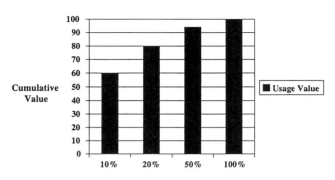

Cumulative Value

Quantities of Products/ Services Bought

- 20% of suppliers will generally create 80% of problems incurred;
- 20% of invoices will generally account for 80% of costs;
- 20% of inventory items will generally account for 80% of usage value.

Purchasers need to focus most attention on the 20% of products or services that represent the highest spend. Added value can be achieved through supply base rationalisation, the process of analysing the supply base and reducing the total number of suppliers. The objective is to weed out the more inefficient suppliers and focus on best-practice suppliers who are cost and quality competitive. By aggregating spend with fewer suppliers, this should reduce the purchaser's costs.

Organisations with uncontrolled purchasing will typically find that there can be a huge number of suppliers for low-cost, low-risk items as there is no co-ordination and control of spend. This is even the case when centralised procurement have been responsible for the placement of orders.

Purchase Portfolio Analysis

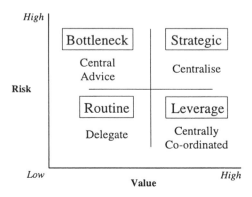

Non-Critical Items

The advice here is that centralised procurement departments should not have any great operational involvement. A number of call-off contracts may be set up by procurement where users can order their requirements directly from the supplier. This saves the procurement department the administrative burden experienced in placing orders for these items. Users should be allowed to procure their choice of items and be accountable for their expenditures.

Bottleneck Items

With bottleneck items, the procurement organisation faces greater risk in the event of the supplier failing to deliver. So, by the often specialised nature of the purchaser's requirements, the centralised procurement department may wish to:

- Standardise the products or services bought. By implementing a standardisation programme, the purchaser will be trying to redefine requirements and question whether specialised products and services are in fact a necessity.
- Central advice/ assistance may take the form of advising users of developments in the supply market, that is new suppliers and improvements in availability. Alternatively, advice and assistance can be given in sourcing suppliers and negotiating agreements.

Leverage Items

Leverage items warrant a higher priority in terms of the commitment of resources by the purchasing department due to the higher proportion of spend consumed in this quadrant. The focus of the procurement department should be to negotiate call off contracts and use the competition in the market to improve the terms of supply.

Strategic Items

This is an important quadrant for the centralised purchasing section. The emphasis here should be to focus on cost drivers aspects of the purchase which drive up cost. This can be achieved by:

- Improving in-bound logistics by simplifying delivery to the purchaser, perhaps by implementing a Just In Time system where the supplier delivers more frequently, in smaller quantities, direct to the user. This should have the effect of reducing inspection and inventory.
- Improving the specification of the requirement. The supplier's expertise can be used to redefine the purchase as they can reduce costs of the purchase without reducing product or service quality.

- Driving down costs on a collaborative basis, so that the costs will not simply be a measure of purchase price. Other aspects of the purchase such as lead times, the service, stock-holding, modes of delivery, etc. can be analysed collaboratively and improved.

Whilst purchase portfolio analysis is a useful tool to guide both purchasing structure and strategy, it should not be viewed in isolation. Consider the implications of the following matrix for example:

Supplier Perceptions Matrix

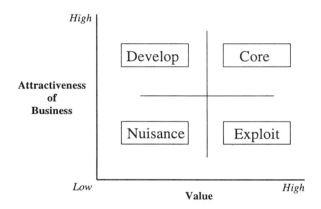

The diagram shown above can be used to represent suppliers' perceptions of purchasers. The y axis measures the attractiveness of the purchaser's requirements; the x axis measures the value of purchases.

Nuisance: when the volume of purchasing is relatively low, infrequent or when the purchaser typically negotiates low prices, then the supplier may regard this area of business as a nuisance. The supplier will not generally allocate any significant amount of resources to the purchasing organisation in terms of sales effort or prioritisation in production. Should a purchaser try to develop a partnership-style arrangement with a supplier who may view the purchaser's business as falling into this category, then it is unlikely to be an effective arrangement.

Exploit: this category is again typified by low attractiveness of the purchaser's business but spend is significantly higher in comparison to nuisance sales. The supplier is likely to exploit the situation by a mixture of premium pricing or inadequate allocation of resources to achieve quality output.

Develop: the third quartile denotes an effective strategy for the supplier where the attractiveness of business is high, yet value of sales is comparatively low. The supplier is likely to want to develop these sales from the customer. A supplier may typically pursue a partnership relationship with the purchasing organisation, and try to provide convincing evidence of the need to work together to achieve a win-win scenario. In this way, the spend of the purchasing organisation may increase over time, if the supplier is provided with such an opportunity. The supplier is likely to allocate significant marketing effort in the form of calls made to the purchaser, promotions and discounted pricing to help develop these sales.

Core: the final quadrant refers to core business. This represents sales which are attractive to the seller and the purchaser's spend is significant. The aim of the seller is to ensure that a greater part of its turnover is accounted for by such sales.

The supplier perception matrix helps to develop the purchasers strategy by a further degree. The purchaser needs to assess, when performing an appraisal of a supplier organisation, which of the quartiles it is likely to represent. Whilst the matrix is a subjective tool, it can be a useful means of evaluating the likely motivation of the supplier in dealing with the purchaser.

Lead Buyer Structures

Earlier in this chapter, the advantages and disadvantages of centralised and decentralised purchasing were discussed. Purchase portfolio analysis helps identify which products and services can best be centralised or decentralised. A key issue of purchasing performance is the need for collaboration and sharing of information throughout the purchasing units in order to improve effectiveness.

Centralised procurement functions will typically have specialist, or as is often referred to, commodity buyers. The commodity buyers will normally be experts on a narrow range of related products or services. These experts develop knowledge of the product or service in question, as well as a range of information about the supply markets. On the other hand, decentralised buyers are likely to be a 'jack of all trades, master of none'. Their work will be varied and, over time, the specialisation of their skills is likely to emanate from a knowledge and understanding of local needs and requirements. Product knowledge can be at a relatively high level if the buyer is able to see at first hand the product in the local environment.

The creation of 'lead buyers' can help to overcome the disadvantages of both centralisation and decentralisation. The lead buyer network is also called a centre-led action network. The essence of the lead buyer network is that it allows for purchasing activity to take place on a decentralised level while purchasing accountability, policy and best practice are generated from the small central team. The following diagram illustrates such a structure.

The Lead Buying Process

B u s i n e s s	U n i t	B u s i n e s s	U n i t

Lead Buyers for Group Wide Purchasing are Established in the Different Business Units

The lead buyers are based in the decentralised business units. The centre is a small team responsible for aspects such as setting strategy, analysing supply markets, writing procedures and initiating training and development plans. The lead buyers are themselves commodity buyers, specialists in particular fields such as the procurement of facilities management, stationery, equipment, advertising, direct marketing, etc. The purchasing effort remains at a local level. Lead buyers can take on responsibility for the creation of call-off contracts which other buyers throughout the organisation may make use of. In some organisations, the use of such agreements by other buyers is mandatory. In others it is not, and the decentralised buyers can choose whether or not to make use of the call-off agreements. Buyers can also make use of each other to gain specialist help and advice.

Advantages	Disadvantages
Allows specialisation	Interaction between different buyers needs to be nurtured
Decision making is retained at a local level and reflects the requirements of the business	There can be a reluctance on the part of lead buyers to create call off unit contracts. It represents an added responsibility.
The benefits of the aggregation of spend can be reaped	Communication between the different buyers can be time-consuming process

Centre can concentrate on purchasing strategy and other key aspects of procurement

Centre may become remote from the purchasing effort which takes place at the business unit level

In a number of organisations, the lead buyer structure utilises a system of internal transfer costing whereby, if one department makes use of another, there is a charge made for the time spent. This can be made on a general daily charge-out rate. Such an arrangement is particularly applicable to large organisations consisting of different subsidiary companies.

The diagram illustrates the use of a sliding scale of uses of the lead buyer. This can range from full responsibility for the procurement process to the mere provision of advice.

An important goal in the development of strategic purchasing and supply management is to link the strategy adopted by the function with the corporate-level strategy.

The Lead Buying Process

Lead Buyer Acts on Behalf of the Customer & Carries Out All Parts of the Purchase-Contract Strategy, Sourcing, Negotiation & Performance Monitoring

Lead Buyer Provides Assistance with Aspects of the Purchase Such as Sourcing, Negotiation and Contract Formation- for example

Lead Buyer Maintains Data on Supply Markets and Supplier Performance. Advice Is Offered to the Lead Buyer Receiver

Lead Buyer Provider

Lead Buyer Receiver

Business Unit Delegates the Whole Procurement Process to the Lead Buyer Provider. Lead Buyer Receiver Retains Responsibility for Approval and Contract Performance

Lead Buyer Receiver Uses Expertise on an Ad Hoc Basis for Aspects of the Purchase

Business Unit Uses its Own Purchasing Operation to Carry Out the Purchase. Lead Buyer Receiver Shares Information with the Lead Buyer Provider

Functional strategies obviously should not be developed in isolation and there needs to be integration of both sets of strategy.

There are many different terms which attempt to define the nature of strategic management, such as corporate strategy, business strategy, business policy and strategic planning. These terms all address the same issue, however, and that is how an organisation is directed in a changing environment.

Gerry Johnson and Kevan Scholes have produced an authoritative text on corporate strategy: *'Exploring Corporate Strategy: Text and Cases'*. They emphasise that strategic decisions are concerned with the following aspects of business planning, as shown in the chart below.

The Nature of Corporate Strategy

Strategic Decisions Are:

- Concerned with the Scope of the Organisation's Activities
- Involved in Matching these Activities to the Environment
- Involved with the Matching to its Resource Capability
- Significant in their Effect on Resources
- Likely to Affect Operational Decisions
- Shaped by the Values and Expectations of those Having Power in the Organisation
- Likely to Affect the Long-Term Direction of the Organisation
- Usually Complex in Nature

The products and services an organisation provides are shaped by the organisation's strategy. A perfect example is provided by IBM who decided in 1981 to concentrate on what they perceived to be their core business – the design and production of IT systems. The production of the operating system was outsourced to Microsoft. Microsoft are now one of the richest and best performing companies in the world as their Dos and Windows systems are the operating software used in 95% of the world's personal computers. This must have been a strategic decision that IBM very much regret!

Microsoft are currently not content to merely consolidate their market position. Their corporate strategy deployed over the last few years has been to invest in new technologies that can further develop their share of the global information technology (IT) industry. Between 1994 and 1996, Microsoft spent $1.5 billion on acquisitions, as well as providing a significant share of finance in a new company, Teledesic, a company that will launch 288 satellites into orbit for high-speed Internet access.

Strategic decisions should match the organisation's capabilities with its environment. In the example of the IT industry, the pace of change is of course characterised by continual change and improvements in technology. The shelf-life for IT personal computers is now a few months as the product lifecycles become increasingly shorter.

The Lifecycle Model

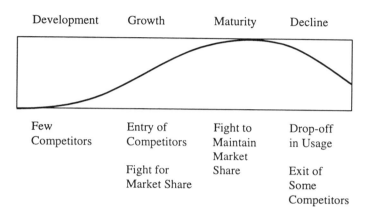

With a new product (or service) there will usually be few competitors in the development stage of the product lifecycle, particularly for new, innovative products or services. If the product or service is successful, it can gain market share and marketing effort can of course help find new markets and customers to buy it. At this growth stage, other organisations may compete and so there can be a fight to obtain sufficient market share. This continues into the maturity stage of the product lifecycle, as competitors will try and differentiate their products or services to gain market share. In the decline stage, the product or service becomes dated and may need to be redesigned or replaced by a new product or service. In this way, the organisation needs to plan successors to its current product or service.

An automotive company knows that the cars produced have a shelf life of probably five to seven years, and the individual car designed will generally succeed through the various stages of the model.

The decisions made by companies like Microsoft to invest and develop in new technologies will have a significant impact on the organisation's strategy. These decisions will have a significant effect on the long-term direction of the company, and will also affect decision making at an operational level. Operational purchasing decisions are those concerned with the day-to-day procurement of bought-out products and services needed for production.

So the decision to invest in a new product, for example, will mean that the purchasing function should be involved in the planning and negotiation of likely sources of supply for the component parts needed from external suppliers.

The strategic decisions are likely to be made by those holding the most power and influence within the organisation. In the case of Microsoft, for example, Bill Gates is the founder of the company and, as such, the culture of the company is very much guided by his values.

In larger organisations, particularly multi-national enterprises, size can lead to diversity in terms of strategy and values. This diversity generally leads to a lack of cohesiveness in the organisation, with different people pulling in different directions. Mission statements are therefore used by organisations to produce a shared vision – a set of beliefs, norms and values. According to Johnson and Scholes, a vision statement will state the desired state of the organisation. As such the vision statement should be able to persist for a significant period of time and it provides an influential backcloth against which more detailed strategies can be developed. A vision should be 'challenging' and even 'exciting'.

Tom Peters, a foremost management consultant and writer, claims that organisations should develop an inspiring vision. This, he argues, is the very essence of sound leadership. Leaders influence the behaviour of employees and so it is vital that the vision statement is to produce a cohesive corporate culture, no matter what size the organisation is.

An example of a strategic visioning statement is provided by Rover Group, now part of the German company, BMW. Their vision as a company is simply to be: 'Internationally renowned for extraordinary customer satisfaction'. Their vision statement is stating that, in today's fiercely competitive market, merely satisfying the customer is not enough as car companies tend to achieve this with the supply of a new car. A goal for many companies during the 1980s was to produce a quality product or service in order to satisfy customers. It is therefore more difficult to secure a differential advantage over competitors on the basis of quality alone; this means to delight customers.

TASK

Taking the example of a car, what aspects of the performance (acceleration, smooth gear operation, etc), reliability (starts first time, no faults, etc) and service (the retailer's focus on the customer etc) would delight you as a customer?

A mission statement will, according to Johnson and Scholes, on the other hand, state the 'overriding purpose of the organisation in line with the values and expectations of the organisations stakeholders (employees, shareholders, customers etc)'. For example, the corporate mission statement of Rover Group was as follows:

Rover group's business is to produce and sell distinctive and desirable vehicles, known for their robustness and driver appeal. Our aim is to improve continually our products and services, to satisfy our customers and make a profit. This will allow us to prosper as a business to the benefit of our customers, dealers, suppliers, shareholders and employees alike.

The Rover Group purchasing function created separate vision and mission statements to comply with those at corporate level.

Rover Group Purchasing

Vision Statement

> Purchasing's Aim is to Provide World Class Products and Services at the Lowest Total Cost in Support of Rover's Commitment to Extraordinary Customer Satisfaction

Mission Statement

> We Are Committed to Excellence, through Investment in our People, Added Value Working, and Constancy of Purpose. By Proactively Developing Supplier Partnerships which Are World Competitive, we Will Secure Preferred Customer Status

TASK

Does your organisation have a vision or mission statement? What is its content?

The Basis of Corporate Strategy

The vision and mission statements of the organisation should state the goals and aspirations of an organisation. The organisation can adopt various ways of achieving corporate success. The basis for corporate strategy will be discussed and is shown in the following chart.

Basis of Corporate Strategy

1. Cost Leadership:
Low cost producer in the industry

2. Differentiation:
Provide features of the product or service that are different to the competition

3. Focused Differentiation:
Provide a higher value to the customer at a premium price

Cost Leadership

The first of these is to gain competitive advantage by being a low-cost producer . This means that the organisation establishes its position in the market by being very price competitive and providing value-for-money products or services. For example, the Eastern European car manufacturer Lada for years adopted this position in the market place. The company sold cheap, low-cost cars. Their designs were simplistic in comparison to the cars produced by Western manufacturers, and purposefully did not include more sophisticated instrumentation such as anti-lock brakes, electric sun-roofs or air conditioning. Other good examples of companies following this strategy are the German grocery chains, Aldi and Netto, operating throughout Europe. Their stores are basic, their merchandise range is relatively limited with few speciality or luxury products, and their prices are very low.

Differentiation

A second choice of strategy that an organisation can pursue is one that seeks to provide products or services that are different from competitors. The aim in this case is to achieve a higher market share than competitors by offering better products or services at the same price, or at slightly higher prices to improve profit margins. According to Johnson and Scholes, this strategy may be achieved through:

- Uniqueness or improvements in the product or service provided by, for example, investing in the design of the product or service. This is often the basis for products like cars or personal computers, as manufacturers seek to compete by investing in technology or design to achieve greater performance and/or reliability.

- Increased marketing effort to demonstrate that the product or service is better than competitors'. The strategy will be based on promoting the brand. Coca-Cola is a

branded product that has appeal world-wid
drink to be superior to its competitors sur
marketing.

With the first of these, purchasing can h?
organisation to produce more innovativ
from suppliers. Tom Peters, a leading consu
writes in his book, *Thriving on Chaos: A Handu*
innovations made in the production of the Ford Taurus
for the development of the car as saying:

Tom Peters argues that these small differences can help differei.
competitor's. When the Ford Taurus, for example, was first produceu,
because it had a coffee cup holder! Attention to small details such as tı.
advantages in a market. He argues that suppliers must become partners .
development process from the start and that:

> Much, if not most, innovation will come from suppliers, if you trust them (show them all information from the start) and they trust you. This is one of the most important instances of the urgent need for a shift from adversarial to cooperative relationships, and 'The uniqueness in a particular product or service often comes from the accumulation of thousands of tiny enhancements.'

Differentiation and Supply Innovation

"With the Ford Taurus, we brought all disciplines together, and did the whole design process simultaneously. The manufacturing people worked with the design people, engineering people, sales and purch -asing, legal, service and marketing.

The common way of doing business is to choose the lowest bidder on advertised specifications. For Taurus, Ford identified its highest quality suppliers and sought their advice in the beginning stages. In return for their contributions, Ford pledged to make them, as far as possible, the sole supplier.

One lighting firm developed louvered interior lights that cut down on reflection on the driver's side when they were on elsewhere in the car. Another firm produced a carpet in which all the fibres lay in the same direction for uniform appearance. These are little attention to detail items we've never done before through the assistance of suppliers."

...to aim to offer higher-value products or services to the customer at a ...e saloon car market is a very competitive market as most car producers ...ract market share for similar products. Ford, Nissan, Toyota, Peugeot, etc. ...this market and try to demonstrate that their product has differential ...ver the competition. Rover Group was taken over by BMW in 1994 and, whilst ...made significant improvements in its portfolio of products, the company was still ...le. BMW are following a focused differentiation strategy with Rover as their cars ...g priced slightly higher than their competitors whilst their marketing aims to ...ce customers of the exclusiveness of the Rover brand.

...ore focused strategy is likely to involve the targeting of a particular market segment. ...r example, a company may have various brands that are aimed at different types of customer. In the UK, for example, the Burton Group is a large clothing retail company. The shops Top Shop and Top Man are aimed at teenagers, whilst Principles is aimed at fashion conscious young men and women. In the clothing retail industry, the vast majority of designs for new fashions are produced by suppliers.

Developing a Strategy for the Purchasing Function

The purchasing function has to ensure that it is supporting corporate strategies. The function needs to provide added value which is the process of improving business performance. The added value that purchasing can bring is shown in the following analysis.

Cost Reduction and Avoidance

One of the main elements of the ability to produce value-for-money products or services is the efficiency with which the organisation undertakes its activities. An organisation's cost efficiency is influenced by supply costs, such as the costs of bought-out products and services. These clearly influence the organisation's overall costs. Purchasing needs to collaborate with suppliers to reduce the total costs of supply.

Costs of supply can be reduced by:

Economies of Scale: these are a traditionally important source of advantage since the high costs of capital need to be recovered over a high volume of output. The higher the output, then the more quickly these fixed costs will be recovered.

Experience: this is another key source of cost advantage and there have been many studies concerning the important relationship between the cumulative experience gained by an organisation and its unit costs. An organisation undertaking the supply of a product or service over time will learn to do it more efficiently over time, and hence costs will reduce over time. Long-term contracts with suppliers can help to increase experience. Studies in the aircraft, electronics and electromechanical sub-assembly fields suggest that experience over time can have a dramatic impact on unit costs.

Product/ Service Design: this is also a key element of cost and how costs can be reduced. Over-specified products or services bought from suppliers will add additional, unnecessary costs to the purchase. Standardisation programmes can be adopted by purchasing organisations to reduce costs of bought out products and services.

Purchasing's Added Value

- Business performance can be improved by:
- Cost reduction and avoidance
- Reducing defects from bought out supplies of products and services
- Risk reduction
- Supply innovation
- Rapid responses to market changes

Reducing Defects

A purchasing department needs to work with suppliers to reduce the numbers of defects produced by a supplier. Japanese companies demonstrated how a concerted effort to reduce the quantities of defects over a period of time can bring about a change in reputation. From being regarded as suppliers of poor quality products, often of cheap copies of those supplied by Western manufacturers, they are now regarded as world- class leaders. Especially during the 1980s, phrases such as 'right first time' and 'zero defects' became widely used in campaigns to promote changes of approach in Europe and America.

In many progressive organisations, the design of new products or services is conducted by a team representing a number of functional areas – planning, design, operations, purchasing, finance, quality and marketing.

Sources of Cost Efficiency

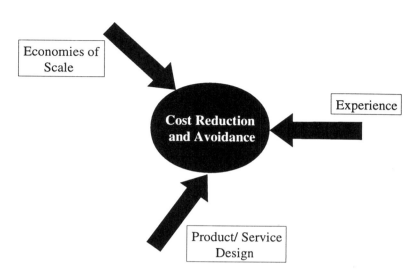

It is important for suppliers to be involved. This process is known as early supplier involvement (ESI). Cost overruns and foregone cost savings can occur if suppliers are not involved. For example, during the 1980s design engineers at the American company, General Electric's Jet Engine Division, frequently designed materials to be purchased from outside suppliers under the mistaken belief that these suppliers had the same manufacturing capabilities as General Electric. Suppliers did not, and the results were increased costs and delays to the new designs as suppliers attempted to meet GE's specifications through a trial and error process. Ultimately, all designs had to be changed, and this produced further delays to the design and subsequent production.

Purchasing therefore needs to devise ways of including suppliers in the development of new products or services. This can lead to savings in cost and improvements in designs through innovation. As John Carlisle and Robert Parker state in their book *Beyond Negotiation: Redeeming Customer-Supplier Relationships*: 'Suppliers must have access to product design as early as humanly possible in the design process to assure optimal use of any special skills or processes they can contribute.' According to Roger Hale in *Made in the USA, the Tennant Company* (1991):

At Tennant we have found that involving our suppliers at the design stage has improved our products. Since they are experts in their fields, they prevent us from making mistakes, help us save money and time, and help us do it right the first time.

Cross-Functional Teams

Representatives from:

- Planning
- Design
- Operations
- Purchasing   **+**   **Suppliers**
- Finance
- Quality
- Marketing

Rapid Responses to Market Changes

Today's business world is characterised by rapid changes to markets and ever-increasing levels of competition. Product lifecycles are becoming ever shorter in many markets. Personal computers become out of date within a matter of months, such is the level of innovation in this industry.

In the late 1970s early 1980s, it would typically take five to six years to design a new car. European and American manufacturers now take about three to four years. The Japanese, on the other hand, are steadily reducing the time it takes to a little over 12 months. Early supplier involvement can reduce the total time it takes to design new products or services,

Purchasing can also contribute to greater flexibility by reducing lead times with suppliers. A lead time is the period taken to obtain a requirement from a supplier and comprises of the following operations:

Lead Times

- Preparation of Requisitions
- Forwarding of Requisition to Purchasing
- Processing of the Requisition by Purchasing
- Supplier Selection
- Transmission of Order to Supplier
- Execution of Order by the Chosen Supplier
- Transportation and Delivery of Order by the Supplier
- Receipt of Order
- Issue to the User

Reduce Time

Increase Flexibility

Actively working to reduce total lead times, which includes internal processes as well as supplier delivery times, will help purchasing provide 'the right product or service in the right place at the right time' and help increase responsiveness to customer requirements.

The main elements of a strategy could include the following:

Review of Purchasing Procedures: an organisation's procedures may be in need of updating. This process itself could concentrate on ways of reducing internal lead times, and help make purchasing more responsive to fulfilling the needs of its customers. The review may take many months to perform adequately.

Implementation of a Standardisation Programme: an initial starting point would be to investigate and find examples of products or services where there are a large number of varieties of products or services being bought. This investigation can take months, but the starting point should be to analyse supplies of products or services according to the procurement targeting model which categorises products and services bought on the basis of value and risk. A standardisation programme should attempt to tackle the high-value high-risk items first, as these will produce the greatest gains.

Reduction in the Number of Suppliers: this element of strategy can be linked to the standardisation programme, as the adoption of common products or services can lead to the sourcing of one supplier for each item. This may, of course, represent too great a risk to do immediately since a single supplier may not be trusted to ensure supply. The standardisation programme could therefore be linked to a dual sourcing policy, whereby two suppliers can be selected for the product or service in question.

Strategy for Individual Products and Services: the use of the procurement targeting model leads to a strategy for each product and service bought. The model of course positions purchases into four separate categories, and the approaches to procurement varies according to these categories.

Implementation of a Supplier Development Programme: collaborative links with certain suppliers may give rise to a supplier development programme, where the purchasing organisation helps to improve aspects of the supplier's business operations. A supplier development programme may again be implemented with a few key suppliers initially.

Encouragement of the Adoption of Total Quality Management by Suppliers: linked to the use of a supplier-development programme, certain key suppliers could be given guidance on the use of Total Quality management if they have not yet taken these philosophies on board.

Supplier Involvement: suppliers can make significant contributions to the designs of products and services, and help reduce costs and risks. A number of key suppliers with whom you may have already developed good long-term relationships could be approached to see what improvements they may be able to suggest. A pilot project could be implemented using perhaps two key suppliers at first, before asking for greater involvement from a larger number of suppliers at some point in the future.

Development of IT Systems: a strategy will also need to address planned improvements for IT capabilities both internally within the organisation, as well as interfaces and improvements to communications with suppliers.

Development of a Code of Ethics: business dealings made by procurement personnel need to be carried out in an ethical manner. Perhaps a first priority of any purchasing manager should be to develop a code of ethics and inform internal departments as well as suppliers of its operation.

There can, of course, be other elements of a strategy affecting an organisation which have not been included above. In particular, personnel involved with any of the above will need to be trained on relevant aspects of purchasing management. In addition, the manager may have limited resources in terms of available personnel, and so a compromise strategy may be necessary, whereby only certain elements will be carried out. What is important, however, is that the strategy is planned out over time. The diagram below shows how the strategy can be mapped out and include targets set for improvement.

Mapping the Purchasing Strategy

Process	1996	1997	1998	1999	2000
Supplier Reduction					
Supplier Development			**Set Targets** ▌◼▶		
Total Cost Management					
People Development					
IT Systems					

References/ Further Reading

Carlisle and Parker *Beyond Negotiation: Redeeming Customer-Supplier Relationships* John Wiley and Sons (1989)

Handy *Understanding Organisations* Penguin Business (1988)

Hay and Williamson *The Strategy Handbook* (1991)

Johnson and Scholes *Exploring Corporate Strategy: Text and Cases* 4th Edition Prentice Hall (1997)

Kraljic 'Purchasing Must Become Supply Management' *Harvard Business Review* September-October (1983)

Lysons *Purchasing* 4th Edition Pitman Publishing (1996)

Minzberg *The Structuring of Organisations* Prentice Hall (1979)

Peters and Waterman *In Search of Excellence* Harper and Row, New York (1982)

Peters *Thriving on Chaos: A Handbook for a Management Revolution* Pan Books (1989)

chapter seven

Sourcing

A key aspect in the procurement of goods or services is defining the requirement. Buyers will need to liaise with their internal customers to focus on their requirements before developing relationships with suppliers (see Chapter 5). Chapters 2 and 3 identified aspects of the specification and contractual terms which may need to be negotiated with the supplier.

Locating Suppliers

Sourcing is the process of identifying suppliers who are able to supply the goods or services purchasers need. There are two main sources of information on suppliers:

- external: through guides, directories, magazines, advertisements, etc;
- internal: through the organisation's own records or by contacting other purchasers.

Identifying Suppliers

Supplier Information File:	The Purchaser May Keep Records of Details of Possible Suppliers
Supplier Catalogues:	Provide a Quick and Efficient Guide to the Availability of Suppliers for more Standardised Requirements
Trade Registers & Directories:	Organisations like 'Kompass' and 'Dunn and Bradstreet' Provide Guides
Trade Exhibitions:	Regional or National Trade Shows May Provide Opportunities to See New Product Innovations and Suppliers
Other Purchasing Organisations:	May also Be Willing to Offer Advice

There are a number of sources of information to find potential suppliers. Possible sources of external information include the following:

Supplier Catalogues

This is a particularly useful means of finding suppliers. Catalogues are usually quick and easy to use and suppliers are willing to send copies. Order and payment details are included in the catalogues.

Trade Registers and Directories

Organisations like Dunn and Bradstreet and Kellys provide directories of suppliers. These generally give information about suppliers and the descriptions of products or services provided. They also provide information on the financial and commercial capabilities of the supplier organisations. They are usually indexed by commodity, manufacturer, and trade name or trademark description of an item.

Trade Journals / Trade Association Journals

Advertisements and articles are often the buyers' first contact with potential suppliers and their products and services. The Chartered Institute of Purchasing and Supply, for example, is the trade magazine for purchasing professionals, and most editions include details of specialist consulting organisations that can provide various services such as training. In the same way, other trade journals will contain both articles and information about suppliers operating in that particular industry.

Trade Exhibitions

Attending trade exhibitions can be a cost-effective means of sourcing and can allow the buyer to:

- see various new products and services;
- make contacts with the sales point for each organisation;
- discuss the products and services with the expertise provided by suppliers;
- expand their knowledge and awareness of products and services of different suppliers.

Direct Mail

It is inevitable that companies will receive direct mail from potential suppliers. This information can be saved and accessed when required.

Sales Representatives

These provide an excellent source of information on product and services, but their obvious bias should always be borne in mind. Sales representatives are keen to stress the benefits and advantages of their products and services and this information needs to be filtered by buyers.

Electronic Sources

An interesting development throughout the 1980s and 1990s is the growth in access to information by electronic means. Rather than rely on printed trade directories in book form for information, many directories are also available on CD-ROM disks holding vast quantities of data that can be accessed by personal computers. Data is stored on a Compact Disk, and vast quantities of data can be held on these. Most computers sold today have a CD-ROM drive which is an integral part of the computer. Dun and Bradstreet for example market such directories on CD-ROM, and the technology provides the added advantages of being able to search for suppliers far more quickly compared to the traditional book form directories.

There are also sector-specific CD-ROMs such as the Technical Indexes produced by the company of the same name. The main CD covers electronic engineering, process engineering and engineering design and manufacturing. A separate CD covers computers and communications. CDs such as these enable highly specialised sourcing into key market areas, and the information is also available in standard book form.

Perhaps the only disadvantage with CDs is their expense: they often cost hundreds of pounds and are only available by subscription so that updated versions are automatically despatched.

Relationship Strategies

Traditional Multi-Sourcing

'There is nothing wrong with screwing down suppliers' argued David Sheridan (1991), a Fellow of the Chartered Institute of Purchasing in Supply. His views typify the traditional view of buying organisations in their dealings with suppliers. Sheridan's arguments can be summarised as follows:

- Buyers should aim to award contracts on the basis of the lowest price.
- Their role is not to question requirements provided by other departments in terms of specifications, delivery or completion dates and quantities.
- There is no such phenomenon as a 'reasonable price'. The purchaser is under obligation to reward the supplier with a profit.

These views represent the traditional relationship buyers forge with suppliers, a relationship based on a lack of trust, and suppliers are dealt with on an 'arm's length basis'.

Traditional multiple sourcing strategies are still widely used, where the buying organisation chooses the source of supply from a number of different suppliers. The benefits would appear to be as follows.

Competitive Pressure: competition between suppliers improves all aspects of the purchase, such as price, delivery and quality. Competition also increases the buyer's negotiating power through better information and threat of loss of business.

Supply Continuity: multiple sources of supply provide alternative sources in the event of supply stoppages.

Market Intelligence: contact with more than one supplier increases the amount of information available. The buyer has direct access to market developments, be they commercial or technical. Multiple sources therefore enhance the buyer's ability to take advantage of market changes such as new technologies, new products, etc. developed elsewhere, and also new suppliers.

Supplier Appraisal: direct access to comparable data from competitors greatly simplifies the task of supplier monitoring and appraisal.

Short-Term Versus Long-Term Sourcing

Whilst we have identified the advantages of short-term, multiple sourcing, these advantages may be offset by a number of disadvantages:

Loss of Economies of Scale: it is quite common for organisations to have little control over their purchasing, particularly when there are no specialist buyers employed by the organisation. As a consequence, the organisation will have a number of different suppliers for the different goods and services which are bought. When this is the case, the supplier will be receiving lower volumes of business compared to the whole, and this will usually be on a short-term basis. The buying organisation will be paying additional costs because of the loss of economies of scale.

Additional Administrative Expenses: more suppliers will inevitably mean more orders, and, therefore, higher administrative expenses. More time will be spent on non-value-added activities, such as expediting deliveries and completing contracts.

Lack of Planning: suppliers have increased uncertainty about expected future levels of business. There can be a lack of planning by both the buying and selling organisations. The lack of planning can lead to panic buying and the inability to meet short-term fluctuations.

Lack of Goodwill/ Trust: because of the short-term adversarial relationships which are characteristic, there is a lack of motivation by both organisations to work together in a cooperative way. This results in a lack of goodwill and trust on both sides. Traditional buyer-supplier relationships are typified by short-term, multiple sourcing. The buying organisation can pursue other long-term strategies.

The following matrix illustrates the options available to buying organisations in terms of the sourcing strategies which can be pursued.

Sourcing Arrangements

Length of Arrangement

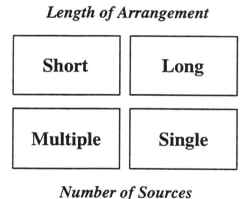

Number of Sources

Long-Term Single Sourcing

The authors Ansari and Modarrass in their book *Just in Time Purchasing* summarise the advantages of single sourcing:

- A minimum investment of resources in terms of the buyers' and engineers' time.
- Consistent quality: when the buyers deal with fewer suppliers and involve them in the early stages of the designs of specifications, suppliers can provide consistently high-quality products.
- Lower costs: overall volume of items purchased from any one supplier is higher.
- Special attention from suppliers, since buyers represent large accounts.
- Minimal amount spent to provide tooling for suppliers.

- Easily scheduled deliveries since all orders are placed with one supplier.
- Long-term relationships, which encourage supplier loyalty and reduce the risk of an interrupted supply of parts to the buyer's plant.

The authors cite E Hennessy, Chief Executive Officer at Allied Corporation as suggesting that: 'Purchasing must cultivate sound relationships with its suppliers so that inventories may be reduced to minimum practical levels and quality of supply may be such that rejection of material is essentially eliminated.'

The adoption of single-sourced long-term suppliers was widely advocated with the adoption of Just in Time. JIT purchasing practices emphasise the importance of product quality, supplier relationship, delivery performance and cost.

However, the adoption of widespread single sourcing has its difficulties. Public sector organisations, for example, have to use competitive tendering due to the enforcement of EC Directives (see Chapter 9). In addition, pursuing a single sourcing strategy will inevitably bring problems when the supplier is a large powerful organisation (see Chapter 8).

Long-Term Multiple Sourcing

An alternative to single sourcing in its purest form, where the supplier could be considered as a life-long partner of the buying organisation, is to select the supplier from competition and then to award a long-term contract. Many public sector organisations are adopting this strategy and placing contracts with suppliers for five or seven year periods, for example.

Advantages of Long Contract Periods	Disadvantages of Long Contract Periods
Development of closer relationship with supplier to reap the advantages of collaborative - win win relationships	Can create complacency
The supplier should improve performance over the length of the contract through the learning curve effect	May be a lack of motivation to continually improve the service provision. Supplier merely works to the letter of the contract
The offering of a larger, longer contract should increase market competition for the work	This depends on the degree of competition present in the market
The supplier may be motivated to produce quality work to improve prospects of repeat business Aggregation of requirements leads to obvious economies of scale	The supplier will typically be motivated at the tendering stage and towards the end of the existing contract - not throughout the greater part of the contract
	Whilst there may be economies of scale, the contract will usually be inflexible and difficult to take advantage of new technologies/changes in the market

The adoption of long contract periods enhances the prospects of improved collaboration between the purchaser and supplier. A key development in the private sector has been the development of partnership sourcing.

Partnership Sourcing

Partnership Sourcing Ltd, CBI/ DTI *Making Partnership Sourcing Happen* (1992) therefore defines partnership sourcing as follows:

> Partnership sourcing is a commitment by customers/ suppliers, regardless of size, to a long-term relationship based on trust and on clear, mutually agreed objectives to strive for world class capability and competitiveness.

Partnership sourcing is therefore a long-term arrangement between buyer and supplier by which the two parties undertake to use their combined resources to better meet the needs of the customer to the benefit of both parties. Lisa Ellram of Ohio University argues that firms are interested in forming partnerships rather than adversarial relationships because of an extensive number of advantages. These are summarised in the following table:

Management

1. Reduced supplier base is easier to manage.
2. Increased mutual dependence lowers the risk of losing supply source and creates greater stability through increased supplier loyalty.
3. Reduced time spent looking for new suppliers, gathering information and obtaining quotations or competitive tenders.
4. Allows for joint planning and information sharing based on mutual trust and benefit.
5. Loyalty may increase supplier attention and customer service in areas such as:
   - lead time reliability;
   - priority in times of scarcity;
   - increased attention when problems arise.
6. Greater cooperation from suppliers to support the buying organisation's strategy.

Technology

1. Partners may be willing to share/ give access to technology.
2. Partners may be more willing and capable of participating in product design based on knowledge and commitment to the other partner.
3. Supplier knowledge/ involvement in design may:
   - improve quality;
   - reduce time to market for new products/ design changes.

Finance

1. Partners may share business risks through:
   - joint investment;
   - joint research and development - sharing of financial risks associated with market shifts.
2. Information sharing/ forecasting may reduce inventory levels.
3. Long-term commitment of a partnership may lead to more stable supply prices.

An excellent example of a partnership relationship exists, publicised by Tom Peters in a business seminar series, between the Body Shop and the Lane Group (a transport and distribution company with particular interests in dedicated contract distribution). A number of Body Shop expectations are set out in the form of performance standards. These cover a variety of different performance measures and include the perception of Body Shop staff of the attitude, helpfulness and appearance of Lane Group drivers, the number of complaints, the number of blameworthy vehicle accidents and the cleanliness of the vehicles. The Lane Group also aim to improve on environmental aspects of performance such as fuel economy and tyre usage. The key performance measure is delivery reliability as the Lane Group drivers are required to deliver stock to the Body Shop retail outlets within a given two hour window of delivery time. The delivery targets are therefore expressed in terms of hours, not simply days. If the Lane Group's delivery reliability exceeds the minimum requirement of 99.4% deliveries on time, bonuses are paid in the form of a higher fee.

The partnership agreement between the Lane Group and Body Shop also provides an excellent example of a cost plus contract. As the partnership agreement states:

> Open book accounting will be applied to the provision of vehicles and staff used on a permanent basis. These costs will be reported to the Body Shop without a margin; a 12% management charge and 8% profit margin will be applied. Should the targets outlined in the (partnership) document be achieved, then the profit margin will increase by a maximum of 14%.

The Relationship Continuum

There is a spectrum of different types of relationships which can be entered into. The diagram below shows these typologies of relationship. A partnership approach may not necessarily be the most favoured relationship type.

Here are some short definitions of each type of relationship.

The Relationship Continuum

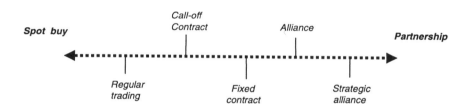

Spot Buy

This refers to the practice of buying individual requirements as a series of one-offs or individual purchases. There is no grouping together of purchasing, and the organisation buys products or services as and when they are required.

Regular Trading

This buying method makes use of suppliers on a regular basis. Whilst the choice of suppliers for each individual purchase may change, the purchasing organisation generally selects suppliers from a known listing or from prior experience.

Call-off Contract (Blanket Order)

Under this arrangement, the purchasing organisation sets up a framework agreement and buys from the supplier on an 'as and when required' basis (described in Chapter 2). These agreements are typically made over a year's duration, or longer.

Fixed Contract

Under a blanket order type of arrangement, there is no promise to buy specific quantities. Under a fixed contract, there is such a promise. A fixed contract offers more continuity than the blanket order type of arrangement. The contract is therefore more definite, as the blanket order only represents an option for the purchaser to buy from the supplier.

Alliance/Strategic Alliance

This refers to an arrangement between organisations to work together for mutual advantage. A strategic alliance makes recognition of the need to work together in a spirit of cooperation. The relationship focuses on wider aspects rather than merely the current purchase. Product innovation, and new ways of improving logistics reducing total costs, for example, may be considered.

Partnering

A partnership is the most advanced form of relationship management. Both the purchaser, the supplier and other organisations involved in the supply chain may be working together to reduce total costs and improve the quality of the product or service. The organisations involved are striving to achieve world-class standards and there is a strong element of co-destiny in the relationship as the purchaser and supplier are working closely together on both short and long-term goals.

The following diagram shows the effect that the type of relationship may have on the negotiation process. The factors referred to on the left-hand side refer to characteristics associated with spot buying. The middle range refers to regular trading, blanket orders and fixed contracts. The right hand refers to alliances and partnering. The diagram shows that there are a significant number of differences between a partnership relationship and a spot purchase.

A partnership relationship emphasises a high degree of trust between the purchaser and supplier. Help, support and information are given willingly by the organisations involved. As we shall see later in this chapter, the trust required for a true partnership or co-destiny relationship is often lacking. At the other end of the continuum, a spot purchase will resort to the written contract to define the basis of the agreement. There is a tendency for little trust, and the contract will define the rights and duties of both parties.

Relationship Continuum and Negotiation

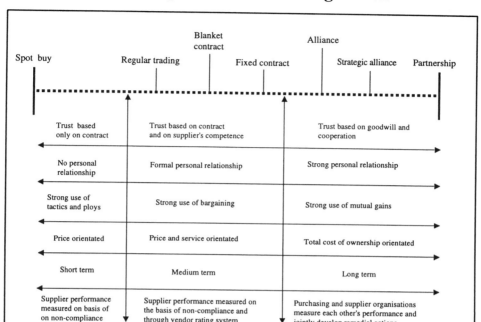

Secondly, personal relationships under a partnership will be common, as joint teams from both the purchaser and supplier may work together to tackle projects. The projects may focus on various aspects of the business relationship, as cooperation can help reduce the total costs of supply, improve product innovations, reduce the time to launch new products or services to external customers, or the organisations may generally work together to improve aspects of quality. Under such arrangements, the people involved from both organisations will develop personal relationships with each other. Under some partnership arrangements, it is common for employees of the supplier to actually work at the purchaser's site location.

In terms of the negotiation styles typically adopted under the various relationships, the emphasis in a partnership will be on obtaining mutually beneficial win/ win outcomes that suit both parties. Under a more short-term relationship, however, the negotiations will be approached in a more adversarial manner, and in face-to-face negotiations. There is likely to be use of deceptive tactics to try and gain an upper-hand over the other party. Information is concealed and the parties will each be trying to make gains at the other's expense.

In *Making Partnership Sourcing Happen* published by Partnership Sourcing Ltd a joint Department of Trade and Industry and Confederation of British Industry initiative:

Sourcing

Partnership Sourcing can improve your competitive position by bringing down costs, boosting quality and making you more responsive to your customer's needs. It means rejecting the 'master servant' syndrome where the supplier is merely told what to supply and the customer told the price. Instead the partners agree on common goals and build the commitment, trust and mutual support necessary to achieve them.

There is no doubt that partnership relationships have become a key development in supply chain management strategies in the late 1980s and 1990s. Ingersoll Engineers conducted a major survey of different types of manufacturing industries in 1996, to survey the organisation and processes organisations were adopting to meet their customer needs. 325 different organisations replied to the survey, and the second most common process improvement sought was through partnership sourcing arrangements.

Approaches now Considered Critical to Future Success

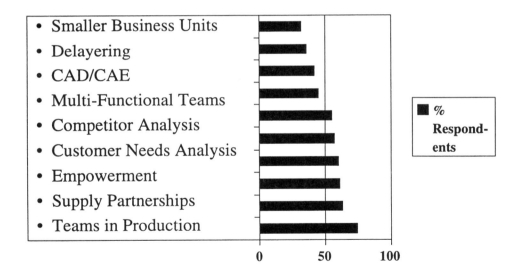

Teams in Production: organising operatives into small teams taking on greater responsibility and accountability for the organisation of their tasks to produce improved quality of workmanship.

Empowerment: giving people greater freedom to express ideas for continuous improvement and responsibility for decision taking.

Customer Needs Analysis: evaluating the requirements of organisation's customers. Often project teams are established to analyse how processes can be improved to improve the provision of product or services demanded by customers.

Competitor Analysis: organisations diverting resources to analyse the product or service provision of key competitors. Often, this is linked to a benchmarking initiative.

Multi-Functional Teams: these are teams created at middle and senior management levels where people who were traditionally aligned by function work together in multi-disciplinary teams.

CAD/CAE: computer aided design/engineering systems which are used to both improve and reduce the times for designing new products.

Delayering: emphasises the reduction in the numbers of tiers in management hierarchies as organisations move towards flatter structures.

Smaller Business Units: creating new structures in organisations where smaller organisations with greater accountability are created from formerly larger groups.

Ingersoll Engineers comment that supply partnerships are particularly prevalent in the automotive component industry. This is principally through the adoption of Japanese-type Just In Time supply arrangements. However, there is plenty of evidence to suggest that partnership sourcing arrangements have been embraced in other sectors.

Partnership Sourcing: Myth or Reality?

In the construction industry, for example, greater cooperation throughout supply chains was advocated in *Constructing the Team*, a review of procurement and contractual arrangements in the UK construction industry (1994). Sir Michael Latham chaired the joint government and industry review. Research by Professor Andrew Cox and Mike Townsend in *Latham as a Half-Way House* argues that:

> It would seem that many in the industry believe that 'partnering' provides the answer to the question of which relationship type should be used in the procurement of construction works.

They cite Bennett and Jayes in their report 'Trusting the Team' which implied that partnering could be based on a single project (project partnering) or on a long-term commitment (strategic partnering). Thus, partnership arrangements could be applied in all situations.

However, Cox and Townsend conclude that: 'There is growing evidence that the fragmented, self-interested and adversarial culture of the industry still persists'. The typology of a partnership, in which the supplier and purchaser adopt a co-destiny approach to their relationship rarely exists in practice.

According to research undertaken in 1994 by the consulting company AT Kearney, over 40% of UK private sector organisations had established customer / supplier partnerships. However, the report concludes that the term 'partnership' had become devalued through overuse and, as a result, was difficult to define and execute. The report states: 'There is no clear evidence that companies which claim to have partnership sourcing behave in any significant way different from companies which do not make such claims'.

The report also states that true partnerships are a rarity. It would appear that the term has been so widely misused in commercial relationships that the term lacks any real meaning, and should best be avoided.

A further study in 1995 by Ingersoll Engineers 'Partnership or Conflict?' of the adoption of partnership sourcing in the automotive sector, analysed the attitudes of both suppliers and purchasers (Original Equipment Manufacturers). Their conclusions were:

Partnership or Conflict?

A Study by *Ingersoll Engineers* (1995) Reveals:

From the Suppliers' Perspective, they Perceive Customers Squeezing them Relentlessly and Being Unwilling to Agree to an Equitable Arrangement... Many Adversarial Attitudes Remain. The Issue is One of Trust - or Lack of It

The Way forward is through more Effective Collaboration up and down the Supply Chain - Areas for Co-operation Are: Price, Quality, Product Design, Delivery Performance and Business Strategy. Objectives Include:
- Creating the Right Culture by Working together
- Increased Supplier Involvement in Design and Support
- EDI Links, CAD and Direct Line Feed

In 1995, Ingersoll commented that there needs to be greater cooperation throughout the supply chain. This is the focus of Chapter 8. Mark Ralf formerly of SmithKline Beecham provides perhaps the best advice on purchasing relationships when he states:

> In many cases, SmithKline Beecham may not want to partner a company in a certain category of expenditure simply because we do not believe that a partnership is relevant for that activity. Whether we have collaborative partnerhips or arms length relationships depends on how SB feels any particular relationship will best assist the fulfilment of the strategic corporate goal. This means that we have many and varied supply relationships and will continue to do so.

Finally, the Ingersoll survey conducted in 1996 of different types of manufacturing industries found that relationships between purchasers and suppliers were generally good. Few purchasers or suppliers claimed to have created full partnerships and the figures show that many relationships with suppliers tended to be adversarial.

Relationships with Customers and Suppliers

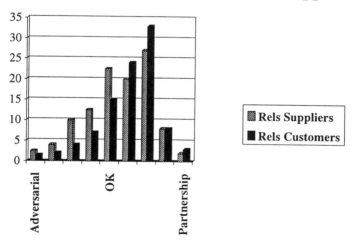

Source: Ingersoll Engineers (1996)

Partnership Sourcing and the Public Sector

A great deal of attention has focused on the utilisation of partnership sourcing in the private sector, particularly in the automotive sector. It explores the principles of partnership sourcing applicable to public sector organisations, and organisations which normally use competitive tendering to select suppliers.

The sourcing strategy for goods and services bought through competitive tender relies on a multiple sourcing strategy. It is illegal not to do so, because of the legislative requirements placed on public purchasers to select suppliers through competition (see Chapter 9 for further detail). Does this mean that public sector purchasers can never take advantage of the benefits of partnership sourcing ? The following table compares the competitive and partnership approaches.

Characteristic	Competition
Supplier selection	Solely tendering
Length of contract	Usually short, < than 2 years
Number of suppliers	Numerous
Contractual relations	Very formal, rigid
Communications with suppliers	Very guarded, infrequent
Negotiation	Adversarial
Join activities with suppliers	Very rare

Characteristic	Partnership
Supplier selection	Direct negotiation
Length of contract	> 2 years, can be life-long
Number of suppliers	1, perhaps 2
Contractual relations	Flexible, informal
Communications with suppliers	Open and continuous
Negotiation	Win/win
Joint activities with suppliers	Extensive

The extreme form of competitive bidding is not only incompatible with the concepts of partnership, but it can also prove difficult to obtain VFM because of the general emphasis on choosing suppliers on the basis of lowest price rather than best value for money. The advice given to government purchasers by the Treasury is that departments should avoid taking an unnecessarily adversarial or unhelpful approach.

Departments will recognise that it is in their own interests to help suppliers develop in ways that make them better able to provide what the department requires, to the desired quality and at a competitive price. The relationship should be one which encourages continuous improvement.

Furthermore, the Treasury unit states that partnership sourcing should be more beneficial than an adversarial relationship; there are important constraints on the use of partnership sourcing in the public sector:

- There must be competition at the outset to select the supplier and periodic re-tendering thereafter.
- There must be a clear definition of the contractual responsibilities of both sides.
- There should be specific and measurable milestones for improved performance as part of the contract with a partner.

According to research undertaken by Erridge and Nondi of the University of Ulster, a hybrid model is now being practised by many public sector organisations.

Characteristic	Mixed Partnership/ Competition
Supplier selection	Tendering & negotiation
Length of contract	3-7 years
Number of suppliers	1, perhaps 2
Contractual relations	Fairly formal
Communications with suppliers	Fairly guarded but frequent
Negotiation	Pragmatic
Join activities with suppliers	Frequent

So, the features of the mixed competition/partnership models include: suppliers selection combining competitive tender with pre- and post-tender negotiation; limited number of suppliers per product/ service; contract periods up to seven years; fairly formal contractual relations but the emphasis is on mutually beneficial terms of business; collaboration on cost reduction and service improvement.

During the period of the contract, partnership can be developed, with an emphasis on improving the quality of service and also on reducing costs during the length of the agreement. Whilst the partnership supplier can not be guaranteed to win the contract on re-tendering, they should clearly be in a strong position to do so.

Supplier Assessment

Suppliers should be assessed both before the award of the contract and during the performance of the contract. The pre-evaluation of suppliers is an important element of sourcing. The purchasing organisation needs to establish whether the supplier is a good risk. Sourcing is the process of identifying suppliers who are able to supply the goods or services purchasers need.

Once the supply market has been established, its ability to perform the contract needs to be evaluated in order to reduce the risk of default. For new suppliers, appraisal can be undertaken by a combination of the following:

- Desk research using secondary data, which is published data already in existence. These sources of information could include company accounts, references or information published in trade journals.
- Primary data can be extracted from field research. This will normally involve a visit to the company where the technical, commercial and financial capabilities of the firm in question are considered.
- A combination of both primary and secondary data could be sought by the completion of a questionnaire sent to the supplier. The questionnaire can request additional information, such as company reports for the previous three years, as well as specific questions about the technical, commercial and financial capabilities of the firm.

The purchasing organisation, in dealing with suppliers which could represent a significant element of risk to the business, may wish to analyse a number of aspects of the supplier. These could include the following.

General Information

The supplier could be asked to make available historical data relevant to present business activities, including growth, diversification, company ownership, supplier and customer base, and its product range; whether they have accreditation to ISO 9000, or other third party certification of their quality assurance processes.

Corporate Management

The supplier could demonstrate that its company has a strategic mission or long-term vision of what the company seeks to do and whether corporate objectives have been set to achieve this long-term vision. The supplier is asked to state its strengths and weaknesses, and the opportunities or threats these create.

Evidence could be sought to clarify whether the supplier has given consideration to the following issues:

- Strategic mission
- Strategic objectives
- Competitive analysis
- Legal/ political factors
- Economic analysis - technological analysis
- Environmental strategy.

Financial Position

The supplier should be asked to demonstrate that it has a financially sound business structure and trading position. Ratio analysis could be used to evaluate:

- Cash flow
- Investment
- Gearing
- Profitability
- Stockholding.

Other questions used could specifically ask the supplier to provide details on:

- The allocation of overheads
- The techniques the supplier uses to eliminate waste
- The cost-effective management of its own suppliers
- The projected wage settlements and their funding
- Whether the supplier is receptive to open book costing (see Chapter 8).

Design, Research and Development

Suppliers could, if appropriate, be asked to demonstrate design, research and development strategy. This should encompass:

- The provision of engineers of sufficient skill and expertise
- Investment in computer aided design/manufacture systems
- Investment in test facilities and resources
- The ability to rapidly respond to customer requirements.

Operations Management

The supplier should have the necessary operations management to enable its strategy, aims and objectives to be realised. The following areas could be considered:

- Production planning and material control
- Capacity planning
- Information technology, including electronic data interchange
- Lead time analyses
- Transport strategy
- Appropriate measures of performance.

Human Resources

The supplier should be asked to demonstrate an awareness of factors affecting human resources and the development of skills in the workforce to support the process of continuous improvement. Examples of aspects of the supplier's human resource management include:

- Management style and company culture
- Training and development
- Motivation and recognition.

Methods of Supplier Appraisal

Method	Appropriate Circumstances
Visit to Supplier	High Value/ High Risk Products or Services
Questionnaire (Comprehensive)	High/ Medium Value or Risk
Questionnaire (Short)	Low Value or Risk
No Appraisal	Negligible Value/ Risk - 'Nuisance' Purchases

These aspects of the supplier's business could be requested by a questionnaire. Many of the areas mentioned would require detailed analysis, and the supplier organisation would find such a supplier appraisal a demanding process which would only really be necessary for strategically important purchases. A simplified version of the questionnaire could be prepared for lesser important purchases requesting basic details of the supplier organisation.

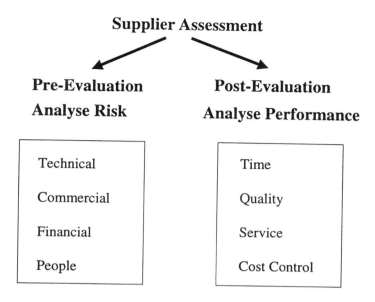

Post-evaluation or vendor rating refers to a system of measuring the supplier's performance. The aims of performance measurement are as follows:

- To compare actual with planned performance.
- To ascertain the causes of poor performance and provide a basis for improvement.
- To identify the contribution of purchasing to the results achieved by the organisation.

Supplier Development Stategies

Strategic Procurement Management In the 1990s: Concepts and Cases edited by Lamming and Cox contains an excellent chapter written by Ian Robertson on 'Developing Lean Supply in the Rover Group'. Rover have deployed a supplier development programme with their supply base.

Rover Group has 34,000 employees worldwide, with a number of subsidiary companies operating throughout the world. Annual turnover is approximately £4.3 billion and purchases from suppliers exceed £3 billion. In 1995, Rover Group was acquired by BMW.

Throughout much of the 1980s, Rover or as it was previously known, British Leyland was perceived as an organisation plagued with industrial relations disputes, unprofitable and hence a drain on the public sector finances. Furthermore, its product portfolio was uncompetitive.

In 1987, Rover commenced a total quality programme. This programme has undoubtedly helped Rover achieve great successes in the automotive market, and the public perception of the organisation is now far more favourable. Rover's vision as a company is to be 'Internationally Renowned For Extraordinary Customer Satisfaction'. As Ian Robertson comments:

> Mere customer satisfaction is no longer enough most car companies now achieve this. Similarly, whereas the goal for many companies in the 1980s was to produce a quality product in order to satisfy customers, the majority now produce quality products as a matter of course. This means that it is more difficult to secure a differential advantage over competitors on the basis of quality alone; different means to delight customers need to be actively sought. Working towards supplier partners, as part of the overall vision and purchasing strategy and objectives, is fundamental to achieving this.

The core of Rover's strategy for partnership sourcing and supplier development is RG2000. This is a part of an overall five-year strategy for the purchasing function. The aims of Rover's purchasing strategy are a number of 'processes'. Linked to each process is a 'process vision'. Each 'process' relates to a particular aspect of the company's push for world competitiveness in the management of their suppliers. The 'processes' and 'process visions' relating to the development of partnership sourcing are as follows:

Process	Process vision
Supplier reduction	Fully-optimised supplier base
Supplier development	World competitive supply base
Total cost management	Maximise material margins
People development	Multi-skilled, satisfied and motivated staff

The supplier assessment scheme is also used to develop suppliers' business systems and supply performance. In this way, RG2000 is a supplier development programme and encompasses the development of partnership sourcing, total quality and total cost reduction. The supplier assessment scheme therefore defines the parameters for selecting partners.

RG2000 seeks to assess suppliers on the basis of their performance. Key performance factors are assessed through a vendor rating system. The assessment survey analyses suppliers' business systems and also measures product and supply performance. The scoring system is shown overleaf:

Rover Group's Supplier Assessment Scheme: RG2000

Weighting System:	
Project Management	30
Total Quality Systems	10
Business Performance	30
Product and Supply Performance	
Delivered Product Quality	10
Delivery Performance	10
Product Warranty Performance	10
	100%

A central feature of RG2000 is the 'Supplier Assessment Questionnaire'. This is a comprehensive questionnaire sent to suppliers requesting information and asking for details on the areas mentioned in the previous section on supplier assessment. This forms the basis of the assessment of the supplier's business systems.

Rover Group's Supplier Assessment Scheme: RG2000

Score	Criteria
0	No Evidence of any Worthwhile System or Procedure Covering the Activity
1	Evidence of Ad Hoc or Unsatisfactory Systems or Procedures Requiring Improvements
2	Evidence that the Activity Is Adequately Covered in Practice, and by Systems and Procedures with Formal Documentary Support
3	Evidence that the Supplier Practices the Activity to Very High Standards with Detailed and Comprehensive Procedures and Records

Evidence of the areas in question are obtained by way of a supplier audit which is conducted by members of the purchasing function. The assessment takes approximately five days and Rover personnel ask for evidence of the factors in question. Suppliers are graded on the basis of a ranking scale 0 to 3, with 3 being the highest grade denoting 'best practice' in the industry. The total assessment aggregates to 70% of the points system. This methodology adheres to the fundamentals of the philosophy of total quality, the need for measurement of performance to provide a basis for continuous improvement.

Supplier development programmes, therefore, are a means of achieving improvements in network sourcing. Network sourcing refers to the forms of relationship taken with external suppliers. As Peter Hines argues:

> The basic starting point for this relationship is not only that the customer firm is focused on the consumer requirement, but that it ensures that its suppliers also have a total quality focus. Hence the strategies that the customer forms to supply the consumers must be translated back through the direct and indirect supplier network.

The assessments at Rover are carried out by a small purchasing team who take a five-day period to assess the supplier. The criteria used to judge each part of the business system is not disclosed to the supplier. In all, there are 242 elements of a supplier's business system which are assessed. These 242 elements are based on the different aspects of the supplier's business referred to in the supplier assessment questionnaire.

The requirements of resources in terms of supplier assessment and management under RG2000 is extensive. This partly explains the move towards reducing the supplier base. An assessment of a supplier will normally take a week at the supplier's premises. In addition to this work is the preparation for the assessment and the analysis of results.

A common theme in many organisations, partnership sourcing strategy is the reduction in the number of suppliers. In 1991, Rover had roughly 850 production suppliers. According to a recent report in *Supply Management*, Rover are now aiming to have no more than 50 to 55 first tier suppliers for each model. Rover and BMW together had 1,560 suppliers in 1995, of which 76 were common to both companies. By the end of the decade, it is predicted that the total will be down to 900, of which 250 are likely to be common.

Another important element in the drive towards a rationalised supplier base is the trend towards reducing the number of first tier suppliers. Professor Richard Lamming mentions the use of first tier suppliers to co-ordinate supply from minor firms.

The process of rationalising the supplier base, weeding out poorly-performing suppliers, eliminating multiple sourcing and creating fewer but more talented suppliers is the company's aim. This aim or process vision is termed a 'fully optimised supplier base' and is part of the Group's strategy referred to earlier.

Central to Rover's vision of creating a world competitive supply base is the adoption of the principles of RG2000 by suppliers. The suppliers' management system is assessed by

Rover's purchasing personnel, in terms of their corporate management, financial position, design and development capabilities, operations management and human resources.

Suppliers therefore receive a rating in terms of a percentage. If a supplier assessed in 1994 had achieved a 65% score, for example, he may be required to improve this score by, for example, 15% improvement one year after initial assessment, so by the end of 1995, the supplier is seeking to achieve a score of 80%; and 10% improvement two years after initial assessment, so by the end of 1996, the supplier is seeking to achieve a score of 90%; or

5% improvement three years after initial assessment, so by the end of 1997, the supplier is seeking to achieve a score of 95%.

Hence, the expectation is that suppliers will be improving their operational performance as well as improving their management systems and capabilities. RG2000 analyses suppliers in both areas. As Ian Robertson comments:

> Initially, when the programme was launched to sceptical audiences of suppliers the inevitable question to arise from the floor was 'Well, what's the pass mark then?' The answer to this question is that there is no preordained pass mark and it took a great deal of work to convey the idea that they were not being measured simply in order to be awarded a pass or a fail. The point of the exercise was not to punish or reward the company for its score on a particular day but to see how the score could be improved through working together with Rover.

> For example, the general attitude is that it is preferable to be with a company that scores 45 and is improving at 20% per annum, than to be with one that scores 50, but is only improving at 2% per annum.

So the aim of supplier development is to concentrate on improving all aspects of the purchaser/ supplier relationship.

Supplier Associations

A supplier association is defined by Compton and Jessop in the *Dictionary of Purchasing and Supply Terminology for Buying and Selling* (1995) in the following ways.

Supplier Associations

> ## *Definitions*
>
> "A Group of Suppliers to a Single Customer Organised, with the Customer's Assistance, to Share Ideas and Information for Buying and Selling."
>
>

David Jessop (1995)
>
>
> "A Mutually Benefiting Group of a Company's Most Important Sub-Suppliers Brought together on a Regular Basis for the Purpose of Co-ordination and Co-operation as well as to Assist All the Members to Benefit from the Type of Development Associated with Large Japanese Automotive Assemblers."
>
>

Peter Hines (1994)
>

Peter Hines in *Creating World Class Suppliers: Unlocking Mutual Competitive Advantage* (1994) provides a different definition stated in the diagram

The Japanese refer to supplier associations as 'kyoryoku kai', founded in parts of the Japanese automotive sector before spreading to the electronics industry. The focus of supplier associations is to improve on aspects of supply chain management – whether it be working together to produce innovative products, reducing total costs, or improving aspects of communication and logistics. Like other developments, supplier associations were founded at Toyota in 1939, when a group of 18 suppliers met under the name of the Toyota Subcontractors Discussion Group. In the 1950s, it appears that Toyota started taking a more active role in developing the capabilities of suppliers. Improvements in quality were achieved with suppliers through the implementation of quality circles and statistical process control methods. In 1953, Toyota's approach to suppliers demonstrated the principles of mutuality and they agreed to:

- share production planning information with suppliers;
- use a standardised approach to purchasing negotiations by using a standard estimation sheet;
- make 80% of payments in cash with the other 20% in 60 to 90 day payable bills.

Other firms copied Toyota's approach of encouraging the empowerment of suppliers. By the 1960s, suppliers were adopting greater responsibility for designing new components and systems. Outline ideas would be given to suppliers in the form of a performance specification, the suppliers would use their skill and capabilities to design an appropriate part or system. This is the key principle of technology transfer which relates to the production of a product or service that improve aspects of another organisation's business performance. Peter Hines cites the use of supplier associations at Mitsubishi Motors, when in 1982 they provided a statement which said:

> We depend on the outside firms which co-operate with us for items which comprise about 70% of the cost of a vehicle. As a result, it is vital for us to maintain their cooperation, to see that Mitsubishi Motors policy is fully understood. The purpose of the supplier association is to contribute to the mutual development of Mitsubishi Motors and its members by building a co-operative system in accordance with our basic policies.

Peter Hines states that the adoption of supplier associations in the UK has only been piecemeal. Business performance tends to be judged on a short-term basis in the West, and supplier associations perhaps produce positive results over the long term. A key difference in the Japanese automotive sector is the very close relationships between the original equipment manufacturer and suppliers. Suppliers tend to depend on one OEM for their sales whereas in Western markets many suppliers are often multi-national organisations who deal with a number of OEMs. There is not the same dependency perhaps as there is in the Japanese automotive sector.

Whilst supplier associations have a great number of benefits, they are mainly active in the automotive sector and whilst the principles of many best practices have originated in this industry, it would be a mistake to think these practices are universally applicable to all industrial sectors.

Technology Transfer

Technology transfer can take place when a supplier passes improvements of the provision of a product or service to the purchaser. The relationship in place with the purchaser must be one where the supplier's ideas will not be divulged to other competing suppliers. It is common to use a contractual clause in the forming of such a relationship either to:

- provide the supplier with an indemnity if the purchaser should breach any aspect of intellectual property rights (copyright, patent, etc);
- allow the purchaser exclusive rights to use the product or service.

Technology has an important role in improving on organisation's product or service offering, and hence its competitiveness. A conference sponsored in 1996 by the Department of

Trade and Industry and organised by the Royal Aeronautical Society focused on technology transfer to other industries. It was estimated that the quantitative value of spin-offs in technology improvements is in the region of £1.5 to £2 billion per year. Examples of technology transfer emanating from the aerospace industry include:

- the development of industrial gas turbines from aerospace engine technologies;
- improvements in adhesive products;
- the shaping of steel rollers used in the manufacture of corrugated paper board;
- finite element analysis (a computer-based technique) used in vibration analysis to optimise the design of structures.

An article in *Supply Management* on technology transfer reported that a consortium involving Cambridge University, Rolls-Royce and GET Alsthom is jointly involved in a project to use computer modelling to design new materials for ultra-high temperatures to increase thrust and efficiency in orangeness. They will also transfer the technology to power generation plants and replace iron components with nickel based alloys. It is predicted that the technology improvement will lead to an increase in thermal efficiency from 40 to 60%.

Many of the improvements brought about through aerospace technologies have been made through the movement of staff once employed in the sector to various technology-based industries including the automotive, marine, petro-chemical, nuclear and railway industries.

An excellent example of technology transfer is the improvement in adhesives used in the welding of aluminium by the aluminium producer, Alcan. The use of an 'aluminum structured vehicle' using adhesive bonding to combine aluminium structures improves the technology of production of aluminum cars. Few OEMs currently use aluminium to produce car bodies, but the development made by Alcan may change buying behaviour towards the greater use of aluminium car bodies because of the advantages of weight saving and thus fuel economy (and environmental aspects).

Another example is the production of a new technology, 'inorganic membrane', a thin film of oxide sheet with a porous structure used in biotechnology industries to separate molecules. This is an example of diversification by Alcan as the production of 'inorganic membranes' represented a new product (one that was totally different to the supply of aluminium) to a new market. The product had the advantage of being an inorganic material and, as such, would not be attacked by solvents and be resistant to acids. Alcan sells the use of technology to a separate organisation who are responsible for the production and marketing of 'inorganic membranes' mainly as a result of Alcan choosing to concentrate on its core business, the supply of aluminium.

Environmental Sourcing

As Malcolm Saunders states in his book *Strategic Purchasing and Supply Chain Management,* environmental concerns are taking on an important dimension: 'As the century draws to a close, one of the most significant issues for society as a whole and for business in particular, is the growing concern for the protection of the environment.'

Purchasing managers have the responsibility for procuring a wide variety of raw materials, components, consumables and packaging materials required in manufacturing and in service industries. They can have a vital role to play in private sector organisations by giving their company the competitive edge in the market place by adopting environmentally sound policies and practices. The following list identifies many of the concerns that need to be covered by the purchasing function:

- The recovery, recycling and reusing of materials and waste products.
- The safe disposal of waste products which cannot be recycled.
- Supplier selection policies to support firms that conform to environmental standards with regard to air, water, and noise pollution.
- Supplier and product selection policies that reflect concern for conservation and the renewal of resources.
- The safe testing of products and materials.
- Concern for noise, spray, dirt and vibration in the operation of transport facilities.

Environmental Purchasing

- Can Purchase Products and Services to Certain Environmental Specifications

- Can Consider Alternative Products and Services and Standardise Environmental Specifications

- Can Evaluate the Commitment and Performance of Suppliers

- Can Undertake Supplier Development to Make Improvements Possible

- Can Help the Organisation Improve Cost Efficiencies

B&Q, the do-it-yourself subsidiary of the Kingfisher Group, has differentiated itself in the market though its purchasing policies. B&Q, under an initiative lead by their environmental controller, Alan Knight, carried full page advertisements in the national press informing the public of their supplier assessment scheme. The scheme provides a grading for suppliers which then forms the basis for an environmental supplier development scheme. A key element of their environmental policy is to ensure that supplies of timber to B&Q suppliers are sourced from certified forestry areas. In 1992, the British Standards Institute published the world's first attempt at providing a model for managing the environmental activities of an organisation when they published BS7750. 200 companies took part in a pilot study implementing the standard. A revised standard was issued in 1994.

The standard is now adopted internationally as the International Standard ISO 14000.

Environmental Standard: ISO 14000

The Standard Specifies the Requirement for Implementing and Maintaining an Environmental Management System

Potential Direct Benefits	*Potential Indirect Benefits*
• Reduction in Resource Consumption	• Enhanced Corporate Image
• Reduction in Scrap or Waste	• Enhanced Marketing Capabilities
• Reductions in Number of Complaints	• Improved Staff Morale
• Avoidance of Accidents or Emergencies	• Better Customer Relations
• Avoidance of Financial Penalties	• Better Community Relations
• Avoidance of Claims for Compensation	

Ethical Issues

Ethics is concerned with the moral principles and values which govern our beliefs, actions and decisions. Naturally, ethical considerations can have a significant impact on purchasers' dealings with suppliers. Kenneth Lysons in his book *Purchasing* argues that ethics is important in purchasing for the following reasons:

1. Purchasing staff are the representatives of their organisation in its dealings with suppliers.
2. Sound ethical conduct in dealing with suppliers is essential to the creation of long-term relationships and the establishment of supplier goodwill.

3. Purchasing staff are probably more exposed to the temptation to act unethically than most other employees.
4. It is impossible to claim 'professional' status for purchasing without reference to a consideration of its ethical aspects.

The Chartered Institute of Purchasing and Supply has a code of ethics which is as follows:

The Ethical Code of the Chartered Institute of Purchasing and Supply

The Ethical Code is in three sections, Introduction, Precepts, Guidance . The following is merely a summary of the precepts and the main areas of guidance. A full version is available from the CIPS upon request.

Precepts

Members shall never use their authority or office for personal gain and shall seek to uphold and enhance the standing of the Purchasing and Supply profession and the Institute by:

(a) maintaining an unimpeachable standard of integrity in all their business relationships both inside and outside the organisations in which they are employed;

(b) fostering the highest possible standards of professional competence against those for whom they are responsible;

(c) optimising the use of resources for which they are responsible to provide the maximum benefit to their employing organisation;

(d) complying both with the letter and the spirit of:

   (i) the law of the country in which they practise;

   (ii) such guidance on professional practice as may be issued by the Institute from time to time;

   (iii) contractual obligations;

(e) rejecting any business practice which might reasonably be deemed improper.

The ethical code was drafted at a time when competitive multi-source purchasing was the rule. The ethical standard perhaps needs to be reviewed in the light of contemporary commercial relationships as organisations move to adopt the greater use of partnership sourcing particularly the wording of paragraph 4 (d) mentioning the prevention of 'fair competition'. In addition, as partnering encourages more personalised relationships between both the purchaser and supplier, one can question the ethical guidance given on hospitality, since joint social events perhaps should be seen as a positive activity.

References/ Further Reading

Ansari and Moderass *Just in Time Purchasing* The Free Press (1990)

CBI/ DTI *Making Partnership Sourcing Happen* (1992). See also: *Partnership Sourcing: Creating Service Partnerships* (1993) and *Partnership Sourcing in Action* (1996)

Professor Andrew Cox and Townsend *Latham Half Way House* IPSERA Conference Paper (1996)

Compton and Jessop in the *Dictionary of Purchasing and Supply Terminology for Buying and Selling* Pitman Publishing (1995)

Nick Edwards 'Here Today, Green Tomorrow' *Supply Management* 11 December 1997

Lisa Ellram 'A Managerial Guideline for the Development and Implementation of Purchasing Partnerships' *International Journal of Purchasing and Materials Management*, Summer (1991)

A Erridge and Nondi 'Public Procurement: Competition and Partnership' *European Journal of Purchasing and Supply Management* Vol 1 Number 3 (1994)

Hines 'Creating World Class Suppliers: Unlocking Mutual Competitive Advantage' *Financial Times/* Pitman Publishing (1994)

Ingersoll Engineers *Partnership or Conflict? The Automotive Component Supply Industry: A Survey of Issues of Alignment* (1995)

Ingersoll Engineers '*The Way We Work: Organisation and Processes to Meet Customer Needs*' in *Manufacturing Industry* (1996)

AT Kearney *Partnership or Power Play* (1994)

Lamming *Beyond Partnership: Strategies for innovation and Lean Supply* Prentice Hall (1993)

Latham 'Constructing the Team:' Final Report of the Government/ Industry Review of Procurement and Contractual Arrangements in the UK Construction Industry, HMSO/ Stationery Office (1994)

Lysons *Purchasing* 4th Edition, Pitman Publishing (1996)

Ralf 'The Strategic Approach to Procurement at SmithKline Beecham' in *Strategic Procurement Management in the 1990s: Text and Cases* Ed Professor Lamming and Cox, Chartered Institute of Purchasing and Supply (1995)

Robertson 'Developing Lean Supply at the Rover Group' in *Strategic Procurement Management in the 1990's: Text and Cases* Ed Professor Lamming and Cox, Chartered Institute of Purchasing and Supply (1995)

Saunders *Strategic Purchasing and Supply Chain Management,* 2nd Edition, Pitman Publishing (1997)

Sheridan *Negotiating Commercial Contracts* McGraw Hill (1991)

Supply Management 'Car Suppliers Hit the Road' 2 October 1997

Supply Management 'Varley Aerospace: Technology Transfer' 15 August 1996

chapter eight
Lean Supply

Chapter 7 concentrated on important aspects and developments in supplier selection. A principle area of focus now for purchasing managers is in supplier development techniques. A proactive purchasing function will continually encourage improved performance from suppliers. This chapter begins with analysing 'vendor rating', the traditional means of analysing suppliers' performance. More recent developments in relationship management will also be discussed, as will the concepts of lean supply, benchmarking and business process re-engineering.

Vendor Rating

Once the contract is underway, vendor rating systems evaluate the supplier's performance in terms of cost control, quality, delivery/completion and service. This helps to provide the buyer with objective information in which judgements on source selection can be based, and the supplier can be provided with their rating which should highlight areas for improvement.

Operationally, it is necessary to continue to appraise the performance of the supplier base on a day-to-day basis and to have in place a mechanism that allows purchasers to evaluate both new and existing suppliers as and when necessary. As an ongoing means of assessing the supply base, vendor rating can measure the overall performance of the base in the areas rated and demonstrate movements, and hopefully improvements, over time, of the entire base. It can also identify particular problems with individual suppliers and provide the objective evidence from which reasonable debate and action can be derived.

Vendor rating schemes which identify the nature of problems encountered can also be used as a diagnostic tool for identifying areas of weakness in the base or of shortcomings in the way the buyers are managing the suppliers.

There are a number of factors affecting consistent vendor rating of suppliers:

Cost Control

Measurement of price performance has proven difficult because of the variability of factors affecting price. Typically organisations purchase a variety of products in differing volumes and demand patterns from a matrix of suppliers selected on grounds of availability, quality and price.

Suppliers sell at prices determined by the cost base they are trading with, the market conditions they find themselves in and their perception of the customer's desire for product. All these factors are in a constant flux and trying to determine what factors affect which price is an impossible task. As we saw in Chapter 7, partnership sourcing encourages the use of open book pricing systems to try to reduce exposure to this volatility.

Delivery Performance

Delivery performance is arguably easier to monitor and appraise. Computer systems may record agreed delivery dates and actual levels of compliance to these performances. More disciplined departments can use these dates and levels of compliance to develop accurate delivery performance monitors. The road to this particular path is however not an easy one to tread. Purchasers frequently change delivery schedules that are communicated to suppliers because of changing market demands. Thus, many a late delivery will have been instigated by the purchasing organisation.

Quality

The measurement of quality performance at its most basic level in terms of recording defects and non-conformance to specifications can provide worthwhile data. Organisations traditionally use sampling techniques which determine the number of items to be checked based on the previous performance of the supplier and the number sent in the batch to be inspected. As performance improves the quantity to be checked reduces and vice versa. In many industries, it was a traditional practice to set acceptable quality levels (which allow for a proportion of defective produce) but the levels of acceptable numbers of defects are reducing significantly as organisations achieve zero defects in terms of their production.

Overall Rating

Organisations often calculate an overall rating of the supplier by aggregating individual performances under one total figure which is arrived at by weighting the respective measures to give them their perceived importance in the rating mix, multiplying the actual figure for a given parameter by the weighting factor and totalling the results.

The use of approved vendor schemes is a common technique used by purchasing organisations. The schemes vary in detailed design but are aimed at producing a list of suppliers vetted by the purchaser. They will typically give approval for supply in accordance with either procedures established for quality (such as ISO 9000) or commercial criteria, evaluation criteria such as their technical, commercial and financial capabilities and perhaps their operational performance in terms of their cost control, quality, delivery/completion and service. Such schemes may therefore combine both 'vendor appraisal' factors (technical, commercial and financial capabilities) as well as vendor performance measurement (vendor rating- cost control, delivery, quality and service).

Professor Richard Lamming et al of the Centre for Research in Strategic Purchasing and Supply at the University of Bath is critical of the use of vendor measurement systems. In an IPSERA conference paper (1996) he wrote:

> While the customer may see the assessment process as a form of developmental co-operation, some suppliers appear to perceive it as an element in a coercive strategy on the part of the customer. If the benefits are not 'sold' to the supplier, its participation will be limited to compliance.

As we saw in Chapter 7 on sourcing, the information received by the purchasing organisation about the supplier's capabilities and performance can be used to help the supplier improve performance over time. This is the principle of supplier development.

Professor Lamming conducted a survey of the use of vendor measurement systems. The Centre's findings are as follows:

Vendor Rating

According to Research Conducted by Bath University:

93% of Suppliers Were Subject to Vendor Rating

85% of Customer Firms Used VR to Improve Supplier Relationships

80% of Customer Firms Used VR to 'Filter Out Unsuitable Suppliers'

Customers Invite the Opinions of the Supplier, but Little is Done to Address their Suggestions

Assessment Criteria and Expected Performance Levels Are not Given to the Supplier Adequately in Advance

Suppliers Are not Given Detailed Feedback on the Assessment Findings. Little Effort is Made towards Developing the Capabilities of Suppliers

Strategic Factors Are Rarely Analysed

Professor Lamming comments that:

> While the majority of customer firms claimed to be implementing vendor assessment as part of a strategy to improve supply relationships, there appeared to be a general lack of genuine involvement of suppliers in the design and development of the schemes. This omission extends to agreement on performance achievements, and active help from the customer to enable the supplier to improve.

Vendor rating systems focus attention on the supplier's performance. Whilst supplier performance does contribute to the satisfaction of purchasing's customers, there are other important aspects which need to be analysed. Research by Christine Harland of the Centre for Research in Strategic Purchasing and Supply (1996) emphasised a mis-match between perceptions of requirements by both purchasers and suppliers in the areas of quality, delivery, service, product range and pricing. Her analysis advocates a model for understanding this mis-match which is shown below.

Harland's model seeks to identify and measure the size of gaps in perceptions between a purchasing organisation and a supplier. Whilst the buyer responsible for making the agreement with the supplier needs to understand the internal customer's requirements, the purchaser's requirements need to be communicated to the supplier. The supplier in turn needs to understand the purchaser's requirements. The agreement made with the buyer will usually be carried out by the sales/ marketing function. Very often the actual performance of the contract is carried out by different business functions, such as by operations and distribution. So, Harland has identified four areas for mis-matches.

Mis-Match One: this represents the gap between what the customer in the relationship claims to require and what the supplier perceives the purchaser as requiring.

Mis-Match Two: this refers to the perception of performance gap, which is the difference between the supplier's view of performance and the purchaser's view of supplier performance.

Mis-Match Three: this represents the purchaser's dissatisfaction as it is a measure of the purchaser's perception of his requirements and his perception of the performance he receive from the supplier.

Mis-Match Four: this refers to the difference between the supplier's perception of the purchaser's requirements and the supplier's performance. This may be significant if the supplier is seeking to improve performance.

Relationship Assessment

Vendor rating and assessment are performed by purchasing organisations and are techniques aimed at analysing suppliers with a view to improving their performance over time. However, these systems which focus on aspects such as the supplier's capabilities and performance (quality, cost, time) do not provide information about the relationship between the organisations. As we have already seen, Professor Richard Lamming (the

The Mis-match Tool

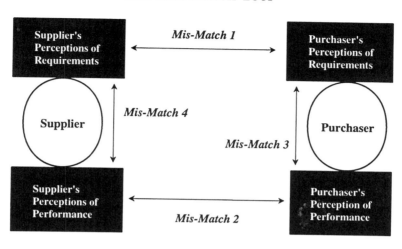

leading authority on purchaser/supplier relationships) is critical of the focus of vendor rating and assessment. The measurements are typically made by purchasing organisations of their suppliers. This all points to a very one-sided view of relationship management. Many of the difficulties experienced in the relationship over operational performance may be just as much to do with problems experienced by the purchasing organisation. The potential difficulties that purchasers could cause are numerous: changed schedules and specifications, poor communication, late payment of invoices and unhelpful adversarial attitudes.

Traditional relationships tend to be characterised by 'power plays' and the 'supplier perceptions' and 'purchase portfolio' models identified in Chapter 6, Structure and Strategy, help to define the position that the purchaser should take when analysing the power relationships associated with any particular purchase.

The following diagram helps summarise the characteristics of the traditional relationship:

Traditional Purchaser/Supplier Relationships

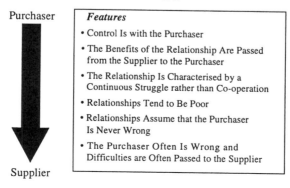

Greater attention needs to be focussed on the relationship itself if the purchaser and supplier are to improve their business performance. Information, help, expertise, value and innovation need to flow both ways between the purchaser and supplier. To enable these to occur, a number of factors which are internal to the organisation need to be analysed and improved. The Department of Trade and Industry produced a guide on 'Supply Chain Development' (1997) and the factors that are analysed as part of the relationship are:

- **Compatibility:** the degree to which the purchaser and supplier's business interests coincide.
- **Trust:** the degree to which the parties open up to each other on sensitive matters such as on pricing and quality problems.
- **Closeness:** how much the parties know and understand each other's businesses.
- **Depth of Relationship:** the depth and breadth of contact between the organisations across different departments (operations, design, planning, purchasing, etc) and at all hierarchical levels.
- **Reliance:** how much the purchaser and supplier actually depend on each other in terms of business output.

The methodology proposed by the DTI to assess the relationship is for both the purchaser and supplier to complete a questionnaire ranking aspects of the relationship from poor to excellent. The results are then plotted on a web diagram (shown below). This will show the purchaser's view of the relationship; a separate web diagram will illustrate the supplier's view.

Relationship Assessment

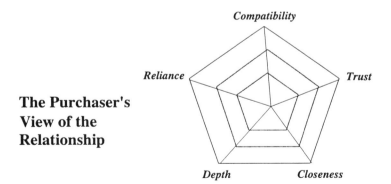

The Purchaser's View of the Relationship

Focus groups consisting of people from a variety of different functions of both the purchaser and supplier organisations should then meet and be facilitated through various exercises aimed at improving the relationship. The results can be improved over time, and should spiral out over time. Both parties will then be embarking on a continuous improvement programme designed to improve their relationship.

Relationship Assessment

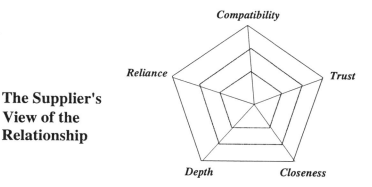

**The Supplier's
View of the
Relationship**

Relationship Assessment

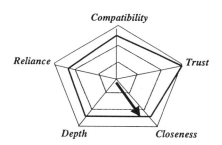

*Continuous
Improvement
Gained in the
Relationship*

Spiral Out the Results

Lean Supply

The concept of lean supply emanated in Japan. The Japanese word 'muda' means waste and refers to any activity which absorbs resources but adds no value. Examples of waste may be rectification of defects, excess work-in-progress, unsold stocks, unnecessary steps taken in processing products or services, or excess manpower. Taiichi Ohno was the head of production engineering at Toyota, and he is widely acclaimed as one of the most inspirational business people in the Japanese industrial boom during the post-war years as he created the Just In Time system at Toyota. The JIT philosophy requires the elimination of waste from any production system, one of the key areas of waste being inventory.

Shortly before Ohno's death in 1990, he was interviewed in a documentary tracing the roots of the massive expanse of the Japanese car industry. In one of the interviews he stated that he would look at a job, and tell those involved to do the same tasks but with half the number of people. When they had accomplished this he would say 'ok, now halve the number again!' Ohno's work at Toyota emphasised more than just cutting the number of people to perform specific processes, as the company were pioneers of the benefits of Just In Time delivery, total quality and employee involvement.

The Machine that Changed the World, James Womack et al, highlights the differences in the world automotive industry. The authors cite Toyota as an example:

> Today (1989) Toyota assembly plants have practically no rework areas and perform almost no rework. By contrast... a number of current day mass production plants devote 20% of plant area and 25% of their total hours of effort on fixing mistakes. Toyota's vehicles have among the lowest number of defects of any in the world, comparable to the very best of the German luxury car producers, who devote many hours of assembly plant effort to rectification.

The principle of eliminating waste present in the Toyota production system was spread throughout the supply chain. The Japanese Ministry for International Trade and Industry intervened to help the supply base improve relationships with the original equipment manufacturers (like Toyota) as well as productivity.

Professor Richard Lamming in his authoritative account of relationships in the automotive sector distinguishes between lean producers and mass production. Mass production emphasised the economies of scale that can be gained from producing large quantities of stocks. Jobs on production lines were de-skilled by being divided into simple tasks. This was the production model devised by Frederick W Taylor.

The characteristics of mass production within the automotive industry were described by Womack et al in *The Machine That Changed the World:*

- Single-purpose machines produce components needed for assembly.
- Specialisation of work tasks occurred at every level of the production system.
- Concentration of the automotive sector in the United States with General Motors, Ford and Chrysler.
- Vertical integration of final assembly and component manufacturing.

The Japanese creation of Just In Time with small batch sizes pulled to feed customer demand reduced work-in-progress and therefore improved working capital. The Japanese did not have the resource capability in the post-war years to invest in single purpose machines, and so their production systems had greater flexibility with reduced set-up times. The Japanese original equipment manufacturers emphasised collaboration throughout the supply chain with the creation of supply associations first established in the 1950s, as we saw in Chapter 7. According to Professor Richard Lamming, lean supply requires such collaboration. He argues that assessment needs to aim at 'optimising relationships' and so lean supply will utilise the relationship assessment techniques referred to earlier in this chapter. The improvements in the relationship lead to the elimination of waste by both the purchaser and supplier and the creation of value which can be gained by improved value to the customer via product innovation, improvements in quality, time to market or reductions in cost.

Lamming claims in his book *Beyond Partnership: Strategies for Innovation and Lean Supply* that lean supply represents a new paradigm (model or approach), one that is different to partnership sourcing since it is argued that the roles of purchaser and supplier are those of master and servant. Under partnership sourcing, the initiative is made by the purchaser and it will generally be an unequal relationship. Lean supply goes beyond partnership:

> The supplier, instead of applying all its efforts to the persuit of price increases and beguiling the customer, directs its attention towards a new strategy of equality – leading its customers technologically, in areas which it knows best and is best suited to explore.

Cross-functional teamwork both internally within the purchaser and supplier organisations as well as with each other becomes essential. Relationship assessment can help improve the efforts of both organisations in both operational effectiveness and strategic improvement. These principles will not merely apply to the automotive sector, but are equally applicable in numerous industries – retail, construction, services etc.

Cost Transparency versus Open Book Arrangements

The practice of open-book costing whereby suppliers provide costing information to the purchaser is used in a number of industries. An obvious example is the automotive sector, but it is widely used in service sector organisations such as in catering, facilities management and logistics. The concept of open-book pricing arrangements is to allow the purchaser the confidence that he will be achieving value for money and that excess profits are not being made by the supplier. In addition, the open- book arrangements tend to be an integral part of supplier development programmes since the purchaser may be able to understand the supplier's processes. The assumption is made that the purchaser is capable of assisting the supplier. This can occur in industries like the automotive sector where there is a degree of commonality in production engineering processes. In general, though, the information supplied on an open-book basis by a supplier may be misleading, and the true costs of processes may not be known by the supplier or these costs may indeed be hiding profits.

The relationship suffers from the same principles outlined in the first section of this chapter: the purchaser is not passing detailed confidential information to the supplier. It is also uncertain whether any benefit found by conducting the open-book costing will actually remain with the supplier. Many purchasing managers will argue that improvements in costings will benefit the supplier and create a win/win scenario because the improvements in costs can help the supplier's competitive position. However, many buyers may expect these cost savings to be passed back to the purchaser, and this can be very much a one-sided arrangement. Cost transparency, on the other hand, refers to more than open-book costing arrangements. Professor Richard Lamming states the following definition in 'Cost transparency: a source of supply chain competitive advantage?'

A practice in supply in which the customer and supplier share detailed information on their in-house activities, pertinent to the supply of goods and services which links them. It can be seen as an extension of open book negotiation , the difference being that the customer shares information on its activity with the supplier in addition to the flow of information in the other direction. The objective of practising cost transparency is to reduce costs through joint development of good ideas, thereby improving the mutual competitive position of both organisations.

Open Book Costing

Purchaser

Supplier

Features
• Information is Passed by the Supplier to the Purchaser
• The Purchaser Claims to Be Able to Assist the Supplier
• The Supplier May Massage Costs
• The Relationship is Characterised by a Continuous Struggle rather than Co-operation
• Detailed Confidential Information Does not Tend to Be Shared
• Dialogue Is not Two-Way

Lamming's research on cost transparency centred on a questionnaire targeting purchasing and sales/marketing managers. It was found that most felt that the practice would significantly benefit their organisation. It should be noted, however, that whilst the principles of cost transparency undoubtedly represent a means of significantly improving supply chain management, current organisational cultures within the vast majority of organisations will hinder the development of the practice. Managers do guard confidential information, and generally feel that such information, whether it be on profitability margins, future plans for sourcing suppliers, or technical details giving the firm a competitive advantage needs to be kept confidential as divulging too much could rebound in the near or distant future. Certainly it would appear that the adoption of the principles of cost transparency would need to be accompanied by workshops aimed at improving the relationships between the organisations affected.

Continuous Improvement and Benchmarking

We have already mentioned the need for organisations to continuously improve their business performance. The definition of quality, 'meeting customer requirements', in customer/supplier relationships is fundamental to the achievement of business requirements. However, business requirements never stay constant and competition is always there. Companies need to be constantly improving their service to customers and developing new products/services to capture market share.

The Japanese call continuous improvement 'kaizen'. It is the attitude of not being satisfied with meeting requirements once, but improving all the time. The principles of kaizen are manifested in the manufacturing sector with continuous improvement in processes. A good example is the ability of the Japanese in the post-war years to reduce set up times for their presses and other items of capital plant. Continuous reductions in set up times enables the manufacturing unit to increase its flexibility and to change supply to meet changes in customer demand. The focus of supply chain management should be to:

- Reduce costs of bought out products and services;
- Improve quality (customer satisfaction);
- Improve time to market and innovation in products and services.

A key development in Western business practice during the late 1980s and 1990s has been the use of benchmarking. The process builds on the principles of kaizen as it involves learning about the best practices of other organisations and subsequently making change for improvement that will enable the organisation to meet or beat the competition. By benchmarking on a continuing basis, the organisation is researching current best practice and the objective is to put improvements into action.

The roots of benchmarking once again lie in Japan, as key Japanese industrialists in the post-war era learnt best practices from Western businesses. The Japanese did not necessarily copy the West, as they flexed Western business practices to suit their own operations. An example is the creation of Just In Time, which was a system primarily created to reduce the costs of working capital. As we saw in Chapter 7 on Sourcing, the best practices were encouraged to be implemented throughout the supply chain by the use of supplier associations: 'kyoryoku kai'.

The roots of the implementation of benchmarking in Westernised organisations is traced to the Xerox Corporation who first used the technique in the late 1970s. Xerox used benchmarking as a means of fighting back against Japanese competition and the company assessed and measured against the standards set by a variety of different organisations, such as American Express for procedures dealing with customer care, the group's Japanese subsidiary for production costs, and Milliken for employee suggestion schemes.

There are numerous approaches to benchmarking, but all methodologies share similar characteristics. Eric Evans, a leading supply chain management consultant, provided one such approach in an article in *Supply Management* magazine October 1994 (formerly *Purchasing and Supply Management*).

What to Benchmark?

The purchasing department can choose a number of internal or external measures of performance to benchmark. The focus should be on choosing benchmarks which will make improvements to relationships with either internal or external customers. A benchmarking exercise might try and identify a range of different processes. These can be categorised

Benchmarking Purchasing Processes

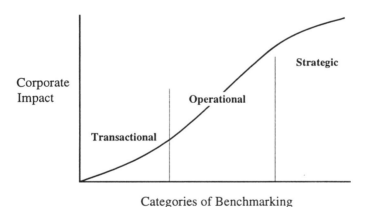

Categories of Benchmarking

into three different groupings, and these will have varying impact on purchasing's impact on the organisation's corporate performance.

Here are a few examples of processes under each category:

Transactional

- Administration process times of requisitions and order placement.
- Numbers of people and steps involved in order placement.
- Response times of queries from internal customers and suppliers.
- Number of orders placed by buyers.

Operational

- Numbers of call-off blanket order arrangements.
- Proportion of financial spend under purchasing's influence.
- Number of suppliers.
- Number of process improvements made.
- Proportion of qualified employees.
- Number of product warranty claims as a result of quality defects per supplier.

Strategic

- Numbers of fully-developed partnership supply arrangements.
- Total cost reductions in terms of reductions in costs of ownership.
- Number of product innovations brought to market as a result of a supplier initiative.

A good example of the use of benchmarking is provided by an exercise conducted in the public sector by the Central Unit on Procurement ('Procurement Practice and Development') in the UK public sector. CUP's methodology analysed the profile and stages of development of the purchasing functions established in central government organisations. The benchmarking tool is called the 'maturity matrix' and is designed to raise awareness of the potential for improvement, as a key objective of the tool was to provide a means of describing procurement's role, and the influence the function may have internally within the organisation with senior management and customers, and also with suppliers.

The maturity matrix is a comprehensive benchmarking tool as it analyses the stages of development of the purchasing function from 'innocence' to 'excellence' across a range of processes. The diagram below shows some examples of the coverage of the maturity matrix tool.

In this way, the maturity matrix analyses the stage of development in the procurement function of the use of cross-functional teams. The use of cross-functional teams can improve the designs of specifications and enable improved procurement by helping to procure products and services that will comply with corporate needs (see diagram Procurement Strategy and Organisationon on next page).

Other aspects which can be benchmarked from innocence to excellence are:

- Influence on bought-out products and services.
- The degrees of strategic planning.
- Roles and responsibilities of those involved in the procurement process.

Customer and supplier management may also be benchmarked. This is a particularly helpful methodology to help improve commercial relationships and is shown in the diagram Customer and Supplier Management on the next page.

Procurment Strategy and Organisation	Innocence	Awareness	Understanding	Competence	Excellence
Cross functional Teams	Procurement handled by procurment unit or others in isolation or with limited input & coordination of complementary expertise	Procurment unit identifies as a source of procurement expertise but little use is made of it by departmental customers or others involved in procurement in the organisation	Benefits of Cross Functional Teams (CFT's) recognised by procurment unit who seek input from key players in the procurement in order to achieve improved business benefits	Procurment unit educates users and key players. CFT's established where necessary to define and agree procurement strategy and plan	CFT's established early for all significant procurement activities. Seen by whole organisation as an essential requirement for efficient and effective management of procurement

Customer & Supplier Management	Innocence	Awareness	Understanding	Competence	Excellence
Supply Base	Large numbers of 'random' suppliers. Need for improved supplier	Large numbers of suppliers, but majority of spend is only on a few	Reduced number of suppliers by volume consideration	Partnership suppliers in key areas, multi-sourcing in others	Positive and continuously reviewed programme to optimise supply base to meet strategy
Supplier selection	No analysis or structured selection	Supplier selection on price & basic service criteria	Suppliers selected on ability to offer best Value for Money	Suppliers selected on VFM, including long term factors & market situation	Proactive research into current & potential suppliers to assist selection based on meeting strategic goals
Customer Satisfaction	Customers not consulted/recognised Procurement carried out in isolation	Aware of customers' needs but no system is in place to routinely take these into account. No attempt is made to obtain customer feedback	Meeting customer needs recognised As important but customer satisfaction only obtained in an informal ad hoc manner	Formal assessment of customer requirements and satisfaction. Feedback mechanism in place Some attempt is made to adjust future requirements based on consultation	Systems in place to ensure customer participation throughout process to satisfy/exceed requirements. Customers included in cross functional teams. Feedback from customers introduced into future activities

The maturity matrix also benchmarks:

- Continuous improvement
- Change management
- The use of performance measures
- Approaches to training
- Contract and risk management
- The use of types of specifications
- Negotiation practices.

Whilst the maturity matrix was developed for public sector organisations, it can also be used in private sector organisations to highlight the scope for improvement to purchasing operations.

Who to Benchmark Against

There are a variety of ways of identifying who to compare against:

Internal Benchmarking: the benchmarks chosen can be compared to another part of the same organisation. At the simplest level, prices paid can be compared as a number of different prices may be paid throughout the same organisation, particularly when there are different sources of supply and little control on purchasing activities.

Industry Benchmarking: an association may be set up with other organisations from the same sector. This is often difficult in practice because firms will rarely give away their competitive edge. The approach is perhaps more common in the public sector, where it is more common for similar buying organisations to collaborate. Examples include the Eastern Counties Group, the Yorkshire Purchasing Organisation and the Wiltshire Consortium. All are examples of consortium purchasing as a variety of buying organisations collaborate to improve their purchasing position.

Best Practice Clubs: the UK Department of Trade and Industry has promoted the development of networks of local firms. For example, in the Thames Valley area a Supply Chain Network was set up at the end of 1994 with the support of the DTI under its 'Managing in the 90s' programme. The aim of the network is to: 'Translate and disseminate information on best practice in customer/ supplier relationships to local firms.' These local associations are capable of carrying out best practice benchmarking.

A recent report entitled 'Benchmarking the Supply Chain' published by *Partnership Sourcing Ltd* in 1996 (the joint CBI/ DTI venture to help promote partnership sourcing in the UK) highlighted that 88% of the 600 organisations surveyed were aware of the benchmarking concept. Partnership sourcing found that 62% of the firms surveyed

UK) highlighted that 88% of the 600 organisations surveyed were aware of the benchmarking concept. Partnership sourcing found that 62% of the firms surveyed practised benchmarking, and found that the take up was lowest amongst small and medium sized enterprises (SMEs). Their research showed that the most common choice of benchmarking partner are direct competitors and other organisations in the same industry. The survey also reveals that:

Customers and suppliers do not feature as popular benchmarking comparators. They would be regarded as relatively easy organisations to benchmark against, if the right relationships had been established...Benchmarking is not yet a significant feature of customer/ supplier relationships.

Choice of Benchmarking Partner

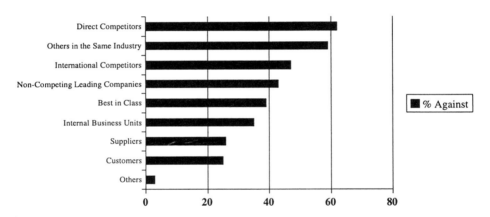

Collect Information

Information can be found from a number of sources. a great deal of information can be found in newspapers, magazines, catalogues and journals, and in specialist databases. The most valuable information often comes through direct exchange of information with other organisations that recognise the mutual benefits of sharing best practice. Partnership Sourcing Ltd in their report highlighted that the three most popular sources of information to be used in benchmarking are:

- Published external data
- Internal information
- Competitors.

This is revealed in the following chart.

Sources of Information

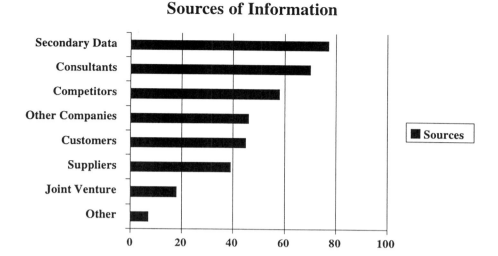

Analyse the Information

Too much information can of course be as detrimental as having too little. Information should be gathered sufficient for making a direct comparison of performance. The higher level best practice benchmark information should be:

- quantified;
- compared on a like with like basis;
- opinions should be gauged from the other organisation's experience.

Use the Information

Sometimes, the realisation that the process is not as good as it was originally thought can make people defensive and resistant to change. The point of best practice benchmarking is to stimulate continuous improvement in the processes that need improving. Management needs to:

- Set new standards for the performance expected and this should be communicated to everyone concerned.
- Delegate to someone or set up a task force to devise an action plan to reach the new standards.
- Provide additional resources for employees to carry out additional research, if at all necessary.
- Monitor progress so that the plan is implemented.

To be really effective, benchmarking is an on-going process, and once benchmarking partners have been established, updating can become a standardised procedure.

Business Process Re-Engineering

The authors who are credited with creating the concept of business process re-engineering (BPR) are Michael Hammer and James Champy whose book *Re-Engineering the Corporation: A Manifesto for Business Revolution* (1993) became a best selling business title. They define BPR as follows:

Business Process Re-Engineering

> ## Definition:
>
> "The Fundamental Rethinking and Radical Redesign of Business Processes to Achieve Dramatic Improvements in Critical, Contemporary Measures of Performance, such as Cost, Quality, Service and Speed."
>
> "Re-Engineering a Company Means Tossing Aside Old Systems and Starting Over Again. It Involves Going Back to the Beginning and Inventing a Better Way of Doing Work."
>
> *Michael Hammer & James Champy (1993)*

They refer to the three Cs of the new business world: customers, competition and change. The three Cs have created an environment where flexibility and quick response need to be achieved by organisations if they are to continue to compete. Organisations will only be able to compete if they analyse their processes to help identify whether they should in fact be operating that process, and, if it is to be performed, how it can be improved. Hammer and Champy argue that organisations should 'radically' redesign their processes to invent new ways of accomplishing work tasks. They imply that BPR should not be associated with making small superficial changes in the workplace. By suggesting that the effects of BPR are to make dramatic changes to the workplace, they are differentiating the approach to that of total quality management (TQM). A central feature of total quality is the concept of continuous improvement which we identified in the previous section. It is argued that the effect of TQM is to make a series of small, incremental changes over time to existing processes.

A process can be defined as a collection of activities that takes one or more kinds of input and creates an output that gives value to a customer. The authors argue that managers tend to focus on the individual tasks in any process. When completing a requisition, passing this to the buyer to source availibility of supplies, etc. managers tend to lose sight of the larger picture therefore, which is basically to get the product or service delivered to the external customer. A number of examples are discussed in *Re-engineering the Corporation* to help illustrate the principles of BPR.

Hammer and Champy's first example concerns IBM Credit Corporation, a wholly-owned subsidiary of IBM. The process of authorising a request for credit from a customer involved a number of tasks.

BPR - IBM Credit

Step 1: Log Request for Credit
     2: Form Taken to Credit Dept for Credit Check
     3: Business Practices Dept Modify a Standard Loan Agreement
     4: Request to a Pricer who Keyed in Data to a Spreadsheet
     5: Administrator Produces a Quotation Letter
     6: Letter Delivered to a Field Sales Representative

Process Would Take *6 Days!*
Re-Engineered by Replacement of Specialists
with Generalists Reducing Turnaround Time to
4 Hours!

1. An IBM field salesperson would visit the office with a request for credit (an arrangement to help the financing of the purchase of equipment and software). Step one of the process would be to log the request for credit on a form.

2. The form would be taken upstairs to the credit department, where a specialist would enter the information into a computer system. The customer's creditworthiness would be checked. Details would be included on the form.

3. The Business Practices Department would then be given the form and they would modify the loan agreement on their computer system. Any special financing arrangements would be attached to the request form.

4. The cost of the arrangement which would be met by the customer in terms of rates of interest, etc. would then be calculated by a 'pricer' who would key this information into a computer spreadsheet. A separate piece of paper would then be attached to the request form.

5. A clerical administrator would convert the information included on the request for credit form into a letter which would then be delivered back to the field salesperson via Federal Express.

It was found that the process took an average of six days to complete. Clearly this was a most inefficient process with many different people involved in performing the various tasks and there were also a number of different IT systems used. The field salespeople were having to wait a long time for the request to be transformed into the written quote, and the result would be that customers would of course get impatient. To compound the problems, there was no means of knowing where the request lay in the supply chain. A field salesperson would have to telephone the various people involved to find out its status.

Two senior managers at IBM Credit took a request and walked it through the system. They found out that the actual work took only ninety minutes. Their solution was to replace the specialists with generalists. One person would process the entire application for credit from beginning to end. To make the change, a new IT system was designed which had the effect of simplifying the process further. The turnaround period was consequently reduced from six days to four hours.

A second example is provided by the Ford Motor company, and is an example that is particularly pertinent to procurement management. In the early 1980s, Ford was considering ways of reducing overhead and administrative costs. Attention focused on the accounts payable department and benchmarked their department against Mazda's as Ford had obtained 25% ownership of Mazda. Ford employed some 500 people in its department whereas Mazda employed five - a slight difference! The procurement process at Fords was re-engineered to achieve the desired improvements in costs.

The process used by Ford is very much a standard process deployed by organisations for the processing of orders from suppliers and their subsequent payment.

1. A purchase order would be sent by purchasing to the supplier. A copy of the purchase order would be sent to accounts payable.
2. The supplier would then send the goods to Ford. A goods received note would be completed by the stores department and this would then be sent to accounts payable.
3. An invoice would be sent to the supplier to accounts payable.
4. Accounts payable would then be in receipt of the three documents: the purchase order, the goods received note and the invoice. If all three matched, the supplier would be paid. However, it was found that the Ford accounts payable personnel would spend most of their time clarifying discrepancies.

To re-engineer the process, the purchasing department would issue a purchase order to a supplier. At the same time, an on-line data base IT system was set up, and so the details of the purchase order would be entered onto the system. The components would be sent by the supplier to the relevant goods inwards section, but the goods inward inspector would check that the shipment corresponded to the purchase order, as the inspectors now had access to the data base IT system. If the components conformed to the purchase order, the inspector would up-date the system and authorise payment to the supplier. If the shipment did not conform, then the components would be sent back to the supplier.

Ford's procurement process had then been re-engineered by:

- taking out the need for an invoice sent from a supplier;
- investing in an on-line data base management system;
- empowering the goods inwards inspectors to make decisions concerning the payments made to suppliers.

BPR - Ford Motor

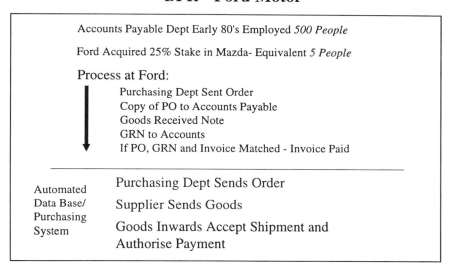

Accounts Payable Dept Early 80's Employed *500 People*

Ford Acquired 25% Stake in Mazda- Equivalent *5 People*

Process at Ford:

Purchasing Dept Sent Order
Copy of PO to Accounts Payable
Goods Received Note
GRN to Accounts
If PO, GRN and Invoice Matched - Invoice Paid

Automated Data Base/ Purchasing System

Purchasing Dept Sends Order

Supplier Sends Goods

Goods Inwards Accept Shipment and Authorise Payment

The Ford example is now, perhaps, a dated one. Further improvements could be made to streamline the purchasing process by, for example:

- A major development in a number of sectors, particularly in retail, is to question the need for a purchase order. Suppliers can be empowered to make decisions over the stocks of goods that can be sent to the purchasing organisation. If suppliers are provided with sales information gained from IT systems like their electronic point of sale systems (EPOS), then the risk can shift to the supplier over inventories that need to be sent to the retailer.
- The principle of consignment stocking can be utilised. Under this principle, the supplier is paid for product that is used or sold. If suppliers take on board decisions over inventory control, they will be paid on the basis of what is consumed.
- Other developments in IT can also have a major effect on the purchasing process. Small value transactions can be processed by the use of corporate purchasing cards which we will analyse in the final chapter.

These changes all involve the availability of more information to the supplier, information over inventory and sales which will traditionally have been seen as being of a confidential nature. Transaction costs will be reduced by improving the procurement process and many organisations are now utilising the principles of BPR to analyse their processes to identify the improvements which can be made. In the Ford example, the number of people employed in accounts payable had been 500, but with the implementation of the new system, this was reduced radically to a little over 100. The economics of analysing these processes will weigh up both the costs and the benefits, which may be numerous.

Processes in an organisation are often very fragmented with many people involved and, as the IBM Credit example highlighted, hidden. Organisation charts do not tend to show the detail in terms of how a process is achieved. Process maps are a tool that can be used to identify all stages involved in any process. These can show various levels of detail from strategic to operational. The following illustration provides a simple example of a process map. The map depicts a number of people involved in the procurement process.

A more detailed analysis can be re-drawn to show a further level of detail. The production controller in our example is responsible for order placement. He or she could be involved in a number of work-related tasks before calculating the quantity to be ordered. The production controller may need to check the call-off or blanket order contract established with a supplier before faxing an order (or using other means to inform the supplier of the requirement).

Process Mapping

People   *Tasks/ Processes*

In this way, process maps can reveal the detailed work tasks lying behind any process. Such information may of course be shared between the purchaser and supplier to analyse how the relationship may be improved, to bring greater commonality between the work processes deployed by both organisations. This will adopt the principles established in the sections included earlier in the chapter on relationship assessment and cost transparency, and hence adopt the principles of lean supply.

Process Mapping

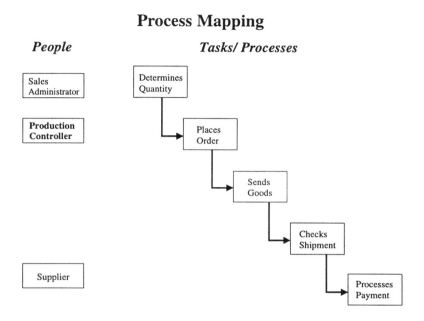

Lean Thinking

The principles outlined in this chapter so far are best summarised by the work of Dan Jones and James Womack in their book of the same title. The authors call for greater collaboration up and down the supply chain between all of the organisations involved. Lean thinking can be summarised in five principles:

Specify Value

This refers to the creation of value as seen by the customer – whether it be fast efficient service or delivery, low cost, reliability of the product or service supplied etc.

Identify the Value Stream

This is a key concept of lean thinking. One needs to map out all the activities required to create a product or service and to search for '*muda*' which, as we saw earlier in this chapter, refers to any activity which absorbs resources but adds no value. Identifying the value stream throughout the supply chain involves a number of the same principles outlined in the discussion of business process engineering. As Womack and Jones state:

> our objective in creating a value stream 'map' identifying every action required to design, order, and make a specific product is to sort these actions into three categories: (1) those which actually create value as perceived by the customer; (2) those which create no value but are currently required by the product development, order filling, or production systems (Type One '*muda*') and so can't be eliminated just yet; and (3) those actions which don't create value as perceived by the customer (Type Two '*muda*') and so can be eliminated immediately.

The Value Stream of a Can of Cola

	Incoming Storage	Processing Time	Finished Storage	Process Rate	Cumulative Days
Mine	0	20min	2 weeks	1000t/hr	319
Reduction Mill	2 weeks	30min	2 weeks		305
Smelter	3 months	2hours	2 weeks		277
Hot Rolling Mill	2 weeks	<1min	4 weeks	10ft/min	173
Cold Rolling Mill	2 weeks	1min	4 weeks	2000ft/m	131
Can Maker	2 weeks	1min	4 weeks	2000/min	89
Bottler	4 days	1min	5 weeks	1500/min	47
Tesco RDC	0	0	3 days		8
Tesco Store	0	0	2 days		5
Home	3 days	5min			3
Total	*5 months*	*3 hours*	*6 months*		*319*

Lean Thinking: James Womack & Dan Jones (1996)

The authors take the example of the production of a can of cola produced for the retail chain, Tesco. The first step is the mining of bauxite in Australia where it is transferred in large quantities to a chemical reduction mill where the bauxite is reduced to powdered alumina. The alumina is then transferred in volumes of 000's tons to Norway or Sweden for smelting before being shipped to rolling mills in Germany or, alternatively, Sweden. Aluminium coils are then shipped to England for the production into the can, where large batches are made. Each promotion and marketing campaign will inevitably require different information to be painted on the cans. These are then transported to the bottler where the cola is poured into the cans. Womack and Jones' analysis of the value stream of the production of a can of cola identifies a total production lead time of 319 days whilst the total processing time which adds value to the product is typically less than three hours.

The data highlights the '*muda*' of waiting and transport. According to the authors, the aluminium and cans are moved through 14 storage lots and warehouses and so it is argued that organisations need to cooperate to look at all the specific actions required to produce specific products. Whilst Tesco have been able to reduce inventory at the downstream element of the supply chain, little has been achieved downstream in the supply chain.

Create Flow

The third principle of lean thinking is to create flow which refers to the lining up of all of the essential steps needed to process a product or service into a steady, continuous run of production with no wasted activities such as queues, handling or other forms of '*muda*'. However, to facilitate flow, the range of organisations involved in the supply chain will need to cooperate and make dramatic changes to their production processes. It can imply the need for more flexible production plant and equipment to be more capable of producing smaller lot sizes. In addition, it will often require the redesign of plant layouts so that they are grouped into the different families of products rather than by grouping according to production process.

Create Pull Systems

In accordance with the principles of Just In Time production, customers should be able to pull their requirements when needed from upstream suppliers. This requires a fundamental change from production in batches which are traditionally pushed out of production, *just in case* the customer requires the stock produced. Pull systems will generally utilise some form of 'kanban', which is a signal to the supplier (whether external or internal) to produce the next requirement.

Seek Perfection

In accordance with the principles outlined in Chapter 4 on Quality, organisations throughout the supply chain need to collaborate to design out all forms of '*muda*' throughout the supply chain. The vision is to create an integrated supply chain focussed on creating value at each stage with the radical redesign necessary to eliminate unnecessary delays, handling, transport, inventory and other forms of waste.

References/ Further Reading

Central Unit on Procurement *Benchmarking: A Practical Way Forward* (1996)

The Department of Trade and Industry *Supply Chain Development* (1997)

Evans 'Benchmarking for the Purchasing Process' *Purchasing and Supply Management* Magazine (October 1994)

Hammer and Champy *Re-Engineering the Corporation: A Manifesto for Business Revolution* Nicholas Brealey Publishing (1993)

Harland of the Centre for Research in Strategic Purchasing and Supply, 'Supply Chain Management: Relationships, Chains and Networks' *British Journal of Management* (March 1996)

Lamming *Beyond Partnership: Strategies for Innovation and Lean Supply* Prentice Hall (1993)

Lamming, Owen Jones and David Nicol *Cost Transparency: A Source of Supply Chain Competitive Advantage?* IPSERA Conference Paper (1996)

Lamming, Paul Cousins, Dorian Notman of the Centre for Research in Strategic Purchasing and Supply, 'Beyond Vendor Assessment: Relationship Assessment Programmes' IPSERA Conference Paper (1996)

Womack, Jones and Roos *The Machine that Changed the World* Rawson Associates New York (1990)

Womack and Jones Lean Thinking Simon and Schuster (1996)

chapter nine
Public Sector Purchasing and the EC Procurement Directives

Purchasing in the Public Sector

Since the late 1970s, there have been major changes in public sector purchasing. The Conservative Party, who were in government from 1979 to 1997, had introduced a number of radical changes with regard to public sector organisations. It is argued that these changes have been motivated by the desire to reduce the total levels of public expenditure and to achieve better value for money in the procurement of goods and services by public sector organisations. Certainly, the Conservative Party have held the view that the public sector was taking up too greater share of Gross Domestic Product (GDP) - the measure of the economy's production of goods and services. This issue looks as though it is set to continue well into the 1990s as politicians and economists debate over the achievement of a reduced welfare state, with the likely solution that individuals may have to pay for services such as health, education and benefits through insurance and other policies. It will be interesting to see whether the current Labour Governement will continue the Conservative policies.

Changes in Public Sector Management

There have been significant changes in public sector management. These changes have impacted on the purchasing operations.

Privatisation of the state-owned monopolies has represented a major change and the examples of BT, the water authorities, British Gas, the rail industry, and the power industry are all well known. In addition, we have seen the privatisation of government functions such as HMSO and the defence research agency, DERA, for example.

Delegation of Managerial Responsibility where responsibilities have been pushed down to lower levels of management, that are dealing more directly with the service user. Perhaps the best-known examples for these developments are provided by the Health Service and local management of schools. Large public sector organisations have also been restructured into smaller 'agency' organisations, such as the Benefits Agency.

Competition, where the creation of internal markets has been a key part of the new strategy for public sector organisations. Quasi-competition has been created in many public sector institutions. Consider, for example, trust hospitals which now compete for funds distributed by general practitioner fundholders and district health authorities. The services in terms of operations and patient care which the trust hospitals provide have to be costed and charged out to the fundholders. In this way, there is competition between trust hospitals for their services.

Competitive Tendering has been extended in the public sector. The Conservative Party had introduced a number of initiatives to enable private sector organisations to compete for services which had traditionally been provided in-house by public sector organisations. Compulsory competitive tendering (CCT) was introduced in 1980 by the Local Government, Planning and Land Act, which introduced controls on local authorities to award contracts to in-house direct work organisations without fair competition. The legislation prescribed the need to obtain tenders from at least three sources above certain financial thresholds.

The Local Government Act 1988 extends the concept of compulsory competitive tendering to include services like refuse disposal, cleaning, catering, garden maintenance and security. In addition, the Local Government Act 1992 further extends the principle of CCT tendering to include professional and technical services like housing management, personnel, finance and information technology services.

The Local Government Acts place a responsibility on local authorities to award contracts on the basis of lowest price. New Regulations and Orders on local authority CCT were first laid before Parliament in November 1997 to empower authorities to move towards a 'best value' approach to contractor selection criteria. Finance, construction, property and housing management CCT will be particularly affected by these changes. 'Best value' seeks to achieve:

- A balance between cost and quality aligned to the public's demand for the services provided by local authorities.
- Economical, efficient and effective service delivery.
- Continuous improvement.

In central government organisations, the principle of competitive tendering has also been promoted through market testing packages of work traditionally performed in-house. Another important development in public sector purchasing is the impact of European Community directives on procurement which are examined in detail later in this chapter.

The rules contained in the directives set out standardised procedures for the award of contracts for requirements in excess of certain monetary values throughout the community. Their purpose is to:

- enable all firms in the EC the ability to compete equally for such contracts;
- promote better use of public expenditures;
- improve the competitiveness of European industry.

The thrust of the directives is, therefore, to ensure competition for contracts.

Market Testing

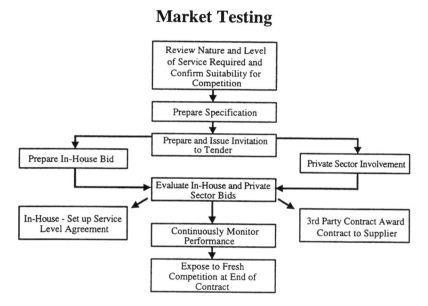

Service Quality has also been a prime concern. There is now greater emphasis on the quality of service outputs and the interests of the customer. This focus on the user/customer is reflected in the drafting of charters for the various organisations in the public sector and the insertion of quality standards in contracts governing the provision of services.

Public Accountability: in the private sector, purchasing staff are accountable to their managers, who in turn are accountable to the directors. Boards of directors are accountable to shareholders, and independent auditors examine their accounts and decisions on behalf of shareholders, and to comply with statutory requirements. Public sector purchasers are also accountable to the taxpayer for the money that may have been spent. A Parliamentary Select Committee, the Public Accounts Committee, examines how public sector organisations achieve value for money.

Organisational Structure: in terms of the form of organisation, public sector organisations are more likely to resemble 'mechanistic' structures with clearly defined:

- specialisation of job tasks and roles;
- lines of authority in a hierarchy;
- procedures which govern decision making.

Confidentiality: public sector employees are bound by the Official Secrets Act and can therefore be prosecuted under criminal law when the confidentiality of government work is breached. In addition to these points, public sector organisations have come under increasing pressure to reduce the numbers of employees. Many politicians and economists will argue that efficiency gains in the private sector should be replicated in the public sector. Productivity gains experienced in the private sector during the 1980s were not, it is argued, matched in the public sector. It can be argued, however, that the thrust of government policy to reduce numbers of civil servants is driven by dogma and that the quality of service can be affected by the degrees of outsourcing and improvements in productivity so far attained.

Government Purchasing

In 1984, the UK Government launched its Government Purchasing Initiative. This initiative sought to improve efficiencies in public sector purchasing. Improvements have been made throughout government purchasing since this time, and we will highlight a number of the key strategies which are now being pursued to achieve better procurement. The government's strategy for procurement is to 'achieve continuing improvement in value for money, based on the whole life cost and quality, and to enhance the competitiveness of suppliers, through the development of world class professional procurement systems and practices.'

The Central Unit on Procurement (CUP) is located with HM Treasury and was created in January 1986 to spearhead the drive to improve performance in central government's procurement activities. In 1997, the CUP evolved to become Procurement Practice and Development (PPD). It was generally accepted that procurement had not been approached professionally in the past. The objective of the CUP was: 'To facilitate the identification, dissemination, and understanding and use of procurement best practice in central government.'

The aim is, therefore, to ensure that departments have in place effective procurement management processes and controls to ensure the delivery of lowest whole life cost and best value for money on all relevant areas of expenditure. Identification, dissemination and understanding is achieved in a number of ways. CUP is comprised of a number of experts who are able to provide advice through:

- written guidelines;
- verbal advice as a result of a specific query or request;
- specific key procurement projects;
- training courses, seminars and conferences.

CUP's role is changing from providing central guidance and advice to one of facilitating and supporting departments in carrying forward a number of new procurement initiatives as a result of HM Treasury's 'Fundamental Expenditure Review' and the government's 'Procurement Strategy' (White Paper May 1995).

- Departmental procurement strategies are now common and all departments have Heads of Procurement, a number of whom have been recruited from the private sector.
- Qualifications such as the Certificate of Competence (equivalent to the CIPS Foundation Stage) were set up, and there has been backing given to increasing numbers of staff trained and educated on specialist procurement programmes.
- Many departments have set annual procurement savings targets which have been monitored by the Central Unit on Procurement and reported to the prime minister.
- The CUP have published an extensive number of best practice purchasing guides as well as a specification for a standard procurement information technology system (PURSUIT).

1995 White Paper: 'Setting New Standards'

The government at that time produced a White Paper 'Setting New Standards- a Strategy for Government Procurement'. The effect of the White Paper was to make the strategy government policy. Best practice procurement should be a central element in departments' businesses at all management levels. Departments should seek to match the cost savings achieved by best practice private sector organisations and collaborate to achieve best value for money. Neil Deverill who was responsible for formulating the White Paper wrote in *Innovations in Procurement Management* Edited by professor Andrew Cox (1996):

Although the performance of the supplier in the delivery of a service, provision of goods or construction is managed and monitored...departments often do not take advantage of the potential cost reduction and value-added opportunities which suppliers can offer. The new way ahead signalled by the White Paper, is that the award of the contract is no longer considered the end of the commercial transaction, it is indeed the beginning of significant cost reduction opportunities. Both the supplier and the buyer/ user can work together to identify and remove inefficiencies within the supply chain. In future, the contract manager needs to understand the commercial realities of the provision, the technical capabilities of the supplier to improve the product or service the real needs of the user (and indeed how to manage all the relationships between the players in delivering the contract).

The White Paper also called for best value for money to be sought through a range of techniques involving procurement, including private finance, market testing and contracting out. The emphasis should be on integrated procurement processes covering the life cycle costs, analysing the costs from acquisition, use to disposal. This requires a focus on the total costs of a product or service to ensure value for money over its lifetime, rather than simply choosing suppliers on the basis of the lowest tender price. For each contract, there should be a contract manager and for each capital project, a project sponsor to allow overall single person responsibility.

There should be greater cooperation between government departments. The CUP called for benchmarking to focus on measurements of effectiveness, and to develop a philosophy of continuous improvement.

A key feature of the strategy calls for relationships with suppliers that combines competition with collaboration. The CUP commented in 'Innovations in Procurement' that traditional commercial relationships in the public sector had largely been adversarial, 'based on price negotiation with very little added value by the supply market.' The White Paper therefore emphasised that relationships between departments and suppliers should be based on cooperation thus allowing suppliers to add value in meeting the department's requirement using their expertise.

Departments will be intelligent customers with well-defined objectives and requirements. For many major service contracts or other large projects, getting objectives and requirements clearly defined is clearly a crucial stage. Those responsible for specifying requirements are expected to have a 'thorough grasp of the department's business needs and sufficient time to achieve the correct specification'.

The Intelligent Customer Role

An intelligent customer, as described in the 1993 report of that name issued by the Government Centre for Information Systems, is a general description applied to a business area rather than to an individual. A business area would be described as an intelligent customer when its culture and procedures successfully enable the procurement of a product or service for value for money. Other key aspects of the intelligent customer include:

- A willingness and ability to be an informed and active customer, demanding the best that suppliers can provide and continuously searching for improvement.
- A good understanding of the supply market and how it can meet the needs of the customer.
- Where an on-going service is being provided, maintenance of the capability to re-tender the department's requirements at the end of the life of the contract.

The roles of an intelligent customer promoted in the public sector are as follows:

Business Needs: the purchaser needs to ensure that the needs of the business are being optimised. The use of purchase portfolio analysis referred to earlier can help identify supplier strategy (see Chapter 6).

What to Buy: the requirements of the product or service have to be specified by the use of a performance or conformance specification.

Value/Cost: the purchaser needs to analyse the full lifecycle costs of the requirement. There will be trade-offs between cost and service levels – very high service levels, such as extremely short and consistent response times for a service, can be very expensive to procure.

Knowing the Market: a knowledge of the market place is necessary, but this can be difficult to achieve in practice. The intelligent customer needs to be aware of what suppliers can offer, and what developments are taking place in the supply market.

The Intelligent Customer

Define Business Needs

Review

What to Buy

Obtain
Performance

Determine Value/
Cost

Manage the
Relationship

Know the
Market

Make the
Agreement

Contracts: contracts form the link between the organisation's requirements and the actual product or service provision. It must be flexible enough to allow change but rigorous enough to give adequate protection. A sound contract provides a useful reference point for both parties and reduces the risk of dispute.

Manage the Relationship: the intelligent customer will have a clear understanding of what the supplier is capable of providing. Experience suggests that a close partnership can be a most successful approach.

Service Quality: the contract should have agreed measures of performance set up. These need to maintained and improved upon.

Monitor/ Review: the effectiveness of the contract needs to be monitored by the intelligent customer, to ensure that the customer is satisfied with the quality of the product or service.

The EC Procurement Directives

As part of the process of creating a single European Market encompassing all member states of the European Community, there have been a number of directives introduced which regulate how purchasing organisations procure their supplies. These directives lay down rules to ensure that purchasers buy goods and services from a level playing field from all those individuals or firms wishing to compete for EC public sector contracts. The directives introduced during the 1980s and 1990s are an attempt by the European Commission to put into legislative effect the original intentions of the Treaty of Rome 1957, and are a key measure to further the development of the 'single market'. Under the Treaty, member states in the Community commit themselves to non-discrimination against, and freedom of movement for, individuals and firms for their goods and services. Purchasers must not, therefore, favour their own domestic suppliers. So, the objective of the directives is: 'To ensure that all companies in the European Community have a fair chance in seeking contracts with public purchasing organisations.' The directives are therefore designed to:

- increase the transparency of procurement procedures and practice throughout the European Community;
- aid the free movement of goods and services between member states;
- develop the conditions of effective competition for public supply and service contracts.

Public purchasers account for about 11% of all money spent in the European Community. This equates to approximately 720 billion ECU. (The 'ECU' stands for the European Currency Unit). Due to the size of spending by these organisations, EC heads of government recognised in 1987 that public purchasing organisations should be regulated more effectively to ensure that no favouritism is given to suppliers operating in their own countries. In this way, the directives help bring about the ideal of a single market where products made in any country can then be sold in other member countries with no barriers to trade. As Professor Andrew Cox comments in *The Single Market Rules and the Enforcement Regime After 1992*:

In theory, there is no doubt that the end to public sector protectionism and parochialism envisaged in the new Directives would clearly go some way to achieving significant efficiency gains if it could be implemented successfully...

If public purchasing authorities are forced to select only the most competitive and best value for money bids for contracts, the Commission expects that this will force a consequential market restructuring to take place. This, it is argued, will lead to rationalisation of un-competitive national suppliers...These reforms are expected to lead to efficiency gains of the order of ECU17 Billion.

The directives operate through:

- setting down financial thresholds above which the directives apply;
- defining procedures for the procurement process;
- defining certain minimum time limits for advance information notices, for the tender period and for the 'contract award notice';
- requiring the use of objective and non-discriminatory critera;
- defining the extent of any exemptions by sector;
- limiting the use of single tender action;
- defining the circumstances where the directives can be overruled in the case of extreme urgency;
- adopting common rules in respect of standardisation in technical specifications.

Cox argues that whilst the aims of the Community are laudable on economic grounds, and are also desirable for the future integration of the Community, their successful implementation are likely to be significantly restrained. He states that the policies of the EC are directed almost solely towards resolving difficulties on the demand side. The main weakness, therefore, is that the EC are overrelying on the demand side without taking full account of the way that its own rules will create a more concentrated market on the supply side. According to recent research undertaken by the UK Department of Trade and Industry and the Confederation of British Industry, 95.3% of the numbers of contracts awarded under the EC directives are awarded to domestic suppliers or contractors. Let us look at the detail of the directives.

Who Are Public Purchasers?

There are four major public sector purchasing areas: central government, local authorities, utilities (private or public corporations in energy, water or telecommunications) and public bodies. Central governments in Europe generally have specialist departments for defence, trade and industry, energy, environment, transport, employment, education and science. There are also departments for regions and, in the case of the UK, there are the Northern Ireland, Scottish and Welsh Offices. Local authorities have responsibilities for education, local highway construction and maintenance, and housing.

Many of the utilities have now been denationalised. Examples include Powergen and National Power, the Regional Electricity Boards, British Gas, British Telecom, and the water authorities. The decision to incorporate the utilities, transport, water, energy and telecommunications industries in the EC to the directives has been controversial as these privatised corporations are affected by the legislation. The Utilities Directive includes utilities which possess 'special or exclusive rights' in the water, transport, telecommunications and energy sectors', whether or not they are private companies.

According to a report in *Supply Management* 26 March 1998, telecommunications companies operating in a competitive market are to be freed from the EC directives. The application of the directives to other utilities (oil, gas, water and transport) is likely to change over the next few years once these organisations are operating in a competitive liberalised market.

EC directives seek to ensure that public purchasers achieve value for money following competition and compliance with good procurement practice. They provide a clear procedural framework which all purchasing and supply provision must follow. The directives cover the following areas:

Works (civil engineering or building services): enacted in the UK as The Public Works Contracts Regulations 1991 (SI 1991/2680).

Supplies (purchase or hire of goods): enacted in the UK as the Public Supply Contracts Regulations 1995 (SI 1995/201).

Services: enacted in the UK as the Public Services Contracts Regulations 1993 (SI 1993/3228).

Utilities (certain operators in the water, energy, transport and telecommunications sectors): enacted in the UK as the Utilities Regulations 1996 (SI 1996/2911).

The Main Provisions of the Directives

- Contracts should be advertised through the *Official Journal of the European Communities* (OJEC).
- Contracts should be put to competitive tender using European standards in specifications to promote wider competition.
- Evaluation criteria used to select suppliers should be clearly stated in the tendering procedure to eradicate any bias and to provide a level playing field for all suppliers competing for the award of contracts. Disqualification from taking part in a tender is permissible only if certain standards are not met by a supplier.

The criteria for the award must be stated in the tender notice. The directive details the criteria that can be used for a contract award. These are the lowest price only or the most economically advantageous to the purchaser. The criteria to be used to determine that an offer is the most economically advantageous include: price, period for completion, running costs, profitability and technical merit. The criteria for economically advantageous selection must be included in the contract notice or in the contract documents in descending order of importance (where possible).

Thresholds

The directives apply when the value of a contract or series of contracts exceeds certain financial thresholds in ECUs. These are converted to national currency values and are rebased every two years taking into account fluctuations in currency exchange. The figures vary according to the type of organisation in question; for the utilities, the thresholds are significantly higher than for central government organisations.

Public Sector

	Supplies	Services	Works
Central Government Bodies subject to WTO GPA	£104,435 (133,914 ECU)	£104,435 (133,914 ECU)	£4,016,744 (5,150,548 ECU)
Other Public Sector Contracting Authorities	£160,670 (206,022 ECU)	£160,670 (206,022 ECU)	£4,016,744 (5,150,548 ECU)
Indicative Notices	£584,901 (750,000 ECU)	£584,901 (750,000 ECU)	£4,016,744 (5,150,548 ECU)
Small Lots	Not Applicable	£62,389 (80,000 ECU)	£779,867 (1,000,000 ECU)

Utilities

	Supplies	Services	Works
Energy, Water & Transport Sectors	£311,947 (400,000 ECU)	£311,947 (400,000 ECU)	£3,899,337 (5,000,000 ECU)
Telecommunications Sector	£467,920 (600,000 ECU)	£467,920 (600,000 ECU))	£3,899,337 (5,000,000 ECU)
Indicative Notices	£584,901 (750,000 ECU)	£584,901 (750,000 ECU)	£3,899,337 (5,000,000 ECU)
Small Lots	Not Applicable	Not Applicable	£779,867 (1,000,000 ECU)

As of January 1998

Award Procedures

The Open Procedure means that any interested organisation is free to submit a tender. This procedure can be very useful to expand a limited existing supply base, for example to gain greater competition in supply markets. It can, however, be costly in terms of transaction cost economics as the purchasing organisation will be bound to provide invitations to tender to all who request them and to consider all the tenders submitted. Additionally it can be a resource intensive and a lengthy process assessing these tenders.

Tendering Procedures

Response Times

Open Procedure:	52 Days for the Receipt of Tenders
Restricted Procedure:	37 Days for Receipt of Requests to Participate 40 Days for the Receipt of Tenders
Negotiated Procedure:	37 Days for the Receipt of Requests to Participate

The Restricted Procedure means that only those suppliers invited may submit tenders. The number of organisations invited must be sufficient to ensure genuine competition. The time limits under the restricted procedure are receipt for requests to be selected for tender 37 days from despatch of notice to OJEC and 35 days in the case of utilities.

A Prior Information Notice (which is also referred to as Periodic Indicative Notice in the case of utilities) published in the *Official Journal* indicates the volume of likely purchases over the next 12 months, or it may state their likely value. Where the sum total of a number of requirements for the same category of goods and services amount to £584,901 (exclusive of VAT) a Prior Information Notice should be issued. The table above shows that different values apply to works contracts in the different sectors.

The following diagram shows the regulations applying to public sector organisations for use of the 'open' and 'restricted' procedures and the effect of a Prior Information Notice. Such requests or queries should be dealt within six days.

Tendering Procedure

Open Procedure:

Allow 52 days for receipt of tenders

Queries/tender documents must be sent within 6 days

Restricted Procedure:

Receipt of requests to be selected 37 days
(15 days accelerated procedure)

Receipt of tenders 26 days*
(10 days accelerated procedure)

Queries/tender documents must be sent within 6 days
(4 days accelerated procedure)

---

* 40 days without a PIN

Accelerated Restricted Procedure is permitted in cases of urgency in rules affecting the public sector, when observation of normal time limits is not practicable. This procedure should be reserved for exceptional cases as the shorter deadlines will naturally mean that fewer suppliers will be able to bid for the contract. Under the directives, the urgency should not have arisen through the fault of the purchaser, for example poor planning, etc.

The closing date for the receipt of applications to tender must be not less than 15 days from the dispatch of the tender notice for publication in the *Official Journal*. The closing date for the receipt of bids must not be less than ten days from the dispatch of invitations to tender. Any additional information concerning the tender documents must be sent not later than four days before the closing date for receipt of tenders. The number of days applying to public sector works, supplies, services for utilities is six days.

The Negotiated Procedure is where the purchaser may negotiate the terms of the contract with selected organisations. As a general rule, there should be a call for competition, but in certain specified cases the procedure may be used without a call for competition. The use of this procedure is more in line with the private sector style of collaborative commercial relationships. On the one hand, public sector organisations need to support the objective of greater access to public contracts in other EU countries but, on the other hand, seek ways of encouraging closer relationships with suppliers within the constraints of the directives.

Utilities have a free choice between the open, restricted and negotiated procedures (provided the negotiated procedure calls for competition). Public authorities may only use the negotiated procedure, with a call for competition, in limited circumstances. For example:

Works and Services: exceptionally, when the nature of the works or services provided, or the risks involved, are such as not to permit overall pricing.

Services: where the nature of the services to be provided is such that specifications cannot be drawn up with sufficient precision to permit the award of the contract using the open or restricted procedure.

Justifications for the Use of the Negotiated Procedure without a Call for Competition

- The Open or Restricted Procedures Have already Been Used and Have Resulted in Unacceptable Tenders
- The Open/ Restricted Procedure Resulted in No Tenders
- Only One Supplier Is Available for Artistic Reasons or on Account of Exclusive Rights
- Extreme Urgency Exists for Reasons that Were Unforeseeable and not Attributable to the Purchaser
- Additional Deliveries/ Services by the Original Supplier Are Necessary

In both the restricted and negotiated procedures, when tenderers are selected, the invitations to tender must contain at least the following detail:

- The address from which the tender documents and any additional information/ documentation may be obtained and the final date for requesting the documentation, the amount and terms of any sum payable for the documentation.
- Reference to the contract notice in the European *Official Journal*.
- The closing date for the receipt of tenders, the address to which they must be submitted and the language or languages in which they must be submitted.

- Any documents to be produced by the tenderer either to confirm the statements about its current standing and past record required under the terms of the tender notice in order to disclose any grounds for disqualification or to supplement the evidence supplied under the terms of the tender notice that the tenderer meets the minimum financial and technical standards.
- The criteria on which the contract is to be awarded, if these were not stated in the *Official Journal* contract notice.

Aggregation and Fragmentation

The aggregation rules relate to the valuation of the requirement. These are complex but it should not be forgotten that the purpose of the rules is to prevent the artificial breaking up of requirements (fragmentation) in order to avoid the rules. If the requirements are split into several lots, with each lot being made into a separate contract, then the value of each lot must be taken into account. In the case of contracts which do not specify a total price, the basis for calculating the estimated contract value is subject to the following principles:

- in the case of fixed term contracts where the term is 48 months or less, the total estimated contract value over the term of the contract; and
- in the case of contracts of indefinite duration or with a term of more than 48 months, the monthly value multiplied by 48.

Should the purchaser enter into two or more contracts at the same time for goods or services of a particular or similar type, then the estimated value of each of these contracts must be added together. This aggregate value is the one which must be applied. If the aggregated value exceeds the threshold, the directive applies and each contract has to be advertised in *Official Journal*, even if the estimated value of the individual contract is below the thresholds. The principle of aggregation can also catch small contracts of the same type for the same requirement at a later date.

Discrete Operational Units

The UK enactment of the legislation includes the use of a regulation which has become known as the discrete operational unit provision. Although there is no reference made to DOUs in the directives, the Commission has supported the position taken in the UK regulations. The provision allows organisations, which have chosen for commercial reasons to break their organisations down into discrete operational units (such as the creation of a government agency organisation), to aggregate at this DOU level.

So, if the goods or services are required for the sole purpose of a separate business area and the decision to purchase and contract has been devolved to that unit, and that decision is taken independently of any other part of the organisation, the valuation methods as described can be adopted. In this case aggregation takes place at DOU level for the purchase and contracting of goods and services of a similar or same type. A DOU does not need to carry out its own procurement or pay the supplier directly. This allows public purchasers greater flexibility in dealing with the directives, as smaller discrete organisations are less likley to be affected by the thresholds set.

Framework and Call-Off Contracts

Call-off or framework agreements, referred to in Chapters 2 and 7, allow purchasers a flexible arrangement as they can buy quantities of a product or service from a supplier on an as-and-when-necessary basis. There is usually no definite promise of quantities which will be ordered from a supplier.

It is considered necessary for framework agreements to include all identifiable fixed and variable, direct and indirect elements of cost, including where appropriate the cost of subcontracted work. The period for which prices are fixed should be included and therefore may be subjected to the EC directives if again, their financial value takes them above the financial thresholds set.

Although provided for in the utilities directive, there is no specific reference to call-off/framework agreements in the public sector directives, and the Commission is known to have reservations about their legality.

Technical Specifications

There are rules governing the use of technical specifications, since the use of certain domestic (national standards) can inhibit fair competition from non-UK suppliers. The directives expressly forbid specifications that include products or services of a specific make or source or refer to specific patents unless the subject of the contract cannot be adequately described in any other way, in which case the references must be qualified by the words 'or equivalent'.

When preparing specifications and calls for competition, European standards must be used. National standards may only be used when the use of European standards:

- creates problems of incompatibility with existing equipment;
- causes excessive cost; or
- limits innovation.

243

The technical specifications for the work and descriptions of the testing, inspection, acceptance (where applicable) and calculation methods to be used must be stated in the tender documents.

Debriefing

Once a contract has been awarded or suppliers pre-qualified under the restricted procedure, the purchaser has 15 days from the date on which any request for debriefing is received to inform the unsuccessful candidate of the reasons why they were unsuccessful. If this was as a result of the evaluation of offers, the name of the successful tenderer should be given. There are rules for the selection of tenderers and the award of contracts. A supplier can be disqualified or eliminated at the selection stage, or before bids are opened, if he or she:

- is bankrupt, being wound up, in arrangement with creditors, suspended from trading or in a similar legal position;
- is convicted of an offence relating to the conduct of business or are guilty of grave professional misconduct;
- has failed to pay taxes or social security payments; or
- is guilty of misrepresentation of information relevant to the contract.

In addition purchasers can request references to check a supplier's financial or economic standing.

Compliance with the Directives

The EC Procurement Directives represent a major constraint on the implementation of the 95 White Paper referred to earlier in this chapter. Cooperative supply chain policies are in many ways impeded by the rules which enforce the use of competitive tendering. Should public purchasing organisations flout these rules, then suppliers have remedies for non-compliance. Individual suppliers can contend that there has been a breach of the rules by a purchasing organisation. Actions may be brought in England, Wales and Northern Ireland in the High Court, and in Scotland, before the Court of Session. Proceedings may not be brought unless:

- The supplier bringing the proceedings has informed the contracting authority (the purchaser) of the breach or alleged breach and has informed the authority of its intentions to commence proceedings.

- They are brought promptly, and in any event within three months from the date when grounds for bringing the proceedings first arose, unless the court considers there is good reason for extending the period within which proceedings may be brought.

A supplier is defined as:

- 'One who ought, or seeks, or who would have wished, to be the person to whom a public contract is awarded'; and
- 'One who is a national of and established in a member state'.

If an action is brought by a supplier, before the award of a contract, the courts may take action in one of the following ways:

- suspend the procedure leading to the award of the contract in relation to the alleged breach of duty; or
- suspend the implementation of any decision or action.

The courts can, therefore, prevent the award of a contract or, when a contract has been awarded, suspend the operation of the contract itself until the alleged breach has been resolved. If the courts are satisfied that a breach has occurred, then the following can be ruled:

- An order to set aside of the decision or action made by the contracting authority. The contracting authority will be ordered to fully comply with the relevant directive, and the current contract entered into with the third party contractor can be suspended.
- An award of damages to the contractor who has suffered loss or damages as a result of the breach of the directive.
- Both of the above.

If the contract has been awarded, the court can only award damages.

The Private Finance Initiative

The Private Finance Initiative was launched by the previous Conservative Government in 1992 and seeks to involve private sector organisations with the financing and operation of projects traditionally undertaken by public sector departments. The Government claims that the PFI has become a main instrument for delivering high quality, cost-effective public services. It aims to bring the private sector more directly into the provision of public services. It is argued that the initiative is not simply concerned with the financing of capital investment of government services, but about exploiting the range of private sector management, commercial and creative skills. The PFI has now been applied to a wide range of assets and services, such as buildings, transport infrastructure, information systems, vehicles and equipment. According to 'Private Opportunity, Public Benefit; Progressing the Private Finance Initiative' a document produced by HM Treasury (1996), there are three types of PFI projects:

Financially Free-Standing Projects

Under this arrangement, the private sector undertakes the project on the basis that costs will be recovered through charges for services to the final user. Public sector involvement is limited to enabling the project to commence, perhaps by the undertaking of initial planning work.

Services Sold to the Public Sector

Under this arrangement, the project's costs are met by charges from the private sector provider to the public sector body who let the contract.

Joint Ventures

This is where the cost of the project is met partly from public funds and partly from other sources of income, with overall control resting in the private sector.

The PFI is therefore geared to increase the involvement of the private sector in the provision of public services. It is different to privatisation since the public sector still retains a substantial role in PFI projects. The Treasury had forecasted that 20% of all government related capital spending will be under the PFI by 1999. It is argued that the PFI secures better value for money through the following:

Better Allocation of Risk

The public sector has a poor reputation for risk management, and it is argued that private sector organisations will be able to improve the management of risks. However, the growth in the number of PFI projects has been hampered by the difficulties associated with the transfer of risks (the *Times* 28/01/97).

Better Incentives to Perform

It is also argued that the transfer of risk improves management incentives. Under the PFI, payment to the private sector contractor only starts when a satisfactory flow of services is provided and ongoing payments depend on meeting performance criteria.

Focus on Responsibilities

The focus should be on the respective strengths of each sector since it is argued that the public sector can concentrate on what service should be provided and the private sector can consider how the service should be best operated.

Continuing Commercial Incentives

The private sector will improve commercial management of projects because of its involvement with the design, asset creation and operation of the project. In terms of risk transfer, there are several risks which need to be considered by private sector organisations:

Risks to Consider in PFI Projects

* Design and Construction Risk (to Cost and Time)

* Operating Costs

* Demand (Volume/ Usage)

* Residual Volumes

* Technology/ Obsolescence

* Regulations e.g. Taxation/ Planning Permission

* Financing Costs

Public sector projects are typified by cost over-runs despite efforts to project manage costs and completion times. Under PFI arrangements, payment levels are agreed in advance of the project being commenced. Should any over-run be experienced, the private sector contractor cannot pass these additional costs on to the government department concerned. Similarly, demand or usage rates may be variable in the future and it is argued that PFI contracts should take account of the variable demand or usage patterns by including protection against such fluctuations.

In respect of the residual value risk, PFI schemes will generally involve an automatic transfer of the asset to the public sector at the end of the contract. By this time, the supplier will have aimed to have recovered the full value of its investment over this period. It can be argued that there will be little incentive for the supplier to leave the asset in a healthy state at the end of the contract since the asset will have been paid for.

Technology or obsolescence risk refers to the point that the provision of the service may cease to be the most effective due to a change in technology during the life of the contract. This could mean that improved performance and value-for-money savings may not be capable of being achieved due the existence of an inflexible contract for the service provision. An example of an area which is typified by fast-changing technology is the provision of information technology services as the PFI would need to incorporate updates in software, for example.

In addition, another risk which needs to be identified is the change in regulations which may be experienced during the life of the contract. There may be changes in law or taxation which could affect the performance of the contract. Finally, there are financing risks as the contractor may experience difficulties with their financiers in raising finance and sustaining cash flow.

Example of PFI

GEC Alstom are providing new trains on the Northern Line of the Underground Network. To initiate the contracts, London Underground published a periodic indicative notice in the OJEC specifying the use of the negotiated procedure. Prospective tenderers were limited to those who could comply with London Underground's pre-qualification criteria. What differentiated this contract from previous leasing deals is that London Underground sought a complete service, so that the supplier would take on full responsibility for the design, manufacture, maintenance and cleaning of both trains and trackside equipment. London Underground also required a guaranteed number of trains for peak service being made available and also reliability of service. This is a very good example of an performance based specification.

The Northern Line contract transfers the following risks to the supplier:

Design and Construction Risk: the supplier carries risk for the design, manufacture and delivery of the trains. However, London Underground are obligated to bear the risk of maintaining a specified environment such as track standard and tunnel profile.

Service Availability: the supplier is responsible for supplying the number of trains against a maximum specified service requirement.

Performance Risk: the supplier carries risk for the performance and reliability of the trains throughout the 20 year primary usage period. London Underground can extend the contract into a secondary period on the same basis.

Residual Value Risk: London Underground is obligated to procure the service for 20 years and this then represents a significant residual value risk to the supplier.

Early Termination: the supplier must achieve a pre-agreed performance and reliability target which is better than the present service level supplied by London Underground. Failure to comply with this requirement will enable London Underground to terminate the contract.

The process of managing a PFI project can be divided into three phases: planning, procurement and contract management.

Planning

The planning phase starts with the recognition of a problem or opportunity for PFI. The first task is therefore to identify the objectives of the project, and it is at this stage that the public sector department or agency decides what responsibilities could be left to the private sector, and the enabling roles of the public sector department or agency. An important aspect at this stage is to draw up a detailed statement of requirements and what is needed in terms of outputs. This is often called the identification of critical success factors which should then be developed into measurable objectives.

Procurement

If the public sector department or agency is the driver of the PFI, it may be necessary to undertake initial exploration of the supply base to find out the willingness of private sector organisations to become involved. Often, a formal request for information is published in the OJEC. Alternatively, private sector organisations may proactively seek PFI opportunities by coming forward with their own proposals.

In line with usual procurement best practice, the public sector body will need to establish the financial, commercial and technical capabilities of the supplier. HM Treasury also encourage the use of the negotiated procedure for PFI projects since the restricted procedure provides inadequate scope for negotiations with bidders. In addition, because of the expense and detail of the negotiations, a maximum of three or four bids should normally be invited.

As has already been mentioned, PFI projects will usually utilise performance specifications, which enables the supplier maximum scope to innovate. Because PFI projects are complex, much time and effort will be needed in the appraisal of bids. The factors of quality, cost and risk will need to be assessed. In addition, project teams will need to be assured that the financing arrangements put in place by bidders is secure. Contingency arrangements in the event of failure will also need to be investigated.

Contract Management

The contract management of PFI projects will have a great deal in common with the management of large service contracts. Contracts management should take account of the following aspects.

PFI Contract Management

* Team Required to Manage the PFI Project

* Variations to Contract Procedure

* Performance Monitoring Arrangements and
  Associated Information Requirements

* Mechanisms for Problem Solving and
  Dispute Resolution

* Contingency Arrangements for Supplier Default

* Preservation of Public Sector Organisation's
  Ability to Re-Tender on Termination of the
  Original Contract

As soon as the PFI contract is awarded , the public sector department or agency needs to establish close working relationships with the supplier. The purchaser therefore needs to be an active and intelligent customer. PFI contracts will typically last a long time and the aim should be to create a relationship in which both sides are open, share information fully and work together to solve problems.

In the 1995 Budget (28 November 1995), the Chancellor of the Exchequer announced a target of £14 billion of contracts to be agreed by the end of March 1999. This announcement confirmed the Government's policy of stepping up the use of private finance to replace public spending, particularly in transport and in health. Since the initiation of the Private Finance Initiative, the previous Government has failed to achieve the targets set. One of the main criticisms levelled in a report in the *Times* newspaper (28 January 1997), is that government departments lack the expertise to negotiate transfers of financial risk to the private sector. According to the *Times*, this is making the tender process extremely time consuming and expensive. The other problem cited is that the UK has 'too few companies willing, able and with the capital backing to put together large PFI proposals – and to shoulder the operating risks once they are finished.'

It is likely that PFI will be continued by the current government, although a re-naming of the policy may be seen as necessary because of its association with the previous administration.

References/ Further Reading

Cox *The Single Market Rules and the Enforcement Regime After 1992* Earlsgate Press (1993)

Deverill Chapter 13 'Public Sector and Regulated Procurement' *Innovations in Procurement Management* edited by Cox, Earlsgate Press (1996)

HM Treasury Procurement Group Policy Paper

HMSO/Stationery Office 'The Intelligent Customer' Market Testing IS/IT Series, The Government Centre for Information Systems, (1993)

HMSO/Stationery Office 'Setting New Standards: A Strategy For Government Procurement' (1995)

HMSO/Stationery Office 'Private Opportunity, Public Benefit – Progressing the Private Finance Initiative' HM Treasury (1996)

chapter ten
IT Applications in Supply Chain Management

Without doubt, perhaps the most significant development in business over the last three decades has been the application of information technology (IT). Most organisations now recognise they cannot manage their supply chains effectively without modern information technology. As Hammer and Champy argued in their book *Business Process Re-Engineering*, IT forms an essential enabler in permitting organisations to respond to the constantly changing industrial environment. IT systems need to take account of the supply chain by integrating processes such as customer service, order processing, logistics and procurement. As Hammer and Champy argued, any organisation should organise its work around its processes. In this way, the service provided can be enhanced and the customer (whether internal or external) can find out the status of the process. So a customer may wish to know about different aspects of the purchasing activity, such as:

- The number of suppliers for a particular product or service.
- Details of similar specifications purchased.
- The track record of current suppliers in terms of their delivery, quality and warranty performance.
- Standard contractual terms that should apply to a particular purchase decision.
- How suppliers can be given a contract in a fast and effective way to help reduce processing times.
- The order status once a contract has been placed.
- Whether the product or service has been provided.
- Whether the supplier has been paid.

These are examples of the types of information which an IT system should help provide, and they mainly concern decision support. IT systems should also support the organisation's strategy, as the net effect of improving the organisation's operations should be to reduce costs, improve time to market, differentiate its product or service provision, etc.

The application of IT in supply chain management during the 1980s developed in the direction of improving decision support and providing improved management information on costs and budgetary control. The 1990s has seen more innovative developments with the use of the Internet for electronic commerce, the use of E-Mail and Intranet, the use of purchasing cards for small-value purchases and a host of expert systems to improve aspects of supply chain management.

A Typical Purchasing System

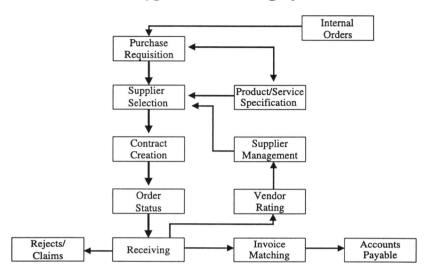

Manual Systems

A manual system refers to a paper-based system and one that does not use information technology. A manual system can be created by maintaining information on suppliers:

Each supplier's address, telephone number and names of personnel to contact on specific

Manual Supplier Data Systems

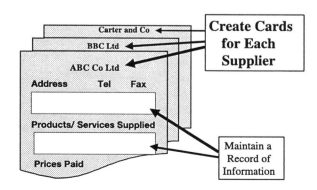

matters can be included in such a record. In addition to such basic information, details may be kept on the supplier's past delivery performance and their quality. Such information can provide a very powerful tool for the buyer as a wealth of information could be recorded on such a system.

Not only will it be useful to maintain information about each individual supplier, but the purchaser may also keep information on a separate card on the products and services bought.

Manual Product/Service Data Systems

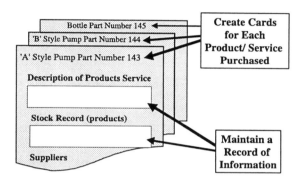

This information may record general stock holding details as well as a brief description of the product or service bought. In addition, there may be information kept on the choice of suppliers.

Whilst such information will clearly be useful, computerisation using master files or databases enables vast amounts of information to be stored and can speed up the retrieval of information.

There are, therefore, a number of disadvantages to the use of manual systems as shown on the table overleaf.

Disadvantages of Manual Systems

- They Tend to Result in Multiple Copies of the Same Document
- Considerable Effort Is Needed to Maintain the Information
- The Files Will Tend to be Held in Different Locations, Rather than in One Single Place Such as on a Single Computer
- A Manual System Will Be Slow to Use and to Retrieve Information
- In Larger Organisations, there Will Usually Be a Lack of Co-ordination of Information Preventing:

    Consolidation of Requirements

    Centralised Purchasing

    Standardisation of Products/Services Bought

Computer Systems

A computer system offers the benefits of being able to:

- Store and retrieve a great quantity of data (for example, information on suppliers and products/ services bought)
- Process the data rapidly (the system should be able to provide information quickly)
- Reduce clerical activities tied up with a manually operated system through the automation of purchase requisitions, orders, acknowledgement forms etc.
- Provide better information to help improve the purchaser's sourcing and subsequent negotiations.

A simple IT system will record the details about suppliers referred to earlier: each supplier's address, telephone number, names of personnel to contact on specific matters. In addition to such basic information, details may be kept on the supplier's past delivery performance and their quality, as well as details of the supplier appraisal.

There are now a significant number of suppliers who provide software for general purchasing systems. A generic purchasing system will be capable of being used for a variety of tasks. An integrated IT system will have a central source of data. Data refers to facts, figures, opinions and predictions from which information is drawn - such as figures relating to products and services purchased in the past, prices paid, delivery performance and so forth. The aim of a supplier data system is to provide a source of information on suppliers to enable people in the organisation to make effective decisions.

Purchasing Systems

A purchasing IT system will comprise of a central data source to which the various system modules attach. This would enable other departments than procurement to access the data and perform specific functions.

The system should be capable of the following functions.

- It would generate orders using internal data relating to records of suppliers, delivery and invoice details, expenditure cost codes related to departmental budgets and product or service code numbers.
- It would match facilities enabling the system to cross-refer orders, suppliers, product codes, expenditure codes. This enables the entry of a detail onto the IT system, and the system will then be able to locate other related files. For example, a supplier's name could be entered onto the system, and the system is able to find current orders and previous orders with that supplier, types of product and service provided (with their related product reference codes), as well as which budget holders they were used by.
- A purchasing IT system will be able to provide an audit trail and so produce a record of all of the events related from payment of the supplier through to the order authorisation.

The Purchase Audit Trail

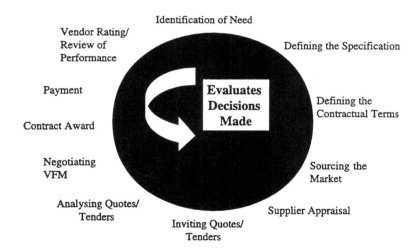

- It would be important for the system to provide an analysis of expenditure by supplier, product code, budget holde,r etc. on a weekly/ monthly/ quarterly/ yearly basis. This helps improve the organisation's ability to control both expenditure as well as assisting it's ability to forward plan expenditure by knowing what costs have been incurred historically.
- Finally, the system has to have in-built security to safeguard order authorisation and access to data.

Contracts Management Systems

In the management of contracts which are more project-specific (contracts for example involved with IT, construction, the procurement of equipment and facilities management), the documentation generated in the administration and management of such contracts will typically be set up by different departments. The purchasing function may generally form the documentation for the invitation to tender and the contractual terms, whilst technical departments will usually establish the specifications. With such contracts, the overall co-ordination and management of the documents becomes a problem both in terms of the flow of information from one function to another, and for the project manager having an overall view of the separate activities undertaken by each department. The management of the procurement will also experience difficulties, since the disparate systems used by the functions involved will generally lead to a lack of co-ordination by the organisation, and the communication problems internally can lead to difficulties in supplier management.

A practical example of an IT system which recognises that procurement activities are devolved to users is provided by the 'UCMS Contract Management System'. The system sees procurement as a process rather than a separate function in the management of contracts. Purchasing, engineering, legal and financial departments are generally integrated into a workflow of activities in the management of a contract. UCMS comprises a number of modules attached via a common control mechanism (the 'Spine') This allows users a degree of flexibility to determine the most appropriate configuration to meet their needs. An example of a version of UCMS might appear as follows:

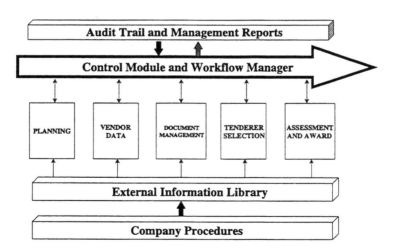

The system recognises that a contract is initiated by defining a series of actions that will need to be performed involving different people from different departments. Not only will there be an internal team involved in the contracts management, but the purchaser may also make extensive use of external consultants. Consequently, the timing and sequencing of activities such as co-ordination with other contracts and payment will also need to be planned. Each activity within the contract would be given a deadline and assigned to a particular user as the activities involved in the management of the contract will be multi-functional. The sequencing of activities continues until all of the actions have been completed. Thus, UCMS incorporates the concept of workflow where the work is seen to flow from one action to the next until completion of the contract. The system can then be used for contract monitoring including reminders given for end of contract, retention monies due, etc. as well as performance monitoring and cost analysis against budgeted costs.

The system generally operates with five screens:

Contract Header | Product/Service | Contract Management | Action List | Award Information

 Contract Header

This is the key data which must be known in order to initiate a contract. Details that could be included here are:

- Contract Number – automatic sequence number of the contract
- Contract Owner – the project manager of a particular contract
- Expected Award Date

 Product / Service

This will list contract requirements as categories of contract type whether for the supply of products, services or works and will assign a product/ service code. There can also be a description of the product or service, and in large value complex projects the system may allow the recording of a detailed specification. The user may indicate which single product / service is the main item of the contract. This will help the system to guide the user towards appropriate standards later in the contract process.

 Contract Management

This screen holds more detailed contract information which should be known before contract award and also detailed contract information needed both during and after the contract award. The principle is to make as much information available from one single screen, allowing a quick overview to be gained of the contract.

- The form of contract such as a call- off/ framwework agreement, one-off requirement, etc.
- The contract's cost code– which may include information about the contract's cost centre, project number
- The contract's estimated value – this is particularly important for organisations affected by the EC Directives as we saw in Chapter 9
- Tender deadline

In addition, information relating to contract award is also contained on the system:

- Award date
- (Actual) Start date of contract
- Actual contract value
- Who the award was authorised by, and date
- End date
- Length of contract
- Account system reference
- Payment terms

 Action List

This screen will typically include all tasks to process the procurement, handle suppliers and produce necessary internal and external documentation. In addition, authorisation tasks and free text tasks may be included. Together with the actions there will be timescales and delegated responsibilities, as well as a recording of each action's current status. The action list will act as the driver of the contract through the workflow management system.

Action Types

'Actions' are the tasks that must be performed in order to achieve contract award. A typical list of actions would include:

- Initiate contract
- Select possible list of suppliers
- Add ad-hoc suppliers
- Conduct a supplier appraisal exercise
- Create technical specifications
- Select contractual terms
- Compile invitation to tender(ITT) documentation
- Authorise ITT pack
- Invite to tender
- Monitor ITT progress
- Open tenders

- Authorise award
- Award contract
- Organisations affected by the EC Procurement Directives will need to create *Official Journal* award notice
- Send rejections
- Review contract performance by continual contract monitoring
- Renew contract

 Award Information

Information relating to contract award will be included on this screen.

The UCMS therefore provides an IT system that co-ordinates the activities undertaken with a contract and also provides full contract documentation and decision support for each of the separate actions (such as the ITT and contractual terms). The system also has the ability to connect with other data systems to help provide improved procurement decision making.

Decision Support Tools

To assist the formulation of commercial relationships with external suppliers, purchasers can make use of systems to assist decision making. In Chapter 9 for example, we identified some of the complexities of the EC directives. An example of a decision support tool for organisations affected by the EC Procurement Directives is the 'Themis' decision support tool. The 'Themis' software is able to guide users through the complexities of the EC directives. Here are some examples of the types of field and information contained on the system.

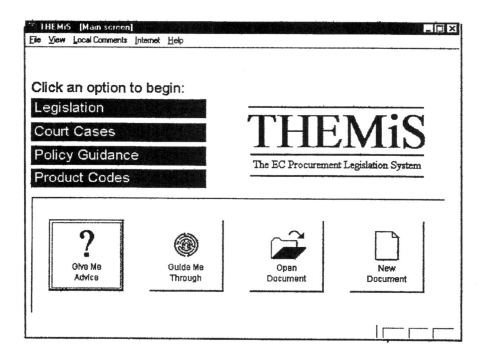

The main menu screen shows that the system provides:

- A library of relevant texts including the directives, and policy guidance published by the UK Treasury department.
- Summaries of important court cases affecting the use of the directives.
- A guide to the procedures with help texts and links to important documents.
- Guidance on the aggregation rules since, as we saw in Chapter 9, the directives apply to requirements in excess of set monetary thresholds.
- A tenderer selection and evaluation system, since there are various rules.

Directives apply to requirements in excess of set monetary thresholds
A tenderer selection and evaluation system- since there are various rules

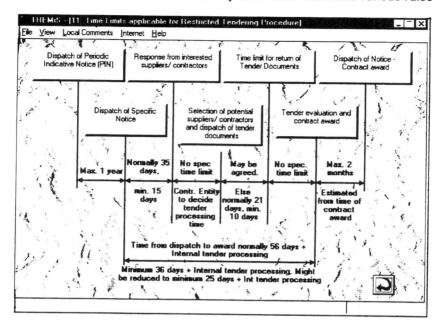

The example of the screen shown illustrates the rules relating to the restricted tendering procedure in the utilities sector. The software is therefore an example of a decision support tool enabling the contracts manager to more easily comply with the requirements established by the directives.

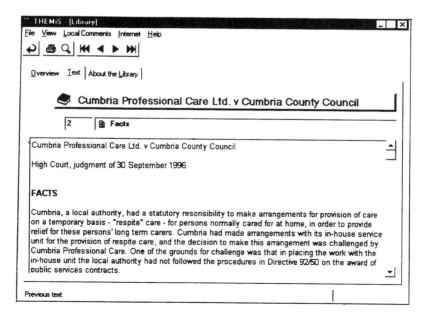

Data Base IT Systems

A computer system offers the benefits of being able to:

- Store and retrieve a great quantity of data (in our case, information on suppliers and products/ services bought)
- Process the data rapidly (the system should be able to provide information quickly)
- Reduce clerical activities tied up with a manually operated system through the automation of purchase requisitions, orders, acknowledgement forms, etc.
- Provide better information to help improve the purchaser's sourcing and subsequent negotiations.

A simple IT system will record the details about suppliers referred to earlier, such as each supplier's address, telephone number, names of personnel to contact on specific matters can be included in such a record. In addition to such basic information, details may be kept on the supplier's past delivery performance and their quality, as well as details of the supplier appraisal.

A computerised data system which keeps information about suppliers could look like this:

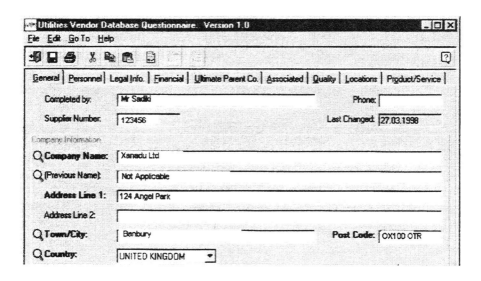

This screen which could be displayed on the computer shows general information about the supplier.

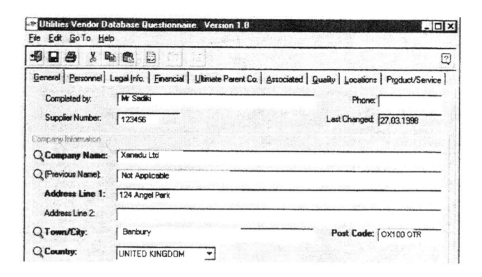

This screen which could be displayed on the computer shows 'general' information about the supplier.

More detailed information can also be maintained:

The pictures of computer screens show how information which is obtained by a supplier appraisal can be stored in a data base system.

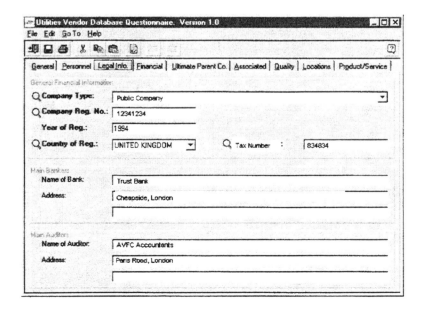

On a sophisticated system, a buyer would be able to find a supplier who matches requirements by keying in to the computer information such as:

- Brief details of the product or service required.
- Stipulations about whether the supplier should have a quality assurance system such as ISO 9000.
- Requirements about the size of the supplier, for example that the supplier should have a minimum turnover of £1,000,000.

The data base system would then locate a list of suppliers who meet these requirements. Such data base systems are used in a number of sectors, such as in the utilities sector, and in the oil and gas industry. Major purchasers of products/ services in these sectors are subscribers to these data base systems, and are then able to access registered suppliers to the data base management system.

This facility would only be available on very sophisticated supplier data base systems, and such systems are normally only available through specialised IT software companies that would offer such a facility on a subscription basis, but it demonstrates the abilities of IT systems. Here is an example of such a system that would be able to search the capabilities of suppliers:

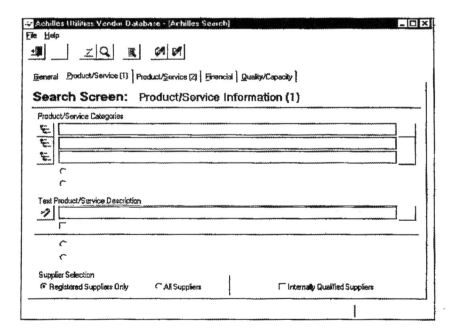

Another advantage of using a specialist data base management company is that it would avoid a considerable amount of duplication in the supplier appraisal process. The diagram below shows that different purchasing organisations would duplicate a great deal of effort in finding information about suppliers. Different purchasers may be using their own versions of questionnaires asking similar questions.

Duplication of Effort

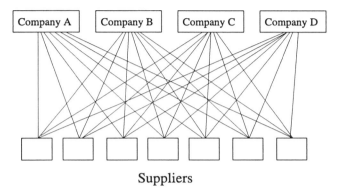

A specialist data base management company would avoid the duplication involved when the purchasing organisations are conducting their own supplier appraisals. In addition, a data base system would allow the different purchasing organisations to rapidly find possible sources of supply by using search criteria.

Vendor Database Management

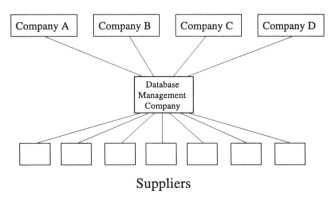

Founded in 1972, SAP (Systems, Applications and Products in Data Processing) has become a market leader in business IT systems. The company, which originates in Walldorf, Germany, operates in over 90 countries and currently has over 7,500 customers and is now very much the standard in industries such as oil, chemicals, consumer products, IT and electronics. The SAP R/3 system manages financial, manufacturing, sales and distribution and supply chain management functions within an integrated data base system. It also enables order processing via the Internet. The software can provide applications for:

- Production planning
- Purchase ordering
- Quality management
- Sales and distribution
- Human resources management
- Financial planning and control
- Investment management.

Corporate Purchasing Cards

The role of purchasing should be to add value to the organisation. A disproportionate amount of time is typically spent by buyers raising orders and dealing with invoice queries. These activities clearly do not add value. What typically accentuates the amount of clerical effort is the time spent dealing with low-value orders in accordance with the Pareto rule – 80% of transactions will equate to roughly 20% of total expenditure. What constitutes low value will vary organisation to organisation, but the following chart illustrates data from a plant site of a major organisation in the UK, and the results it shows are not untypical.

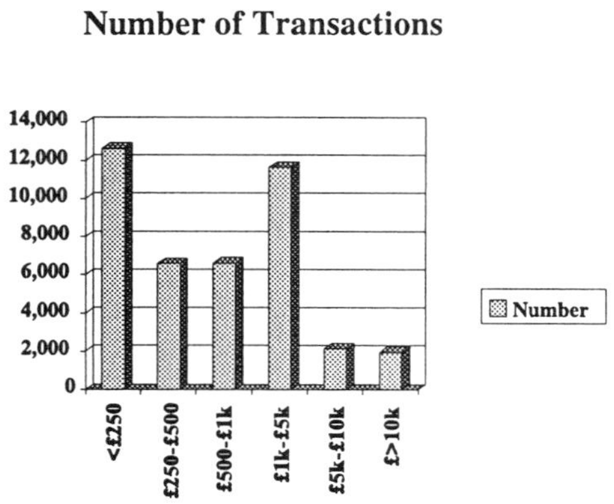

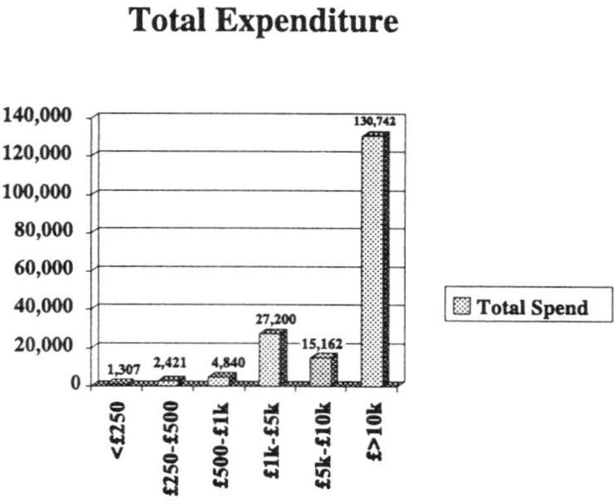

Number of Transactions

Total Expenditure

If the number of orders less than £1,000 were grouped together, these would have totalled 25,850. This can be compared to the volume of orders in excess of £10,000 which add up to a total of 1,950 over the year. The figures for the number of transactions can be contrasted with the total expenditures for the same groupings.

IT developments in the financial sector have led to the creation of corporate purchasing cards. These are particularly useful as a mechanism for streamlining the clerical activity necessary for low-value orders. Under a conventional order placement process, the internal customer will raise a requisition which is then passed to the buyer. Purchasing will source the product or service required, and subsequently raise an order, passing a copy to the accounts department. When products are supplied, a goods received note will be raised, and a copy of this will be passed to accounts. If the purchase order, goods received note and invoice received from the supplier all match, the supplier is paid. However, this can be a time-consuming process, particularly when the invoice does not match either the purchase order or the goods received note.

It is usually estimated that the internal costs of the order placement process vary between £50 to £100. The actual figure will vary from organisation to organisation as there will be differences in the overheads in terms of people and the related costs of communication.

A corporate purchasing card works in a similar way to personal credit cards. For a card transaction to be made possible, the purchaser and the supplier need to be capable of using the cards. On the buying side, organisations will enter into an arrangement with a bank, who will issue cards to selected personnel. The banks usually charge for this facility either by a fixed annual fee, or by an amount charged per transaction. On the seller's side, the bank or card company will help the supplier to set up a payment facility by the use of the cards.

The ordering process is made considerably simpler – the card holder (usually the internal customer) simply orders the products or service required quoting details of the card and the transaction is processed electronically via the supplier's terminal.

There are numerous advantages to the use of corporate purchasing cards. These in brief are as follows:

To Purchasing:
- More time available to spend on value-added activities.
- Potential for discounts due to better terms given to suppliers.

To Internal Customers:
- Improved speed of ordering process.
- Mistakes reduced since communication is made direct to the supplier.
- Delivery lead times reduced.

To Accounts:

- Invoice matching no longer performed by accounts but outsourced to the banks.
- Individual customer code enables the monitoring of expenditure by each user.
- Management information can focus on analysing expenditures made by personnel.

Extensive management information can be provided by the banks to the purchasing organisation. Data can highlight the expenditures made by departments with suppliers. There are limits built into the use of the cards too, to control individual transactions and monthly expenditure limits can also be set for each individual cardholder. In addition, suppliers are given a category code and so the purchaser may prevent the purchase of supplies from certain types of supplier. For example, a cardholder may be barred from buying stationery with the cards if there is already a corporate-wide stationery agreement in place with a single-sourced supplier. Another example may be the barring of travel and entertainment. There is inevitably the risk of card misuse which may be committed innocently or fraudulently (one could easily select the wrong card for making payment in a supermarket for example, especially after a trip to the pub!). However, this risk needs to be balanced against the usual disciplinary procedures which can be enforced if mis-use does occur.

In terms of the implementation of corporate purchasing cards, the following points can influence the success of such schemes:

- Internal resistance is to be expected from budget holders and other affected personnel, particularly accounts payable. Their involvement with the projects implementation would be important.
- A major drawback to the effectiveness of the system is the lack of numbers of suppliers capable of accepting payment by this means. The numbers are growing, but their take-up has been a disappointment for the banks.
- The use of purchase cards needs to be incorporated into existing purchase procedures and training given to the card holders. Whilst the cards will only account for a small proportion of overall expenditure, it is still important that the card holders are made aware of the basics in terms of the buying process.
- The use of such cards requires a degree of trust and empowerment of those individuals entrusted to use the facilities. The organisation's culture will often determine whether there will be a great deal of resistance to change or an ease of its acceptance.

Corporate purchasing cards should be seen as a positive development and a useful aid to off-load the clerical responsibilities of low-value order purchasing.

CD-ROM Technology

A dramatic development throughout the 1980s and 1990s is the growth in access to information by electronic means. Rather than rely on printed trade directories in book form for information, many directories are also available on CD-ROM disks holding vast quantities of data that can be accessed by personal computers. Data is stored on a compact disk, and vast quantities of data can be held on these. Most computers sold today have a CD-ROM drive which is an integral part of the computer. Dun and Bradstreet for example market such directories on CD-ROM, and the technology provides the added advantages of being able to search for suppliers far more quickly compared to the traditional book form directories.

There are also sector-specific CD-ROMs such as the Technical Indexes produced by the company of the same name. The main CD covers electronic engineering, process engineering and engineering design and manufacturing. A separate CD covers computers and communications. CDs such as these enable highly specialised sourcing into key market areas, and the information is also available in standard book form.

Perhaps the only disadvantage with CDs is that they often are expensive and are available by subscription so that updated versions are automatically despatched.

The Internet

Much business information can now, of course, be found on the Internet. The Internet is literally a worldwide web of computers that makes a great deal of communication possible more easily. The Internet can be used to research information, to watch a video, listen to an audio broadcast, or even to broadcast yourself if you set up an Internet site. To link into the Internet requires a computer, a modem link which will connect the computer to a phone line and a 'browser' (a software package that enables movement around the Internet.) Netscape produced the first Internet browser, but now Microsoft dominates the world market with its browser 'Internet Explorer'.

It is argued that the Internet is fast becoming as integral to business as the telephone and fax machine. It provides an invaluable business tool for everyday correspondence, the marketing of products and services by suppliers, a means of providing customers with information and a way of obtaining customer feedback.

The Internet can be used to provide details of supplier organisations. For example, the address for the Chartered Institute of Purchasing and Supply's Internet site is http://www.cips.org and this is their 'home' page:

IT Applications in Supply Chain Management

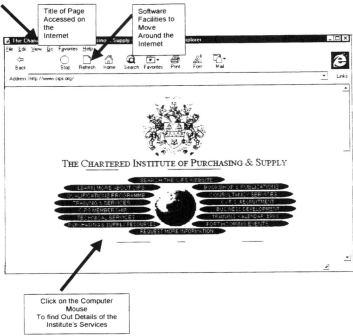

Information can therefore be found out about the CIPS via the Internet. By clicking the computer's mouse control on any of the categories (e.g. 'Learn More About CIPS'), then further information can be revealed.

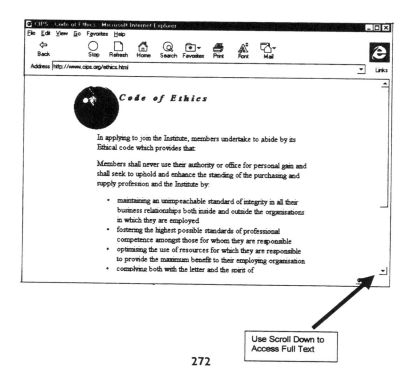

For example the CIPS 'Code of Ethics' can be found on their Internet site. You can see that it is incomplete. On the computer, the full text would be accessed by scrolling down the icon bar where marked.

Other professional institutes for purchasing and supply can be found on the Internet. While accessing a vast number of sites is its advantage, it is also simultaneously its weakness. A search on the Internet under the words 'professional institutes of purchasing' will typically reveal over 35,000 Internet addresses- since the three words used – 'professional + institute + purchasing' throw up Internet addresses and titles using those words. The professional institutes around the world will probably be within those 35,000 (if they have set up an Internet site) but would involve the job of scrolling through all those 35,000 entries just to locate the equivalents to CIPS around the world! However, 'search engines' enable the user to search for something specific by submitting key works, or search terms. Each search engine has a 'read me' page providing tips on its use, and it is well-worth spending a few minutes studying these as they can save considerable time!

The advantage of the Internet is that it is costed as phone calls. In addition, the Internet Service Provider such as Demon, I-Way will make a charge for the connection to the network. This can be in the form of a fixed price per month or year, or an hourly rate. In choosing the service provider, there are a number of important considerations besides pricing structure:

- Whether the phone call costs will be at an local rate.
- The choice of E-Mail system (for example, POP3 E-Mail is currently seen as a superior system).
- The service provider's support hours (24 hours, for example, or limited to normal working hours).
- Each service provider exchanges data with a network of other providers. A positive sign is that the provider will have its own inter-continental and international links with multiple routing options.
- Start-up costs and the software supplied and compliance with Netscape or Internet Explorer and Windows 95.
- Whether there is a discounted costing structure to allow cheaper access to the Internet at certain times.
- The charges for registration of E-Mail addresses and whether there are limitations on the number of these that can be set up.

The Internet enables electronic commerce. Datamonitor's report 'Business to Business Electronic Commerce- Opportunities in the Extranet Age' (1997) predicts that over 60,000 European companies will be doing business over the Internet by the year 2000. Electronic commerce over the Internet opens up access to a global market. It means that products and services can be sourced from anywhere in the world.

However, there are barriers to the use of the Internet as a means of purchasing from suppliers. There is still a lack of skills and the use of electronic commerce is dependent on an educated workforce. A recent survey commissioned by the Department of Trade and Industry (1997) found that 52% of businesses felt that their employees did not have a sufficient understanding of the technology.

A second barrier is the reluctance to use the Internet due to possible breaches of security through crime. There are inevitably risks associated with the use of the Internet to send information concerning sensitive commercial details.

A solution has been for organisations to set up an 'Intranet' which is a mechanism that enables information to be passed between approved trading partners. Many organisations now use Intranets to distribute internal documents- in effect publishing Internet pages for their own private use. So Intranet is the descriptive term used for the implementation of Internet technologies within a corporate organisation and their approved trading partners, rather than for external connection to the global Internet.

Intranet sites can be used by purchasing organisations in a variety of ways:

- To publish documents relating to policies and procedures which can then be accessed by personal computers.
- To provide a means of broadcasting information quickly.
- To encourage closer relationships with approved suppliers who can be sent orders/ specifications and other information over the network.

Intranets certainly provide a means of centralising procurement policies and expenditures. All departmental requirements can be more easily collated, especially when there are different sites operating in different locations, and routed through to the central purchasing manager. Such an arrangement can work most effectively when expenditure approvals are made first before submission to the purchasing manager.

The Chartered Institute of Purchasing and Supply's journal, *Supply Management,* often focuses on the development of electronic commerce. A survey of opinions was published in the 9 April edition, asking how useful and widespread it is in practice. Here are some useful quotations from the article.

At the moment, electronic commerce is barely used on the supply side, other than a few electronic data interchange (EDI) links and e-mails. But we want to set up an Intranet with our top 20 or 30 suppliers such as fleet, stationers, furniture and caterers so that we are a family and can talk to each other. Also we want to introduce electronic forms for orders...

The Internet has massive potential to cut out the supply chain and I see many risks for purchasers. We offer information on suppliers and sourcing, but the Internet makes it just as easy fro customers to find it themselves. Purchasing needs to move away from the requisitioning and ordering process and get close to internal customers so that we can get ahead of them and add value...

Alan Fenwick, Head of Group Purchasing, Thomas Cook Travel

...I'm not yet convinced of the potential for the Internet for commercial buyers, but for individuals it is very attractive. Buying very large, expensive products like computer systems is not possible on the Internet so its use for us is very limited...

Keith Holland, Group Purchasing Director, Midland Bank

...People can see the potential of the Internet, but there are still concerns about security of transaction and information which will hold up progress until the medium is seen as follproof. In the immediate term, I find E-Mail a very useful way to communicate both internally and with suppliers.

Simon Jones, Purchasing Controller, Rank Group

...I think electronic commerce has huge potential for procurement- in fact, it is one of the best things to happen to it. As technology advances, its usefulness will become greater, as will its speed. You will be able to investigate orders, and suppliers will be able to look at inventory, delivery dates and lead times instantaneously. It will be possible to make better purchasing with more up-to-date information.

In the short term, our relationships with suppliers will change immensely. I think it will gravitate to those that have electronic commerce and others will lose out.

Theresa Nash, Purchasing Manager, University of East London

Year - 2000 Compliance

'The 'Millennium Bug' is one of the most serious problems facing not only British business but the global economy today. Its impact cannot be underestimated...' stated Tony Blair in a speech on the scale of the problem. As well as computers, all manner of business equipment, production and control systems, management systems, etc. are at risk. The technical shortcoming of such equipment is now well-known, as many software programmes and computer memory systems only acknowledge the last two digits of any year. When '99 turns to '00, it is argued that there is an inherent risk in such systems as they will fail to cope with the change and revert to the year 1900, corrupting data or closing down. Companies are already experiencing problems with systems that stretch beyond the Millennium, such as credit card expiry dates which stretch into the year 2000.

The possible effect on organisations' supply chains and, therefore, commercial relationships can be potentially catastrophic! An entire supply chain could be disrupted if a single supplier has failed to make his system compliant. To help eradicate the problem, the British Standards Institute has provided a definition of requirements that must be satisfied to achieve year - 2000 compliance. This definition was prepared by BSI- 'DISC', the arm of the BSI which purports to 'Delivering Information Solutions to Customers'.

The Definition

Year 2000 conformity shall mean that neither performance nor functionality is affected by dates prior to, during and after the year 2000.

In particular:
- No value for current date will cause any interruption in operation
- Date-based functionality must behave consistently for dates prior to, during and after the year 2000...

Amplification - general explanation

Problems can arise from some means of representing dates in computer equipment and from date-logic embedded in purchased goods or services, as the year 2000 approaches and during and after that year. As a result, equipment or products... may fail completely, malfunction or cause data to be corrupted.

To avoid such problems, organisations must check, and modify if necessary, internally produced equipment and products and similarly check externally supplied equipment and products with their suppliers...

Where checks are made with external suppliers, care should be taken to distinguish between claims of conformity and the ability to demonstrate conformity.

Rule 1

1.1   This rule is known as general integrity

1.2   If this requirement is satisfied, roll-over between all significant time demarcations (e.g. days, months, years, centuries) will be performed correctly

1.3   Current date means today's date as known to the equipment or product

Rule 2

2.1 This rule is sometimes known as data integrity

2.2 This rule means that all equipment and products must calculate, manipulate and represent dates correctly for the purposes for which they were intended

2.3 The meaning of functionality includes both processes and the results of those processes....

Rule 3

This rule is sometimes known as explicit/ implicit century

In all interfaces and data storage, the century must be specified either explicitly or by unambiguous algorithms or inferencing rules

The standard can be used to seek clarification from suppliers that they are year-2000 compliant. However, the statement of requirements does make an interesting point in that 'Where checks are made with external suppliers, care should be taken to distinguish between claims of conformity and the ability to demonstrate conformity.' It is regularly the case that suppliers are required to complete questionnaire sent by purchasing organisations with little concern over their validity. It is clear that purchasing organisations are not paying significant concern over suppliers' ability to demonstrate conformity.

The following advice is provided by the UK Department of Trade and Industry on their Internet site recommending a 7-step plan for year-2000 compliance.

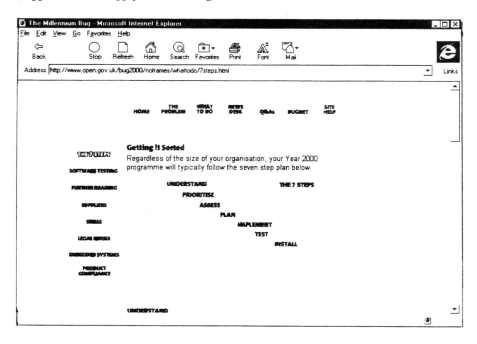

278.1

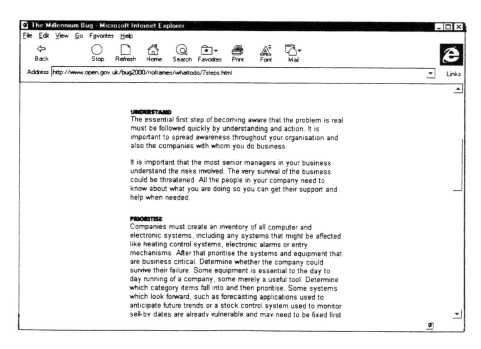

278.2

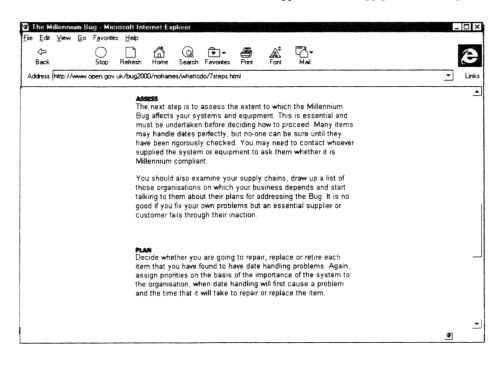

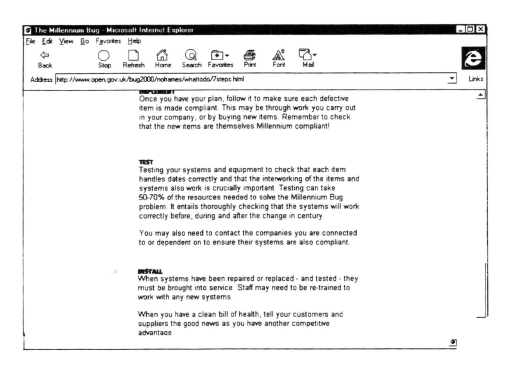

In addition, its Internet site http://www.open.gov.uk/bug2000.htm provides a useful listing of books and other publications for further reading on year-2000 compliance.

There is plenty of evidence that larger organisations are spending vast resources to deal with year-2000 compliance. For example, BT are spending £300 million to ensure that there is a smooth transition. Barclays Bank has set aside £250 million, and Tesco is spending £30 million. However, the main threat is with organisations lower down in supply chains, as they do not have the same financial resources to investigate the problem.

Let us all hope that the threats posed by the millennium bug are exaggerated - for all of our futures!

Further Reading

The following are useful Internet addresses which provided excellent sources of information for a number of topics covered in this book.

For information about IT systems and services provided by Achilles Information

http:/www.achilles.co.uk

For information from the British Standards Institute about ISO 9000, ISO 14000 and DISC

http:/www.bsi/disc

For information about the Chartered Institute of Purchasing and Supply

http:/www.cips.org

For information and assistance on year - 2000 compliance from the Department of Trade and Industry:

http://www.open.gov.uk/bug2000.htm

For details about the European Commission's regulations affecting public procurement

http://europa.eu.int/comm/dg15/en/publproc/index.htm

For information on HM Treasury's policy guidance discussed in Chapter 9

http://ns.hm-treasury.gov.uk/

For details about Partnership Sourcing Ltd and other initiatives geared towards partnership sourcing discussed in Chapter 7

http://www.brainstorm.co.uk/cbi/publi/partnership.dir/pshome.html

For the newspaper, the *Sunday Times* and *Times* publications

http:/www.sunday-times.co.uk

For full information and data base search facility on the work of IPSERA (the academic research body in purchasing and supply)

www.wbs.warwick.ac.uk/ipsera/search.html

Index